COLOUR FOR COLOUR
SKIN FOR SKIN

COLOUR FOR COLOUR SKIN FOR SKIN
Marching with the Ancestral Spirits into War Oh at Morant Bay

Clinton A. Hutton

IAN RANDLE PUBLISHERS
Kingston • Miami

First published in Jamaica, 2015 by
Ian Randle Publishers
11 Cunningham Avenue
Box 686
Kingston 6
www.ianrandlepublishers.com

© Clinton A. Hutton
ISBN: 978-976-637-906-3

National Library of Jamaica Cataloguing-In-Publication Data

Hutton, Clinton A.
　Colour for colour, skin for skin : marching with the ancestral spirits into War Oh at Morant Bay / Clinton A. Hutton.

　　pages ; cm.
Includes bibliographical references and index.
ISBN 978-976-637-906-3

1.　Jamaica – History – Insurrection, 1865
2.　Insurgency –Jamaica – History – Morant Bay Rebellion, 1865
3.　Jamaica – Politics and government
I.　Title

972.9204 -　dc 23

All rights reserved. No part of this publication may be reproduced, stored in a retrieval system or transmitted in any form or by any means electronic, photocopying, recording or otherwise, without the prior express permission of the author and publisher.

Cover image © Clinton A. Hutton
Book and Cover Design by Ian Randle Publishers
Printed and Bound in the United States of America

Dedication

For Tamayo, Jada, Syre and Ru

In memory of Paul Bogle, James McLaren, Letitia Geoghegan, Rosanna Finlayson, Arthur Wellington, William Bowie and hundreds more who died at the hands of the British and the Jamaican elites for freedom, justice, sovereignty and dignity.

Table of Contents

List of Illustrations	...	viii
List of Tables	...	ix
Acknowledgements	...	xi
Introduction	...	xiii

1. 'Liberty of Person Liberty of Land':
   The 'Morant Bay Rebellion' – its Socio-Economic and Political Bases ... 1

2. 'It is Money They [Planters] Want, and Not Labour':
   Free Trade, Cane Sugar and a Post-Slavery Economy in Free Fall ... 13

3. 'Buckra Has Gun, Negro Has Firestick':
   Post-Emancipation Political Struggles ... 27

4. 'Their Very Independence is an Evil':
   Cane Sugar Elites Creating Inflammable Materials in Post-slavery Society ... 48

5. 'Legal Redress is Shut out from One Class Altogether':
   Magisterial Oppression in St Thomas-in-the-East ... 63

6. 'Colour for Colour, Skin for Skin':
   The Intellectual Foundations and Leadership of the 'Morant Bay Rebellion' ... 77

7. 'You Are No Longer Slaves, But Free Men':
   George William Gordon: The Brown Link Ideology and Politics ... 120

8. 'Buccra Can't Catch Duppy, No, No':
   Marching into War Oh with the Spirits at Morant Bay ... 147

9. 'Take a Thousand Black Men's Hearts for One White Man's Ear':
   The Suppression of the Black Jamaican Masses in 1865 – A General Survey ... 172

10. 'He set my house on fire, and I was in Childsbirth':
    The Suppression of the Black Woman ... 184

11. Factors Which Accounted for the Defeat of the People's Rising ... 204

12. The Nature of the 'Negro Character' Determined the 'Character of Negro Insurrections':
    The Philosophical and Ideological Justifications for the Suppression of the 'Morant Bay Rebellion' ... 227

References	...	241
About the Cover Image – *Communion with the Spirits*	...	247
Index	...	249

List of Illustrations

Figure 1. Sugar cane plantations still dominate the Plantain Garden River District of St Thomas. ... 50

Figure 2. Ruins of the Bath courthouse. ... 66

Figure 3. John Willis Menard – Edith Menard – 'John Willis Menard' – Negro History Bulletin 23–No.3 (1964). ... 81

Figure 4. This photograph is believed to be of Paul Bogle. ... 99

Figure 5. George William Gordon. ... 121

Figure 6. Remains of the Steps of Paul Bogle's Chapel in Stony Gut. ... 151

Figure 7. The cutlass is still pervasively used in Revival and Kumina rituals in Jamaica today. ... 164

Figure 8. Morant Bay Massacre. ... 172

Figure 9. Col. Francis Hobbs. ... 175

Figure 10. One of the three canons at the fort behind the Morant Bay courthouse where persons were tied, stripped of their clothing and whipped. ... 179

Figure 11. The spot where Arthur Wellington was executed and decapitated. ... 183

Figure 12. Morant Bay after October 1865 with the burnt out courthouse in the background. ... 193

Figure 13. Governor Edward John Eyre. ... 205

List of Tables

Table 5.1.	Status of Complainants and Defendants in Civil and Criminal Cases Heard in Petty Sessions at Bath, St Thomas-in-the-East, 1863–65	...	64
Table 5.2.	The Economic Links of Justices of the Peace in St Thomas-in-the-East	...	66
Table 5.3.	Planter-Magistrates vs Labourers in Civil and Criminal Cases Heard at Bath, St Thomas-in-the-East, 1863–65	...	67
Table 5.4.	Judgments Handed Down Against Tax Offences in Petty Sessions at Bath, St Thomas-in-the-East, 1863–65	...	68
Table 5.5.	Labourers vs Labourers, Civil and Criminal Cases Heard in Petty Sessions at Bath, St Thomas-in-the-East, 1863–65	...	70

Acknowledgements

My deepest appreciation to the staff of the National Library of Jamaica, especially Ruby Burton and her colleagues who worked in the section housing newspapers, manuscripts and maps. I must also express my profound appreciation to the staff of the University of the West Indies Main Library, especially Patricia Dunn, Frances Salmon, Anthony Bushay, Nolda Thompson, Ann-Marie Long and Walter Gordon, and others, from the West Indies and Special Collections, whose interest in my work and assistance sometimes went beyond the call of duty.

To the supervisors of my PhD Thesis, Rupert Lewis, Department of Government, and Verene Shepherd, Department of History, many thanks for your advice, the discussions, the confidence shown in me and the freedom to let me imagine and be myself.

To Linette Vassell, Anthony Harriot, Patricia Thorpe (dec.), Swithin Wilmot, Colin Moulton, Joseph Pereira, Colin Morrison and Disraeli Hutton, who have consistently shown interest in my study and helped to keep the fire burning.

To members of the Department of Government, especially Carl Stone (dec.), Gladstone Mills (dec.), Edwin Jones, Brian Meeks, Robert Buddan and Trevor Munroe, who showed more than a passing interest in my work.

To Brother Grey, Brother Haye and other members of the International Peace Makers Association who have become my friends. They have carried the gem of Africa and pride and intellect of post-emancipation fighters in their hearts. Their modus operandi gave me a peep into what aspects of the movement led by Paul Bogle might have been.

My appreciation to Yvonne Wallace for her technical advice, and the typing of my thesis and to Yvonne Davidson for translating early nineteenth century Haitian constitutions for me, many thanks.

To my dear son, Tamayo Sandino, who was seven years old when I began my thesis. We prevailed. Love.

Introduction

> War is at my black skin – war is at hand
> From today to tomorrow.... The white people
> Are now cleaning up their guns for us, which
> We must prepare too
>
> — *Paul Bogle, B. Clarke, J.G. McLaren,*
> *P. Cameron and E.K. Bailey*

> Oh General Jackson!
> Oh General Jackson!
> Oh General Jackson!
> Oh you kill all the Black man dem!
> Oh what a wrongful judgment!
> Oh what a wrongful judgment!
> Oh what a wrongful judgment!
> You kill all the Black man dem!
> Oh what a awful mourning!
> Oh what a awful mourning!
> Oh what a awful mourning!
> You bring on St. Thomas people!
>
> — *Folk song on the suppression of the people in*
> *St Thomas-in-the-East in 1865*

The year 2015 marks the 150th anniversary of what the British colonial authorities and their allies called the 'Morant Bay Rebellion', which they put down with a 'reign of terror!' But this 'reign of terror' or 'the killing time,' which choreographed its demise, failed to destroy what ontologically amounted to be a definitive emerging national complex. The rising of the people in Morant Bay on October 11, 1865 contained in its making the spiritual, creative, emotional, psychological, ideational, linguistic and political signatures of this emerging national complex. So too did the Great Revival of 1860–61 which nationalised Myal (Myaal) in two manifestations of Revival, Zion and Poko (Poko-Kumina), denoting a prime source of the cosmological architecture of this emerging national ethos.

Perhaps then, the significance of Morant Bay to Jamaica's post-emancipation history is that it reflected the development of a deeper inner national dynamic that not even the butchery performed by the

British military and their allies directed by Governor Edward John Eyre could turn back. That mood, which led the people into violent conflict in 1865, was not confined to the parish of St Thomas-in-the-East but constituted a national feeling among an important segment of the black population across the island. This national feeling was not just associated with the activities of the masses of the black population leading up to the Morant Bay outbreak. The careful documentation of the responses of the people to the supression by Heuman (1994, 100–109), also reflected that feeling.

And that mood would return in 1938, 73 years later. It came in the midst of a Revival/Kumina upsurge and a well spring of Garveyite consciousness which saw the emergence of Rastafari – reminiscent of the emergence of Zion and Poko in the early 1860s. Then, the economic context that framed this development was the removal by the British authorities of the protection of cane sugar by unleashing a most robust historical free trade regime as well as the deliberate policy of former slaveholders to prevent people of African descent access to the means of production.

The fundamentals of the early post-slavery economic structure did not change in the early twentieth century. Added to this came the Great Depression and many of the thousands of Jamaicans who were forced to seek employment abroad returned to the island. By this time, the nationalising factors became more mature culturally, politically and organisationally. The realm of communication became significantly better and social cohesion and the tenure of alliances formed became stronger. Moreover, the regional and international climate provided the context that made radical struggle from below, more permissive. The 1938 outbreak began in January at Serge Island in St Thomas and, by May, it became a national uprising and swept away some of the colonial plantocratic vestiges of 1865.

'Colour for Colour Skin for Skin': Marching with the Ancestral Spirits into War Oh at Morant Bay, a rework of my 1992 PhD thesis, examines aspects of the ontological, cultural and ideological complex and political motives of people of African descent who clashed with the colonial political authorities and cane sugar elites and their allies in Morant Bay, the chief town of the parish of St Thomas-in-the-East, on October 11, 1865. This confrontation was called the 'war' at Morant Bay in the language and meaning of the Jamaican folk. Paul Bogle and other leaders associated with it referred to it as such.

This study unearths, discusses and applies the inner logic of the world view, culture and action of the people in St Thomas-in-the-East/Jamaica in recreating their world, just 27 years removed from slavery. The persons who put their shoulders to the wheel in Morant Bay were thus mostly formerly enslaved Africans and the first generation of their descents born after slavery. This partnership was perhaps best exemplified by Paul Bogle the leader, who was at least 16 years old when slavery ended, and James McLaren, the secretary of the movement which Bogle led, who was born about four years after slavery was abolished.

In crafting *Colour for Colour Skin for Skin*, I was mindful that the world view and epistemic culture fashioned by blacks who emerged from slavery did not disappear but exists today as the principal basis of the world view of the Jamaican folk. It is here that the world view of Revival: Zion and Poko is located. It is here, too, that notions of freedom and justice in Jamaican popular music such as the Wailers' *Concrete Jungle* and *Catch A Fire*; Bob Marley and the Wailers' *Crazy Baldhead*, *Babylon System* and *Redemption Song*; and the Itals' *Ina Dis Yah Time*, are located.

Here, the extent of freedom and justice in post-colonial society is measured by the extent to which it is believed that the social, material, mental and cultural basis of slavery exist in free society. This method of defining, measuring and articulating freedom and justice is not a post-colonial construct. It was a method used by Paul Bogle, James McLaren and others in their campaign leading up to October 11, 1865. More has been written about the outbreak at Morant Bay than any other historical moment articulated in the historiography of Jamaica. '*Colour for Colour Skin for Skin*': *Marching into War Oh with the Ancestral Spirits at Morant Bay*, when introduced in 1992, broke new ground in articulating the significance of the 'Morant Bay Rebellion' socially, politically, culturally and philosophically. More than 20 years on, and on the 150th anniversary of the event, the publication of this work to reach a much wider audience will hopefully yield a greater understanding and appreciation of a still very young nation.

1 'Liberty of Person Liberty of Land': The 'Morant Bay Rebellion' – its Socio-Economic and Political Bases

> [T]he prosperity of the Labouring Classes, as well as of all other classes, depends, in Jamaica and in other Countries, upon their working for Wages, not uncertainly, or capriciously, but steadily and continuously, at the times when their labour is wanted, and for as long as it is wanted; and that if they use this industry, and thereby render the Plantations productive, they would enable the Planters to pay them higher Wages.
>
> *– Edward Cardwell, Colonial Secretary*

October and November 1865 were two of the most crucial months in post-emancipation Jamaica. The most serious crisis in the relationship between former enslaved Africans and former slaveholders culminated in a bloody clash and a brutal suppression. British troops from Barbados, Nassau, and Halifax, along with US military personnel, fresh from victory in that country's civil war, and Spanish forces from Cuba, descended on the island to expunge the 'Haytian virus'. In Halifax, 'upwards of three thousand volunteers tendered their services to Sir James Hope' to assist in the suppression, while in Panama, 'Jamaicans under Mr. Benjamin Scott, organized themselves into a body ready to come [to the] "assistance"' of the island's colonial government, according to the *Gleaner* (November 17, 1865).

The Iron Bar Broke

What has become known to history as the Morant Bay Rebellion, but to the Jamaican folk as the Morant War, erupted at about mid-afternoon, October 11, 1865, in Morant Bay, the chief town and administrative centre of the parish of St Thomas-in-the-East. On that fateful afternoon, an estimated 400 to 1,200 small farmers, labourers and others clashed with a detachment of St Thomas-in-the-East militia in front of the Morant Bay courthouse. They were led by Paul Bogle, an influential black leader of the parish.

In the first round of that clash, one report put the number of Bogle's followers shot and wounded, some mortally, at about 20. The crowd recovered from that deadly volley and surged with machetes, a few old muskets, and a variety of home-made weapons upon the troops who desperately tried to reload their rifles. Six were killed. Others were wounded, some critically. Of those who could, some assisted in barricading themselves in the courthouse. The local state officials, including the Custos, Baron Maximilian Augustus von Ketelholdt, were also bottled up in the courthouse.

Cross-firing/sniping continued between the belligerents for some time until forces from the Bogle camp, led by a woman, set the schoolhouse and the courthouse on fire. The siege of the courthouse ended after 9:30 that evening when its occupants, unable to bear the heat and smoke, alighted and made their last stand. Over 20 of them were killed. Among them were Baron von Ketelholdt, Custos; Revd V. Herschell, Curate of Bath; H.A. Alberga, Inspector of Police; Charles Price, Contractor and the second black person to be elected to the Assembly; Captain E.W. Hitchins, Commander of the Volunteers and Deputy Clerk of the Peace and John Walton, Justice of the Peace and proprietor of Retreat Estate. Others escaped, some undetected, while some were set free. About seven hours after the fighting commenced, Morant Bay was in the hands of the black masses.

For the next two days, the uprising spread across the parish of St Thomas-in-the-East and neighbouring parishes of Portland and St David. St Thomas-in-the-East was in the hands of Paul Bogle and his followers. However, that did not last long. British colonialism and the Jamaican plantocracy and its allies wrote one of the bloodiest pages in the history of Jamaica and the Anglophone Caribbean.

The making of the Morant Bay uprising commenced several weeks before the outbreak when Governor Edward Eyre refused to meet a deputation from St Thomas-in-the-East. The deputation, which was led by Paul Bogle, was composed at a public meeting in Morant Bay on August 12, 1865. It was mandated to go to Spanish Town, the island's capital and seat of the Governor, to present a set of grievances to Governor Edward Eyre. Bogle and the other members of the deputation made the journey for nothing. He went back to Stony Gut, his St Thomas-in-the-East district and shifted the political gear.

This shift manifested itself in an organisational, instructional and psychological mode of operation denoting the politics of violent confrontation. Men were organised in detachments of 50 and drilled in semi-military fashion in Stony Gut. Those so organised had to swear by their ancestors' names/grave, kiss the Bible, drink a mixture of (grave) earth and (human/animal) blood and or gun powder and rum, among variations of combination of elements that symbolised the oath-taking rituals historically associated with anti-slavery insurrections in Jamaica, the Americas and anti-colonial struggles in Africa.

Saturday, October 7, 1865, saw a dramatic change of events. Over 250 men and women, some carrying staves, marched on the Morant Bay courthouse in support of one of their numbers who was to be tried that day for trespass. These marchers were led by Paul Bogle. Trouble broke out when Alexander White, who was being tried, was found guilty of assault and ordered by the Court to pay a fine and costs. Two members of Bogle's party vociferously advised White to pay the fine but not the costs, and the presiding Justice, John Walton ordered the arrest of James Geoghegan, one of those advising White. His arrest was thwarted by Bogle and some of his followers.

On Monday, October 9, 1865, a warrant was issued for the arrest of Paul Bogle and 27 of his colleagues for disturbing the peace in Morant Bay. The following day, eight policemen went to Stony Gut to execute the warrant. On Bogle's orders, the policemen were detained and some of them roughed up. They were told that the people would no longer put up with oppression and injustice. They were freed only after they took an oath to 'cleave from the whites and cleave to the blacks'. Moreover, the policemen were told by their detainers to tell their superiors that Bogle and his people would come to the Bay the following day to proclaim their innocence.

When the policemen were freed that evening, Bogle and 19 of his men wrote a letter to the Governor informing him of the 'mean advantages that has (sic) been taken' of them, especially the 'outrageous assault' 'committed' upon them 'by the policemen of this parish, by order of the Justices' and called upon him 'for protection...which protection, if refused' would compel them 'to put [their] shoulders to the wheel' as they 'have been imposed upon for a period of 27 years'. The writing of this letter was backed up by an all-night vigil in Stony Gut of hundreds of Paul Bogle's supporters.

During that time, Custos Ketelholdt also wrote to Governor Eyre requesting protection in the form of British troops. He also mobilised the No. 1 Volunteer Troops of St Thomas-in-the-East for deployment in front of the courthouse. Both sides, it would seem, were expecting/anticipating a clash.

The Industrial Capitalist Triumphed

The crisis, which came to head in Jamaica in 1865, had its roots in fundamental reforms in Britain and the socio-economic and political regime that emerged in the island colony after the abolition of slavery. The period in which 1865 fell was characterised on the international scene by the growth and increasingly decisive power and influence of the industrial bourgeoisie over the economic and political life of Britain. The rise to prominence of the industrial bourgeoisie simultaneously meant a serious decline in the power of the mercantile forces and their allies associated with the old slavery system of colonialism. One sterling recognition of this fact was the passage of the Reform Bill by the House of Commons in 1831 and ratified by the House of Lords in 1832.

The passage of the Reform Bill was a clear indication that the new thinking, developed with the evolution of the industrial bourgeoisie decades before, was becoming official thought, as the manufacturing and middle classes gained strength over the country's political, social and economic life. This new thinking can be summed up as the 'Free Trade Ideology'.

The rise to power of the industrial bourgeoisie in Britain and the adoption of its policy of Free Trade as the national and international policy of the world's number one industrial and colonial power had a profound impact on developments in Jamaica.

One of the first consequences of the policy of Free Trade for British colonial policy was, to an important degree, the abolition of slavery in the British West Indies between 1834 and 1838. The termination of slavery also had to do with the consistent struggles of enslaved Africans to free themselves, thus rendering slavery increasingly unprofitable[1] as it had to do with the need of the industrial bourgeoisie to remove policies and institutions that were fettering free trade.[2] The social forces which derived their wealth, status and political power from the institution of slavery and other pre- and semi-capitalist forms of agricultural production and commerce had to be defeated. They had to be defeated because the power which allowed them to fashion Navigation and Corn Laws, guaranteeing them unchallenged privileges in trade, was now fettering the ability of the industrial bourgeoisie from expanding, and assuming hegemony over world trade, despite possessing the means to do so.

The restrictions of the political and economic power of the landed mercantile and banking aristocracy associated with slavery, was a significant step forward for the freedom struggles of the black population in the British West Indies when slavery ended. The route to emancipation and the form it took, however, had profound consequences for society's development in the post-slavery period.

Firstly, the abolition of slavery did not mean the abolition of the power of the plantocracy over the colony. The old slave owners were to become the new masters of contract peasant labour. The task of building a new Jamaica was handed over to those who were the architects and motive forces of the late colonial slave state.

The industrial bourgeoisie, who could not maintain British colonialism by themselves, did not want the total rout of the mercantile forces, especially in the colonies dominated by non-European populations. This position was stated by Lord Stanley, Secretary of State for the Colonies, when he was piloting the Abolition Act through the British Parliament in May 1833:

> I would not, by one single hasty step, at once remove all the shackles by which the slaves were now bound; I would not, at once, turn them forth from a state of hopeless slavery into one of unrestricted freedom for which they may be yet unfit (Robotham 1981, 99).

If the black masses were to make emancipation a practical freedom constructing reality, they would need to have a certain level of independence from the ex slave-owning classes and their allies. This independence would, of necessity, mean that blacks should be free to sell their labour power for wages for specific periods of time and place, as well as have a certain amount of freedom to determine the purchaser of their labour. That independence would also mean having a right to self-employment and cooperative employment, along with the freedom to employ and exploit labour. It would have meant, as well, that the freedom of Africans to employ labour necessitated their right to own means of production as it would mean that blacks be guaranteed a certain level of legal, political, social and civil rights, such as freedom of movement, assembly and association.

Liberty of Person, Liberty of Land

Therefore, the idea held by many former enslaved Africans that 'liberty of person' must be connected with 'liberty of the land' was a basic call for emancipation to be made a material reality for the black masses. In this respect, Wellwood Anderson, Inspector-General of Immigration and proprietor, who claimed ownership to the disputed Middleton property in St Thomas-in-the-East, said the people told him 'that the Queen had given them the place when she gave them freedom, and freedom would be of no use if they had not their lands and houses' (Royal Commission 1866, 566). In other words, they wanted emancipation with empowerment, with use value.

The extent to which factors necessary for a more independent black population were realisable depended on the extent to which blacks were collectively conscious of their needs and were willing to struggle and throw up alliances to realise them; the extent to which the planter/merchant alliance was able to thwart the aspirations of the black masses and impose their regime of post-slavery development; the extent to which British colonial policy coincided, lent support to and required the ex-slave-owning classes to keep the colony safe as part of the British empire.

The last factor proved to be the most critical during that period; having lost their power to exploit slave labour, the ex-slave owners signalled from early the type of socio-economic and political system they wished to have established in post-slavery society. Their policy could be summed up as grudgingly accepting emancipation without granting the former enslaved the instruments necessary for their empowerment, for making freedom.

As early as 1834, one Lord Sligo, mirroring the sentiments of the plantocracy, sent a letter from Jamaica to the British colonial Secretary, directing his attention to 'the vast tracts of land which remain uncultivated and apparently unowned in the centre of the island.' Sligo thought 'it very injurious that these tracts should remain without owners,' as he felt 'assured that a vast number of apprentices as they get liberated by purchase, or become finally free in 1840 will retire to these tracts, as squatters, in preference to paying rent for land on the estates on which they have heretofore lived' (Robotham 1981, 32).

In 1836, Lord Glenelg, then Secretary of State for the colonies, turned Sligo's concern into a practical colonial policy. He sent a dispatch to all colonial governors in the Anglophone Caribbean, urging them to 'prevent the occupation of any Crown lands by persons not possessing a proprietary title to them, and to fix such a price upon all Crown lands as may place them out of reach of persons without capital' (31).

Instead of becoming self-owning, self-serving, self-employing and independent as the basis for their relations with the former slave-owning classes, the majority of the black masses were forced to become a kind of peasant-serf labourer, subjected to a historically backward pre-capitalist/semi-capitalist plantocracy, whose habits, attitudes and social psychology were shaped by some 200 years of organising and defending slavery. The nature of the social relationships between the formerly enslaved and ex-slave owners which grew out of post-slavery economic realities was revealed by Edward Underhill in the following observation:

> No labourer likes to live on the estates; nor will he do so unless necessity constrains it, for fear of being turned off when any dispute arises, and the whole of his provision grounds be forfeited. Service must be rendered to the planter on whose land he resides; he dares not choose any other master. The rent paid for provision grounds is 20s. an acre; land is rented only for provisions. The people plant their own land with sugar cane, or cultivated coffee upon it, or other exportable articles; for proprietors of estates will not lend land for those purposes (Underhill 1970, 285).

The methods of coercing black people, apparent in Underhill's statement, were obviously different from the shackles, whips and treadmills of slavery, but the results were in many respects similar, or even worse. 'No labourer likes to live on the estates.' Yet, as free men and women, thousands of people of African descent continued to do so, because, although raw brute force and terror kept them enslaved on estates, want of land and employment and being deprived of reparation, led them into a new regime of oppression. Under slavery, they dared not choose any other owner, because, like draught animals, they were the property of their purchaser. Yet, in the epoch of emancipation, many dared not choose any other employer because the want of land and other requirements for the production of life's sustenance, were controlled by people who wanted to maintain a regime little removed from slavery.

The nature of land tenure was such that the planter class rarely failed to use it against the Africans to promote uncertainty, insecurity and instability in the black community. This was certainly an effective way to weaken black resistance to oppression and injustice. Thus, the Baptist ministers, in reporting on the 'uncertain tenure on which rented land is mostly held', noted:

> On very few properties can it be leased for a term of years; and, consequently, the small growers cannot risk the cultivation of produce which stands more than twelve months. Coffee, e.g., which takes three years to come into bearing, and trees of which yield an annual crop, he cannot plant; he would have no hope of reaping the benefit. In most cases the tenant is subject to a six months' notice to quit; and not infrequently, no sooner has he planted off an acre of ground provisions, than such a notice is served upon him, (Underhill 1865, 36).

The aim of the above 'cruel measure', Thomas Harvey and William Brewin noted, was to fulfil the desire of the plantocracy 'to render the people more dependent than before on estate labour for subsistence' (Harvey and Brewin 1867, 43). There was a direct relationship between access to the land and the status of wages for black labour across the island. John Bigelow, the American journalist who visited the island in 1850, noted that 'the planters discourage these sales of lands to the blacks in every possible way, for they say it raises the price of labour by increasing the independence of the labouring classes' (Oliver 1933, 32).

By restricting land ownership to a level acceptable to the planters and colonial officials, the plantocracy increased the dependency of the labouring classes in three main ways. In the first place, the plantocracy was able to contain employment opportunities to estate employment, while simultaneously stifling alternative sources of employment, like freehold self-employment or cooperative employment.

Secondly, the planters were able to create artificial unemployment as a means of bringing down wages by blocking the source of primary self-employment for blacks. In that way, a greater demand for fewer available jobs became the basis for reduced wages and increased abuses of the masses.

Thirdly, restricting access to the land increased black people's dependence on wage labour. The more land the Africans accessed, the more they were able to produce and make ends meet outside of depending on wages. This put them in a stronger position to demand more wages, choose their employer, reside off the estate and develop a more stable abode and family.

Blacks who were able to establish themselves as free-holders tended to be better off materially. They took more initiatives for self-advancement independent of the plantocracy. It was these blacks who were responsible for growing and producing most of the coffee and pimento in Manchester, earning, according to a report, 'the handsome sum of thirty thousand pounds sterling' in 1853 (Ripley 1985, 409). The road to black proprietorship was never easy, because the plantocracy fought against the rise of black enterprise every inch of the way. One typical example of the hostile feelings the plantocracy held for black proprietorship, was revealed in a letter from black American Abolitionist, Henry Highland Garnet, to Louis Alexis Chamerovow, Secretary of the British and Foreign Anti-Slavery Society, October 1854. According to Garnet, who was at that time a Missionary in Westmoreland, Jamaica:

> A black neighbour of mine has a considerable cane field, and he, and a friend of his were about to put up a small boilinghouse; and a still. But the proprietor of the estate to which the poor man's lot was contiguously situated, heard of the arrangement and rode into the yard of the enterprising black, and the following conversation, and results took place. "So you are going to turn planter?" "How so master?" "Why I hear that you are going to grind your canes, and boil your sugar." "Yes master I was intending to do so." "Well I should like to see you doing anything of the kind. You must remember that you have no title for the land you occupy, and I doubt if you will ever get one if you persist in your undertaking." I am informed that the poor man has been completely overawed by the threat, and will proceed no further (409–10).

Against Black Economic Associations

It was not only in the general area of land ownership that the black population was being kept on the periphery of the post-slavery economy. History has recorded that the post-emancipation colonial state machinery was mobilised against blacks who tried to set up various kinds of economic associations.

When slavery ended, some blacks showed keen interest in setting up economic associations. They tended to form cooperative enterprises, especially for bigger economic undertakings. Invariably, mutual benefit and other cooperative societies founded by blacks were seen by defenders of the status quo as seditious or subversive. In one example, the *Falmouth Post* (August 1859) reported of the existence of what it called a 'Seditious Society' in Trelawny and urged the authorities to crack down on it:

> We have to direct the attention of the Authorities of this parish, to the existence of a Society, which is conducted by a number of blackmen in this town, by whom sentiments of a seditious nature are freely uttered. The meetings are held at a place called the Red House, near to the small Iron Bridge on the Rock Road, and with this information, we hope that the Police will be careful watchers of the movements of the members of the Association.

However, societies formed by Jewish and white minority ethnic groups were treated differently. Just five months before it carried the above report on the 'Black Seditious Society', the *Falmouth Post* reprinted an article from the *Jamaica Tribune* on the 'Hebrew Benevolent Society'. The article was full of praise and encouragement for this Jewish society:

> The reports of the growing prosperity of this invaluable Charity are periodically placed before the public, and we are glad to say attract interest beyond the limits of the Jewish community – the institution being regarded, by all who are familiar with its objects, acquainted with its usefulness, as a model worthy of imitation. It extends to a large number of the Jewish poor, who are classed as "pensioners," a money allowance weekly, and to many who are on its books as "recipients," it makes, occasionally, grants according to their necessities. Then there is, worthy of all praise, the Industrial Branch, which secures needle work to those capable of performing it, resulting in an addition to the eleemosynary aid afforded, whilst it enables our store keepers to procure articles of clothing, and our merchants coffee and pimento bags as cheaply as they can be imported. In addition to these advantages, the most necessitous of the poor are periodically provided with stretchers or cots, the value of which, especially to those unfortunates who are stricken with disease, cannot be overrated (*Falmouth Post* March 29, 1859).

The *Hebrew Benevolent Society* which was founded eight years previously by rich Jewish merchants, planters, legislators, newspaper proprietors and religious leaders, was partially funded by the colonial government.

Independently founded black societies like the one above, were treated differently. Harvey and Brewin noted that:

> A few intelligent young men of T. Lea's[3] congregation, [Trelawny] living a few miles in the country, had been reading some of Cassell's publications, and had taken from them the suggestion of forming a "Mutual Benefit Society." They posted up a written placard inviting a meeting of their own class, to be held on Good Friday (a general holiday), to consider the project. The announcement caused a flutter among the authorities. It was said appeal was made to the King's House for troops. The Custos did not acknowledge this, but he admitted that police had been sent out to attend the meeting and watch the proceedings; but he said, they had returned without finding the place (Harvey and Brewin 1867, 51).

In yet another example, the 'Mercantile Agency Association', founded in Black River, St Elizabeth, by black men 'to facilitate the exportation of the produce of the small freeholders' came under fire from the ruling classes and the colonial authorities in that parish (41). Each member of that Association 'was to subscribe five pounds, and the money was to be taken to England by a local magistrate named Brydson. There he would purchase a vessel, load it with goods wanted by the small settlers, and return to Jamaica to pick up a cargo of settlers' produce for return to England' (Hall 1959, 200–201). They wanted to better their lives on their own account. Harvey and Brewin noted that:

> The humble blackmen who started it invited the Custos of the parish to become its honorary president. Instead of acceding to the request, he forwarded the rules to the Governor, inquiring if the Association was not seditious, and one that should be suppressed by authority (Harvey and Brewin 1867, 41).

Custos John Salmon's request to the Governor was soon acted upon. Governor Eyre submitted his request to the coloured Attorney General, Alexander Heslop, who saw no need for 'legal preventive measures' but ridiculed the founders of the Association and reserved the right to use military force to crush the people, whom he felt, might become disaffected and disturb the peace when their project failed as he believed it must fail. Helop said:

> By foolish or wicked counsels the small producers seem to have lost confidence in the Mercantile Capitalists. I know no better way of enabling them to find out their own blunders than that they should try their experiment... And no better than the present... when there is a strong Force in the Country to preserve the peace against any attempt against it which should arise from dissatisfaction of the Industrious producers as the result of their own folly (Hall 1959, 201).

The efforts of Custos John Salmon, President of the Legislative Council and de facto Deputy Head of State; Governor Eyre, Head of State and the coloured man, Attorney General Heslop in suppressing the black entrepreneurial efforts in this case, showed that the determination to keep Africans out of business found their highest expression at the summit of state authority. In most cases, black people's efforts failed, because a climate conducive to them becoming self-governing economically and politically after slavery was prevented from growing by the former slave holding classes who continued to hold power after slavery. Yet, despite the enormous odds against them, they never gave up. Some went as far as appealing to Queen Victoria for help to realise their desire for self and cooperative employment through land acquisition, the formation of a company to export their produce, the guarantee of a reliable export market in England and access to investment capital. These people were not looking for hand outs. In their petition to the Queen, the St Ann's residents, with a proto-reparation vision, said:

> We are blessed with a good Island, but we require a much larger extent of cultivation. If our most Gracious Sovereign Lady will be so kind as to get a quantity of land, we will put our hands and heart to work, and cultivate coffee, corn, canes, cotton and tobacco, and other produce. We will form a company for that purpose, if our Gracious Lady Victoria our Queen will also appoint an agent to receive such produce as we may cultivate, and give us means of subsistence while at work...
>
> We, your humble servants, will thankfully repay our Sovereign Lady by instalments of such produce as we may cultivate (Harvey and Brewin 1867, 103).

The reply to the people's petition through Edward Cardwell, the Colonial Secretary, repeated in no uncertain way what former enslaved blacks consistently heard from the Jamaican plantocracy, viz, prosperity can only come to the Africans through hard work as labourers:

> the prosperity of the Labouring Classes, as well as of all other Classes, depends, in Jamaica, and in other Countries, upon their working for Wages, not uncertainly, or capriciously, but steadily and continuously, at the times when their labour is wanted, and for so long as it is wanted; and that if they use this industry, and thereby render the Plantations productive, they would enable the Planters to pay them higher Wages for the same hours of work than are received by the best Field Labourers in this country [England] (40).

Several other attempts were made by Africans at establishing agricultural, commercial and mutual loan societies. Among them was 'the Labourers

Club', which was essentially a mutual loan society. The capital accumulated, chiefly from profits, amounted to 700 pounds (40). This club was founded in St Elizabeth. There was also 'The St. David's Joint-Stock Company and Society of Arts'. Writing briefly about this Company, Douglas Hall noted the following:

> In 1857 "The St. David's Joint-Stock Company and Society of Arts" had been formed by small farmers in the Yallahs Valley district. The plan was to raise £1,000 in 200 shares of £5 each, but in this case it was to finance production and not marketing. The enterprise was intended "to regulate by means of co-operative labour, certain schemes of cultivation upon such lands as the Company might be able to purchase." By early 1858 the association had bought about 450 acres, but what was done with the land and what happened to the Company remain a mystery (Hall 1959, 202).

This company of which Hall spoke coincided with the growth of the social, entrepreneurial and political activism of the black freeholders in the parish of St David. Freeholdership generated its own political path and was in the vanguard of the struggle against the plantocracy and its racist ideology in post-slavery society.[4]

The persistent efforts by the plantocracy and the post-slavery colonial state to keep the African as a perpetual labourer in the economic system by denying the black person access to the means of production, was motivated by a belief that long justified slavery. In this belief, the European was endowed by nature to be master and the African his servant. This profoundly racist belief, which constituted the essential epistemic wellspring of plantation ideology and praxis became the guiding principle on which relationships between blacks and whites were based and which the freeholders in the vanguard of the black masses, were desirous of destroying.

Notes

1. See Richard Hart, *Slaves Who Abolished Slavery* 2 Vols. (Jamaica: Institute of Social and Economic Research, University of the West Indies, 1980 and 1985).
2. See Eric Williams, *Capitalism and Slavery* (Chapel Hill: University of North Caroline Press, 1944).
3. In other sources T. Lea is spelt T. Lee as in Revd Thomas Lee.
4. For a case study of this, see Swithin Wilmot's essay 'The Politics of Samuel Clarke: Black Political Martyr in Jamaica 1851–1865,' *The Jamaica Historical Review* XIX (1996): 17–29.

2 'It is Money They [Planters] Want, and Not Labour':
Free Trade, Cane Sugar and a Post-Slavery Economy in Free Fall

> [N]o black man, who will not work according to what ability the gods have given him for working, has the smallest right to eat pumpkin, or to any fraction of land that will grow pumpkin, however plentiful such land may be, but has an indisputable and perpetual right to be compelled, by the real proprietors of said land, to do competent work for his living.
>
> – Thomas Carlyle

While the post-slavery economy went into free fall with the passage of the Sugar Duties Act in the British Parliament in 1846, the plantocracy was unfurling measures to prevent and restrict black proprietorship, which objectively fettered new areas for economic renewal in the post-emancipation colonial Jamaican state. The passage of this Act and the catastrophic effects it had on sugar and rum, the island's leading export products brought to an end the emancipation honeymoon, if there was any such period for the planter class.

The few years leading up to 1845 (relative to the late slave epoch) brought the most rapid progress in the lives of the black population. That period brought wages that were to be cut later by over 50 per cent. That period saw a rapid increase in the accumulation of personal property – like clothes, household articles, buggies, domesticated animals and tools. There was a rapid increase in facilities for elementary education and children attending school. Many people were able to set up their own house on their own 'buy land'.

The Sugar Duties Act removed the favoured position British West Indian sugar interests held on the British market over sugar coming from other sources. The high duties placed on foreign sugar guaranteed British West Indian interests preferential treatment on the British market up to 1845. The drastic altering of the duties under the 'Free Trade' regime, and its ultimate equalisation, ensured similar opportunities for British and foreign sugar on the British market. British West Indian sugar, and especially the Jamaican quota which constituted the bulk of the sugar exported to the United Kingdom, could not compete on the free open British market. Anglophone West Indian sugar was just not competitive enough and a more serious decline hit the already declining industry.

The number of sugar estates operating in Jamaica, in 1844, fell from 664 to 330 in 1854 (Hall 1959, 82), a drop of 49.6 per cent. As a result, costs for lease and sale of estates going out of business became quite cheap. George William Gordon, for example, acquired three properties in Portland and St Thomas-in-the-East for £5,200 in 1847 and 1848. This represented only 3.2 per cent of the original cost of £160,000 (112).

Sugar exported from Jamaica fell from 900,000 cwts in 1847 to under 500,000 cwts in 1865 (117). Meanwhile, increase of foreign sugar imported into Britain moved from 480,000 cwts in 1831–40 to 4,600,000 cwts in 1861–63 compared to 3,400,000 cwts in 1831–40, with no movement (3,400,000) in 1861–63 for British West Indian sugar (85). At the same time, sugar imported from Mauritius and the British East Indies increased from 790,000 cwts to 1,700,000 cwts (85).

Of course, the decline in sugar cannot be attributed to the consequences of the Sugar Duties Act alone, although its passage, and the response of the plantocracy to it, became the primary cause of the serious deterioration in the island's sugar industry at that time. While the abolition of the old slave state and the creation of the new post-slavery state became the foundation of new socio-economic and political relations, the consequences of the passage of the Sugar Duties Act became a catalyst for the plantocracy adopting even more extreme positions in their relations with the black population. The planters conducted a bold and determined economic, political and ideological struggle to extract as much as possible out of the black masses. This, it was hoped, would help to compensate for their losses due to the removal of British protection from West Indian sugar.

The passage of the Sugar Duties Act was a logical follow up to the Emancipation Act. The abolition of slavery and the significant reduction of the power of the plantocracy was one of the first and clearest indications that the historic role that West Indian sugar played in the development of the British economy had come to an end. Britain had become the world's industrial giant and its manufacturing class needed to get British manufactured goods into foreign markets. If the industrial bourgeoisie hoped to get their products on the foreign markets they would have had to open their market to foreign competition. In this Free Trade regime, the British industrial bourgeoisie had few competitors in a world still dominated by agricultural production. Therefore, the British plantocracy had to become more competitive or become redundant.

It is Money They [Planters] Want, and Not Labour

The desire by planters to compensate for their economic losses led them to unleash a most oppressive tax regime on the black Jamaican population. This regime included drastic increases in tax on consumer goods such as saltfish and cloth. These were increased by 366 to 1,150 per cent between 1840 and 1865 (Robotham 1981, 46). There were also dramatic increases on tax on each horse, mule or donkey used by the masses for agricultural purposes and travel. Tax on a horse increased by 1,220 per cent and on a donkey by 1,580 per cent (46). The law required that a person possessing a donkey should pay three shillings and sixpence tax. If he/she owned a horse he/she was obliged to pay ten shillings plus one shilling licence. On the other hand, tax on horses and mules on the estates was reduced by 40 per cent to sixpence per head. A planter's horse working on roads outside his/her estate was not required to pay any tax. The harshness of the tax on poor people's horses, mules, donkeys and oxen were lamented by Baptist minister Henderson: 'It...is hard to make poor and old people who use their horses only to go to their ground... pay 11s., when Planters' stock used for working on roads are not so taxed' (Underhill 1865, 85). Cartwheels were also subjected to a tax of six shillings each.

There was a general reduction of tax on items used by the materially better off classes. Wood and imported lumber, for example, 'had their tax rate reduced by 52 per cent from 25s. to 12s. per 1,000 sq. ft.' between 1862 and 1865 (Robotham 1981, 47).

There was also the broadening of the range of taxable items to include once tax-free articles such as canoes and carts not used for plantation purposes. By 1865, the tax on canoes was 20 shillings each and on carts 18 shillings each (46).

General taxation was primarily used to finance projects from which the upper classes mostly benefited. By 1865, for example, over £40,000, or just about ten per cent of the national budget, was allocated to the official state church. At the same time, only one per cent of the budget (i.e., £3,000) went to education for over 100,000 children upwards of age five to 15. The official policy of taxing the population to finance the minority Anglican Church came in for bitter criticisms from ministers of the dissenting churches. Ministers Henderson and Reid opposed the scheme which 'contributes largely to the support of a Church Establishment, which is emphatically the church of the rich' (Underhill 1865, 86).

Another area for which public tax was imposed, but hardly benefited the labouring masses, had to do with the construction and/or repairs of roads and bridges. According to Revd Henderson:

> Vast sums are spent on the main roads, and on those which lead to estates, or pen, or to gentlemen's country mansions, whilst those which lead to the villages and freeholds of the people are sadly neglected, and many of them are dangerous to travel over (86).

This oppressive tax regime was complemented by steep rises in the cost of land rented or sold to blacks, even though land value was in continuous decline due to the massive losses suffered by the sugar industry. In 1854, for example, while the Tharp Estates comprising 20,000 acres of land were being leased yearly for £800 by a 'Mercantile Firm in Falmouth' (Hall 1959, 112), black people were 'compelled to rent land from the large proprietors at the rate of £2.8s.0d. per acre for one year' (Harvey and Brewin 1867, 102).¹ Thus, while the 'Mercantile Firm' in Falmouth was getting land to lease at the rate of 9.6 pence per acre per annum, a black person was paying £2.8s.0d. or 60 times more for lease/rent for an acre of land per year. The extremely high lease/rent that the black labouring classes had to pay to secure use of small plots of land was widespread throughout the colony (Harvey and Brewin 1867, 102) (Underhill 1865, 77–79). As with leased or rented land, acquisition through purchase meant one price for the black person and another price for the white or 'refined coloured' person. In addition to the high cost for land, the black purchaser had to come up with other sums for fulfilling the legal ramifications for ownership. In this way, the real cost of land could be more than doubled. The Baptist Ministers' Report to Governor Eyre highlighted this problem thus: 'The expensiveness of CONVEYING LAND is a great hinderance to the purchaser. The surveying, the titles, the stamps and the recording, often cost more than the original purchase' (Underhill 1865, 45).

The excessive taxes, the exorbitant rentals and cost for land severely fettered the ability of the labouring classes to create wealth and earn money on their own account. At the same time, the wages they earned from working on the estates, were steadily decreasing since 1864. Wages were cut from 25 to 50 per cent, according to the Baptist Ministers' Report (32). However, there were many other reports which suggested that wage reductions were as high as 60 per cent (33), (Harvey and Brewin 1867, 101).

The 25 to over 60 per cent cut in wages represented only part of a bigger reduction in wages. In reality, the cut in wages to the labouring classes was much higher because a tendency developed among the planters to increase the employment of women and children over men, while overall employment was drastically falling. Since women and children were traditionally paid far less than men, a 25 to 60 per cent cut in their wages meant that the overall take-home pay of the labourers represented less than the actual cut in wages because less men were being employed, while relatively more women and children were assigned to work in the rest of available jobs (Underhill 1865, 71, 61).

The massive unemployment was primarily due to the widespread bankruptcy in the sugar industry, the largest employer of labour in the island. In Trelawny, for example, the Missionary Report said 'the cultivation of several sugar estates has been suspended, throwing numbers, directly and indirectly dependent on them, out of employment' (51). The large amount of surplus labour, coupled with the high cost of living and the restriction of access to land, left the labouring classes humiliated and vulnerable. According to the *Anti-Slavery Reporter,* a correspondent in St Thomas-in-the-East wrote, in 1859, the following observation:

> You can have no idea of the number of people turned back from different estates every Monday morning because there is no work for them. The poor people often go away with tears in their eyes for the want of employment. These planters who are from time to time complaining that the people are lazy and won't work must know why they are uttering a downright falsehood. The truth is they cannot afford to employ the people. It is money they want, and not labour. Besides, many of them treat the people like brutes, especially those that are living upon the estates, and who rent provision grounds. If they do not submit to the bad treatment they are turned off the properties (Robotham 1981, 23).

Employers, especially on the estates, became engaged in a set of practices which undermined the principle of wage payment, a vital necessity to move the island away from coercive labour and pre-capitalist development to free labour and free enterprise. There was the widespread practice of employers withholding or stopping wages from their labourers 'for the merest trifles, under pretext of damage done to the estates' (Underhill 1865, 66). Labourers were sometimes not paid 'for weeks and months' and had to walk for their pay 'many times in rain; and sometimes, on some pretext or other, are kept out of it altogether' (67).

Not satisfied with withholding the labourers' meagre wages, the majority of planters shifted the method of allocating work. They moved from day's work to task work and increased the task while decreasing or continuing the original rate of payment. By increasing the task while maintaining the same wage, the planter ensured that the labourer produced more without additional compensation. By increasing the task and decreasing the wage, the planter ensured that the labourer produced more while having his wages cut (32).

The decline of sugar and the massive redundancies associated with it, was directly or indirectly responsible for lay-offs and redundancies in other sectors. Thus, many domestic servants, seamstresses, carpenters, masons, bakers and other skilled labourers and artisans could find little or no work. At best, they could only find occasional employment (90, 92).

While the vast majority of labourers earned less than £12 per annum in wages, government and state church officials were paid up to £5,000 per year. At the higher and lower poles of post-emancipation society, the gap in earnings between state officials and the labouring masses was more in the region of 1,000:1. While wages were cut for the labouring masses, government officials voted themselves increased salaries. In 1850, for example, the Assembly made into law 'an Act to provide an adequate salary to support the honour of Her Majesty's representative is this island' (*Laws of Jamaica*, Chapt. 1 of 1847 to Chapt. 45 of 1855. 'C' MDCCCLXIV, 235–36). In another example, the Assembly enacted another law in 1864 'to provide an adequate salary for the agent-general of immigration.' This salary was made adequate when it increased to £500 per annum (*Laws of Jamaica* Vol. IV, AD 1857–66, 395).

The cost of the social and economic policy of British colonialism and the plantocracy began to reveal itself in the acute social deterioration in the living conditions of the people by the early 1850s. Reports from across the island gave vivid descriptions of poverty and distress never experienced by the people since emancipation. From Montego Bay, Revd Henderson reported that:

> The peasantry are decidedly worse off. I never knew them so poor. Indeed, while at work many of them are half naked,... It will not, perhaps, be far wrong, speaking of them as a whole, to say that they now come to church in clothing similar to that in which they used to labour, and work in old things, in which formerly they would not have appeared out of doors. Many of the children are not clothed at all, and are therefore kept indoors and from school. The aged are also in many cases without decent clothing (Underhill 1865, 61–62).

In another report from Stacey Ville and Paradise in Clarendon, Revd Dalling said:

> I have been residing in this district twelve years, and never knew the times more severely felt by the labouring people than now.... It is a common thing now to meet with grown up young men and women who are as good as naked, so as to shock the eye of decency. Great numbers of the people have to be eating their meals without fish of any kind, not having the means of procuring that article, especially as it is so very dear at present (64).

Poverty and Man/Woman Relations

Women suffered more poverty and distress than men since they were the primary organiser and provider for the family and the black household. Many women who usually made their living from needlework, found themselves out of work, because the masses of people could no longer afford to dress as before (65).

The many instances of neglect of the aged and the emergence of large numbers of children roaming about would suggest that women, as well as men, were losing control of many households. Accordingly, the Baptist ministers noted that:

> Many persons mournfully fail in the discharge of parental duties, and neglect to bring up their children in habits of obedience, industry, self-respect, and honesty. Parents too often lose all proper control over their offsprings at an early age. In numerous cases children forsake the parental roof at eleven or twelve years of age, and frequently find too ready a welcome in the yards of vicious neighbours, under the influence of whose bad advice and example they give way to a reckless, lawless and roving disposition: become indolent and insolent (39–40).

The instability of the black family, a direct result of the extreme material degradation of the masses, also led to what the Baptist ministers called 'reckless sensuality which is now subverting social order and religious progress to an alarming extent' (65). This 'reckless sensuality', the ministers noted, was giving birth to 'helpless offspring of illicit connections from the heartless neglect of vicious parents' (45–46). Of course, many of these 'vicious parents' who were said to be 'subverting social order and religious progress to an alarming extent' were once churchgoers who could no longer attend services because of extreme poverty. This 'reckless sensuality' also reflected itself in the rise in prostitution, a signal that sex and sexual relations were in some respects becoming more transactional. Many women turned to prostitution. In this regard, the *County Union* (October 17, 1865) noted the following: 'In every town there are hundreds of females who cannot obtain work – who are actually starving unless they ply the harlot's trade' (qtd in Royal Commission 1866, 1,161).

In Kingston, the island's chief commercial centre, 'the shameless scenes of prostitution' was in full swing (qtd in Robotham 1981, 82). This 'reckless sensuality' was also evident when women had to give their bodies to 'officials who solicited sexual favours from women in lieu of taxes which the women were finding it difficult to pay' (Wilmot 1987, 13). Within the context of this 'reckless sensuality', the ministers, with much sorrow, said that 'Few marriages take place; and young men and women live in open concubinage' (Underhill 1865, 27).

The abject poverty and distress under which the people had to live was a main factor generating and/or heightening conflicts between black males and females. One case in point had to do with Samuel Bailey and his wife. Bailey, a resident of Hampden in Trelawny, was serving time in prison as an insolvent debtor when his wife was said to have slept with Alexander Reid. According to the *Falmouth Post* (February 25, 1848):

> [Reid] had an improper intimacy with the wife of Bailey, and that intimacy was encouraged by the parents of the abandoned woman. Bailey had been imprisoned at the Montego Bay Gaol, as an insolvent debtor: on his return home, he was told his wife had conducted herself in a lewd manner, and when he taxed her with having wronged him, she left his house, and went to reside with her father and mother, where males and females are in the habit of assembling night after night, for infamous purpose. He became exceedingly jealous, and having set a watch, soon discovered that his suspicions were well grounded.

Bailey allegedly responded by physically attacking Reid. In another case, one 'Mrs. Anderson' was arrested for attempting to poison her husband, Edward, a tailor residing at Jackson Town, Trelawny by putting 'pounded glass' in his soup (*Falmouth Post* May 24, 1859). According to a report, the couple had a 'very serious quarrel...arising from jealousy' (*Falmouth Post* November 18, 1859). There were also several reports of rapes or assaults with intent to commit rape by poverty stricken men on their female counterparts (*Falmouth Post* July 28, 1865). On Monday, August 7, 1865, for example, two rape cases were brought up in the Home Circuit Court, Precinct of Kingston. The *Colonial Standard* (August 8, 1865) reported on one of the cases in the following manner:

> The girl alleged to have been ravished is young – not, it seems, above 16 or 17. The medical evidence will, however, satisfy you that, though so young, she was certainly not deflowered by the prisoner, but had been accustomed to sexual intercourse with men... The want of chastity in a female is no answer to a charge of rape, which might be committed on a common prostitute; only to substantiate such an offence committed upon such a person, you would naturally require proof much stronger than in ordinary circumstances.

So bad had this state of affairs got that the authorities passed 'an Act to consolidate and amend the law relating to offenses against the Person' in 1864. This law increased the penalties for 'aggravated assaults on women or children' (Law of Jamaica Vol. IV, 1857–1865. 1912, 204).

The Bill also looked at 'Rape – Abduction and Defilement of Women'. It considered rape a 'felony' punishable by 'penal servitude for life, or any other not less than 3 years' (*Laws of Jamaica* Vol. IV 1857–1865, 204). The Act spoke about 'Procuring defilement of girl under 21' and 'Carnally knowing girl under 9' (*Laws of Jamaica* Vol. IV 1857–1865, 204). At the same time, it was not uncommon for men to desert their wives and children, thus increasing the number of broken homes. Accordingly, the editor of the *Falmouth Post* (August 22, 1865) noted that 'At present, we hear frequently of wives and children being deserted by husbands and fathers'.

Outside of sexual and family conflicts, broad relations between male and female took on an increasingly antagonistic character. Between 1863 and 1865 in St Thomas-in-the-East, for example, 39.4 per cent of criminal cases (heard in Bath) involving labourers had to do with conflicts between men and women. Fifty-seven per cent of these cases had to do with abuses and assaults in which men and women were complainants and defendants.[2] Common assaults of women by men also grew into major assaults. In the parish of Vere, for example, two women were murdered by three men whom the victim caught slaughtering a stolen ox. According to the *Morning Journal* newspaper, 'three men were discovered slaughtering an ox, which they were supposed to have stolen. The two women who made the discovery, were instantly seized and decapitated, and their bodies buried.' In another incident, two men were reported to have been detained and charged with murdering a 16-year-old girl on Slipe Pen Road.

Women who were prepared to kill their babies to save them from growing up under slavery and who, it would appear, never had to resort to such a measure under 'freedom', found themselves killing their infants. Several reports from different parts of the island of women killing their children were carried in the island's press throughout that period (*Falmouth Post* October 20, 1865) (*Colonial Standard* March 2, 1865).

That the level of crime was becoming exceedingly high did not escape the press and state officials, including the Governor and the Inspector of Prisons. An editorial in the *Falmouth Post* (August 18, 1865) noted that 'The progress of crime in the island is admitted by all persons who are careful observers of passing events.' More than a careful observer, the Inspector General of Prisons presented a report to the Executive Committee and the Assembly on October 1, 1864 which noted among other things:

> In my last Report it was my painful duty to remark on the increase of Crime throughout the island; but I did not expect it was to have increased to the enormous ratio it has done during the past twelve months. The number of persons in the General Penitentiaries have been greater than for many

years back, the District Prisons and Jails have had a like increase in numbers (*Falmouth Post* August 18, 1865).

The number of people sentenced to the General Penitentiary in Kingston, for example, increased from 283 in 1861 to 629 in 1864, a jump of 181.7 per cent (Royal Commission 1866, 809). Speaking more generally of the prisons across the island, Harvey and Brewin noted the following:

> In the general state of the prisons of the island there was much that was painful,...The working of prisoners in chains in the streets of Kingston; the reintroduction of the treadmill into the General Penitentiary; the use of old rice-bags for clothing in all the prisons – a costume needlessly degrading and incompatible with personal cleanliness; the mingling of all classes, criminals of a deep dye with those whose offenses are of a kind not declared simply but created by law, such as the plucking of fruit, growing in open or forest land (1867, 6).

Governor Eyre was acutely aware of the serious crime problem in the colony. He placed the rise of crime squarely on blacks who committed themselves and proposed 'stringent measures' to deal with the offenders (*Falmouth Post* August 18, 1865). In spelling out some of these 'stringent measures', the Inspector General of Prisons 'strongly advocates the infliction of corporal punishment, the use of the crank, the thread-wheel, and shot-drill, with recourse "to diet merely sufficient to keep a man in health"' (*Falmouth Post* July 18 1865).

The call for the return to standard torture methods used under slavery was seen as the only effective way of combating these crimes. Magistrate Robert Walcott, in expressing the feeling of the governing classes, said 'the fear of corporeal punishment is the only thing that has any effect upon the Negro' (Royal Commission 1866, 845).

Fear of a Return to Slavery

So bad had the conditions of the people got that it was widely believed among many of them that the ruling classes were about to reintroduce slavery. In St Elizabeth, for example, Archdeacon Rowe said: 'the greater portion of them (blacks) with the exception of a few, the most intelligent, was firmly convinced that they were going to become slaves again (645).

Roman Catholic priest, Joseph Woollett, made a similar observation: 'At Negro Hill, in Westmoreland, and afterwards in St. Elizabeth, it was reported that the people were to be made slaves, this I heard from the poor black people (547).

In a letter from 'a Negro' written to the *Watchman* newspaper, May 1859, the author voiced his/her fears of the possible return to slavery. These fears were generated by local and international factors. He/she said:

> Our liberties and our lives are endangered by the way how things are carried on in this island, and we fear that unless something is done to alter the present oppression that upwards of 300,000 of Her Majesty's subjects of this island will be starred or sold into slavery, and, no doubt, we may have the mortification of seeing the much dreaded and hated American stars and stripes flying over our head (qtd in *Falmouth Post* May 24, 1859).[3]

Slavery was the worst thing to happen to the black race in modern history. The 'present oppression', of which this 'Negro' wrote in 1859, appeared to him/her to be edging back to slavery. Indeed, it can be argued in some ways that the people were worse off under emancipation than under slavery. In many ways, the use of taxes, wages and land, extracted more value from the black masses for the governing classes than the use of the whip and shackle did under slavery. Simply put, under emancipation, former slave owners were putting less in the process of production and extracting more value than they did under slavery. Under the whip and shackle, enslaved blacks were given clothes, food rations, and a plot of land to do farming to supplement the food rations. They paid no taxes, medical bills or rent nor did they have to buy the tools they needed for agricultural purposes. Under emancipation, the blacks had to find everything – at costs ten times higher than what planters would have had to pay. On top of that, the labouring classes were required to pay a higher percentage of taxes than the plantocracy, while earning wages that rendered their labour almost similar to serf labour. Overall, slavery was comparatively worse, especially respecting the issue of freedom.

The fears that slavery was coming back stemmed from other factors as well. The passage of a series of bills into laws in the colony's parliament convinced many blacks that steps were being taken to reintroduce slavery. The 'New Immigration Bill' of 1858, for example, was viewed by the *Watchman* as the 'opening of a slave trade under the fictitious name of Immigration (qtd in *Falmouth Post* March 12, 1858). On February 15, 1865, two laws were passed. One, called 'An Act to Authorise the Infliction of Corporal Punishment In Certain Cases of Larceny, and Other Offenses', reintroduced whipping; that hated symbol of slavery (*Laws of Jamaica*, Chapts. 1–45 or 1864–1865 MDCCCLXIV, 731-33). The treadmill, another instrument of the torturous past, was also reintroduced. Importation of several of the implements of torture was resumed in 1865. The *Gleaner* reported the arrival in the island of the aforementioned implements: 'We learn that, the treadmills for the General Penitentiary have arrived by the Barque Westmoreland; and that they will be speedily erected, to serve all who may require their use (qtd in *Falmouth Post* December 5, 1865).

The second law was called 'An Act to Empower Justices of the Peace to Apprentice Persons Who Shall be Respectively Under the Age of Sixteen, Convicted of Petty Larceny.' This law made it:

> lawful for any two Justices of the Peace of this island, exercising summary jurisdiction, to apprentice to any householder carrying on business or trade, handicraft mystery or calling, or to any proprietors of estates, pens, or plantations as labourers, to look after live stock, or to families, a domestic servant, willing to take them for five years, any person or persons who, being under the age of sixteen years shall be convicted of stealing, or of destroying, or damaging with intent to steal, any tree, plant, root, fruit, or any other vegetable production growing in any garden, orchard, provision ground, or cane, or coffee, or pimento field, whether enclosed or not, or of the larceny of articles, or produce, or small stock, the value where of shall not exceed the sum of ten shillings (*Lasw of Jamaica* Chapts. 1–45, 1864–65, 733–34).

With the passage of this law, nothing could convince masses of black people in 1865 that the return to slavery was not imminent. In St Elizabeth, for example, the Revd John Seilas said there was 'Great excitement', a 'mournful excitement' among the people because 'they were [afraid] of being enslaved again.' Seilas said one black teacher said 'he believed there was danger,... that the people would be again apprenticed for five years'(Royal Commission 1866, 637). This minister of religion noted that the widespread fear in that parish of a return to slavery might be due to the fact that 'a number of boys had been received from a reformatory, and they were apprenticed for five years on an estate in St Elizabeth' (637). He said the people looked upon that as a recurrence of slavery.

The passage of the 'Whipping Bill' was viewed in a similar manner. The *Anti-Slavery Reporter* saw this as proof that 'the pro-slavery spirit does exist in the island' and gave notice that the Anti-Slavery Society of England would not allow 'that issue to be pushed aside' (qtd in *Falmouth Post* August 15, 1865). The real and imagined perceptions of the black masses about the re-imposition of slavery in Jamaica dangerously heightened the antagonisms between the labouring classes and its allies on the one hand, and the ruling classes on the other hand.

The abolition of slavery formally ended Jamaica's role as a strategic capital accumulating outpost for the development of the British economy.

Consequently, the importance of the island to Britain after emancipation fell in that country's list of colonial priorities. Meanwhile, the planter/mercantile forces who were still administering the colony, continued to regard Jamaican sugar as their number one priority. The significant lowering of Jamaica's importance to Britain on the one hand, and its continued importance to the plantocracy on the other hand, led to a determined effort by the planters to strengthen their hold on the local state power. This determination was hastened by the fact that emancipation opened up new prospects for the black masses to struggle for self-determination.

The abolition of slavery speeded up the process of Jamaicanisation, that internal development giving rise to peculiar feelings, attitudes, and language that were distinctly Jamaican. Because of the unprecedented prospects that emancipation allowed for the black people to struggle against their historic enemies, the ruling classes were forced to reorganise and strengthen the organs of state power to meet the new challenges. The new situation, it would appear, required a state possessing the capabilities to act more like a national power rather than a loose power of estates under a governor, assembly and military.

Which Direction – The Colonial State?

While the Jamaican interest section of the ruling classes and the British Colonial rulers saw the need to keep former enslaved blacks on the periphery of power in the colony, they disagreed on how political power should be wielded in the island. The Jamaican planters and merchants felt that they should play the leading role in exercising state power. The colonial authorities, however, felt that the ex-slave owners were incapable of doing so. They felt that if state power were wielded by the plantocracy, the planters and merchants would continue to use their position in the Assembly to frustrate British policy objectives vis-à-vis the island colony. More importantly, the colonial authorities felt that the black masses and their allies would, in a short period of time, become the majority in the island's parliament, posing a far greater threat to British rule in Jamaica. As early as 1838, Henry Taylor, a senior civil servant in the Colonial Office, proposed the abolition of West Indian Assemblies to save the colonies from too much control by the plantocracy and especially from potential black legislators who would be intolerable (Hart 1974, 13). Meanwhile, on June 1, 1847, Earl Grey, Secretary of State for the Colonies, wrote to Charles Grey, Governor of Jamaica, expressing the deep fear the Colonial Office felt for the safety of the island – under the plantocracy.

> From all I can hear it seems certain that before long the negro population will obtain a preponderating influence in the Assby., & considering their ignorance and the degree to which they are under the influence of persons who would not I fear use power very discreetly, it seems most important that before this change takes place, the authority of the Crown should for the protection of the higher classes be somewhat strengthened (13).

By August of that same year, the Secretary of State repeated his assertions and fears in another letter:

> It is perfectly clear that the acquisition of property by the blacks and the distress of the planters must both contribute to throw in a very few years the power of returning a majority of the Assembly entirely into the hands of the former, and I fear they will not have this power long before the influence of the dissenting missionaries and especially of the Baptists leads them to use it to carry measures most injurious to the planters and as I think to the Colony (13).

Just under two years later, Grey again returned to the question of power in Jamaica. In a letter dated March 16, 1849, he strongly criticised the planters, who, by their unwillingness to give the Executive of the Colony power over the Assembly, would lead to blacks taking over the reins of power (14).

Meanwhile, despite the proponents of direct Crown Colony rule, the planters were determined to remain key players with respect to the question of state power in Jamaica. They took several measures to restrict the elective franchise to the barest minimum to black males of legal voting age. The right of the male to vote depended on the extent of his or his wife's asset, income and tax contribution to the state. The women had no right to the elective franchise. The electoral laws ensured that only a handful of males drawn principally from the upper classes could be elected to the island Legislature. Out of a population of over 430,000, only 1,903 or less than one-half per cent had the right to vote, of which 1,457 exercised that right to elect 47 Assembly men in 1864 (Underhill 1971, 3).

Notes

1. Stated in 'The Humble Petition of the Poor People of Jamaica and Parish of St Ann.'
2. Calculated from statistics presented to the Royal Commission in Royal Commission 1866, 1,083–98.
3. The *Watchman* newspaper represented the left wing of the brown middle class and black own-account professionals, small farmers and labourers.

3 'Buckra Has Gun, Negro Has Firestick': Post-Emancipation Political Struggles

> Whenever they [black people] are brought together they begin to think too much. They are ignorant, and it makes them think above their sphere, and they begin to give opinion upon points that they cannot grapple.
>
> – Alexander Gordon Fyfe

Developments in post-slavery Jamaica were marked by persistent and sometimes acute political struggles between former enslaved Africans and their allies on the one hand, and the ex-slave owners and their allies on the other hand. The African people waged a determined struggle against race and class oppression, never before witnessed in the history of Jamaica. The ruling classes, despite facing many uprisings during nearly 200 years of British imposed slavery, had never been so pressed to defend and justify their position in colonial society.

Forms of struggle that were hardly possible for the African to employ under slavery became real possibilities in post-slavery conditions. The use of petitions, resolutions, the press, letters to newspapers, deputations, election campaigns and canvassing, public mass meetings and strikes became new or qualitatively developed forms of struggles utilised by the black masses in post-slavery Jamaica. In addition, old forms such as insurrectionary means employed during slavery were never abandoned. The new situation allowed black political activists and their allies to discuss and formulate socio-economic and political demands, and publicly agitate and educate the masses to accept and fight for their realisation. The ruling classes, long used to employing the gun, whip, treadmill and shackle to force black people to accept white domination were now faced with the fact that they would have to compete with black, coloured and progressive white leaders for the minds of the black masses. Indeed, they had to send their journalists to meetings organised by black and coloured leaders and use the press, their ministers of religion, legislators, et al. to contend with and refute the viability of the alternatives that were being proposed to the people by their leaders. In this new situation, however, the ex-slave owning classes still had the decided advantage. They had control of the principal means of production, the press, military, legislature and means of communication and transportation. They had the advantage in making use of the deep feeling and psychology of inferiority cultivated in the minds of many blacks for almost 200 years. Above all, the ruling classes had the backing of Britain, the most powerful and experienced colonial power and technologically the most advanced state in the world.

Leaders among the people attacked laws passed by the Assembly as not in the interest of the masses. Consequently, they came under consistent fire from conservative leaders and the conservative press. In one such attack, a *Falmouth Post* editorial (April 8, 1859) said:

> Every opportunity has been seized to inflame the minds of the people. In the month of November 1858, Mr. James Taylor told them at a public meeting, that certain members of the House of Assembly, 'wished to reduce them to a state worse than that of vassalage': and Mr. Johnson, the Editor of the *Watchman*, asserted, 'that the tendency of all legislation during the last twenty years, has been to degrade the people, and deprive them of their rights and liberties as free men.' The reverend agitator added, 'that the Barons, at the point of the sword, wrested Magna Carta from King John': and the language of another reverend speaker, called Roach, was equally strong and inflammatory.

Apart from broad agitation against laws passed by the Assembly, leaders among the people also mobilised the masses against specific pieces of legislation. The new Immigration Bill, for example, became a main issue for which the people were mobilised to oppose. In its opposition to this bill the *Watchman* appealed to 'every sane man' on the island to denounce the proposed law and work to prevent it from receiving the Royal assent:

> Every sane man in the colony must pronounce the working out of such a measure, as simply impossible, the system of serfdom which it contemplates establishing, can never be grafted upon a condition of free society, such as exists in this island... if the Friends of Freedom in Jamaica, allow the act to receive the Royal assent, without protesting against it, then they will virtually admit the failure of Emancipation.... if the labouring people of this country, will tamely and quietly stand by, and allow a law like this to come into operation amongst them, then, they themselves will richly deserve to be made slaves again. [The] labouring people of this country, must be energetic in their movements (qtd in *Falmouth Post* March 12, 1858).

For their part, the conservative press and leaders of the ruling classes had to do what they would never have done under slavery. They were forced to publicly defend and justify their actions before the black masses. They were forced to verbally dismiss those who were opposed to the passage of the new Immigration Bill, among other things. Thus, the *Falmouth Post* (March 12, 1858) stated the following in its editorial:

> The crusade against the new Immigration Bill, has commenced, and the 'Friends of Freedom' are not only up, but doing an immense deal of Mischief... The 'Friends of Freedom are trying to get up 'popular demonstrations,' and these demonstrations should be met by a counter-movement on the part of all who desire the well-being of the island. Above all, there should be a oneness of purpose among the conductors of the Press.

Campaigns were also waged against the Election law and the whole system of representation in Jamaica. On February 24, 1859, for example, a meeting to petition the Queen against the election Law which was recently enacted by the House of Assembly was held at the court house in Kingston. The meeting was chaired by George William Gordon, who called on the people to 'protest against the Act' (*Colonial Standard* qtd in *Falmouth Post* March 1, 1859). Gordon told the meeting that 'There was a strong desire to centralise everything in the hands of the Government, although Responsible Government had done nothing to benefit the country' (*Falmouth Post* March 1, 1859). That meeting passed several resolutions in opposition to the Election Law. Several speakers placed the blame for the concentration of representation in the hands of the ruling classes squarely on the plantocracy who looked at black people as 'they would on dogs'. The *Colonial Standard* reported that:

> Mr Alexander Sinclair, one of the members of the Jamaica Reform Association, moved the first resolution, and declared that the election Law would make serfs of poor men, and attributed this to the plantocracy, who looked on his class as they would on dogs (qtd in *Falmouth Post* March 1, 1859).

The second resolution was moved by Revd R.A. Johnson, Editor of the *Watchman*, who spoke of the importance of representative government for the people. He viewed the gains made by the people with respect to the elective franchise and representation as the product of political struggle waged by men of the liberal party against the ruling classes.

> Under a constitutional form of government, the channel through which the power of the people flowed, was representation, and hence it was that the Assembly made every effort to deprive the people of the elective franchise. Shortly after Emancipation, an election law was passed through the instrumentality of the Honourable Edward Jordan, the Honourable Robert Osborn, James Taylor, and Charles Lake, Esqrs., who were then the strength of the liberal party, but soon after it was found that that law gave too much power to the people, and it was amended by the passing of an act making the

payment of taxes on a certain day, a condition for voting. The object of this act was to deprive the small men of the right of the elective franchise, and the dominant party now with the same view, had imposed a tax of 10s. on every qualification to vote. The object of the last act was to make the people the political slaves of the dominant party, who have perpetrated all the misery in the land (*Falmouth Post* March 1, 1859).

The question of representative democracy was a very important issue for the black population, especially own-account/freeholders and their coloured and white allies. In the normal run of things, they tended to the view that the best or only way to change things in their favour, was to put people in the Assembly who would implement their agenda and repeal oppressive laws. Hence, even if they did not succeed in having broader representation by political means, extraordinary work should be undertaken to ensure that the necessary material requirements set by the Assembly to acquire the franchise were met. In this respect, the Revd James Roach, a participant of the aforementioned courthouse meeting said: 'the only way to remove the Slave Laws from the Statute Book of this country was for the people to work and pay the 10s. fee, and sweep from the Assembly the whole of those who had been oppressing them' (*Falmouth Post* March 1, 1859).

Despite the fact that Revd Roach's recommendation was long practised, it would take a national uprising 106 years after slavery was abolished for emancipation to yield a fundamentally higher degree of representative democracy.[1]

The campaign against the Election Law was only part of a wider struggle for greater representation and democracy in Jamaica. In their struggles for reform, the people and their leaders made several demands which, in essence, were elements of an alternative programme to the policy of the ruling classes. Their varied demands for reforms were present in the passage of resolutions, in speeches at public meetings, in letters to the editors of newspapers, in petitions, through representations in the Assembly and Vestry, etc.

Among those demands was the call for the training of the 'rising generation' in all 'branches of mechanical, commercial and agricultural industry, the arts, science, jurisprudence, religion and political economy' (*Sentinel* January 30, 1865). There was a demand for 'sanitary improvements in the lives of the people' (Royal Commission 1866, 1,156) and a call to increase the education budget along with better training and pay for teachers (*Sentinel* January 27, 1865). There was also a call for the 'abolition of all export duties on produce' and 'the free admission of all agricultural implements and machines used in the cultivation of the soil and in the preparation of its production, and the imposition of only a nominal tax on horse kind and asses used in agriculture, and in the conveyance of produce to the market – as measures which ought to be adopted as soon as possible for the purpose of increasing production by stimulating and encouraging the industry of the country' (Underhill 'C' 1865, 20).

George William Gordon, the most widely known leader of the people, had what could be regarded as the closest thing to moving in the direction of an alternative programme for development in Jamaica. In his election manifesto presented to the people of St Thomas-in-the-East in 1859, Gordon, who was campaigning for a seat in the House of Assembly, proposed to struggle for the repeal of the Clergy Law which levied taxes on the people to support the official state church; a reduction of import duties which were partial and oppressive; a reduction of the rates of stamp duty on conveyances of land...; the amending of the Main Road Act and the building and repairing of roads 'leading to negro villages and settlements'; and the establishment of an 'Island Collegiate Institution, where our youths may be instructed and qualified to fill the highest positions in society' (*Falmouth Post* July 29, 1859).

The masses, their leaders, and the demands they made for reform, were often times ridiculed and treated with scorn, arrogance and contempt by the ruling classes. The *Falmouth Post* (September 13, 1859) provided a typical example of the kind of arrogance and contempt shown to the people. The author of an article entitled, 'Another Popular Demonstration', was giving his assessment of a meeting of labourers, held at Mount Industry, 'Above Rocks' in St Thomas-in-the-Vale:

> There is a property in the 'Above Rocks' district of Saint Thomas in the Vale called Mount Industry; and, in a 'spacious Coffee Store' on this property, 'kindly lent for the purpose, by the proprietor, Mr. Henry Davis', a large number of persons – oppressed labourers, of course – assembled on Thursday, the 1st September, to listen to eloquent speeches about popular rights and privileges, class legislation, and the thousand and one other evils connected with the present government of the country. The WATCHMAN of the 5th instant, contains a report of proceedings of the important occasion, and from this report we learn, that Samuel Rodgers, Esquire, was called to the Chair: that the call was readily obeyed: and that the said Mr. Rodgers, appreciating the high honour conferred on him by the greasy, unwashed citizens, (who, instead of idling away time, should have been profitably employed in digging cane holes or boiling sugar), delivered himself 'of an admirable opening address'; pointing out the 'encroachments which had been made during the last years upon the liberties of the People by the Legislature': denounced certain members, 'who, having obtained seats in the Assembly through the People's support, had basely betrayed the People's interest.'

Whether the proprietor was one who organised the production and distribution of ideas, as was the case with the editor of the *Falmouth Post*, or the proprietor engaged in sugar or coffee production as Alexander Gordon Fyfe, their arrogance and contempt for the masses were unmistakable. Thus, in the spirit of the *Falmouth Post*, Fyfe said of the black masses: 'Whenever they are brought together they begin to think too much. They are ignorant, and it makes them think above their sphere, and they begin to give opinions upon points that they cannot grapple' (Royal Commission 1866, 901).

In 1865, Fyfe would lead a contingent of Maroons to track down and unfurl a carnival of violence against Bogle and his followers in St Thomas-in-the-East as he did in 1832 against Sam Sharpe and enslaved Africans in western Jamaica.

The implications of this racist arrogance and intolerance of persons such as Fyfe meant that major reforms benefiting black people would remain unlikely to come to term unless they literally shook up colonial society. Reforms had no basis for implementation if elective franchise, representative democracy, reasonable taxes, for which the people campaigned, were regarded by the plantocracy as things 'above their sphere' of thinking and 'points that they cannot grapple.' This type of thinking provided a recipe for confrontation and social explosion, since the black masses had nothing to give, because they were the product of a recent past that held them as stocks, and when they were freed they got no reparation.

If the people could not think, if they were incapable of grappling with the operation and organisation of society, then obviously, they needed people of superior intellect (white or near white people) to do it for them. Such was the logic of white supremacy. These leaders of the people were regarded by the ruling classes as evil men, 'nigger worshippers', 'sedition-mongers who travel from county to county for the dissemination of dangerous, revolutionary doctrines' (*Falmouth Post* April 8, 1859). The struggles of the people were, therefore, regarded as something imposed from without, rather than their intrinsic response to post-slavery oppression and injustice.

The efforts of the people to bring about reforms could thus be shown no leniency. In this respect, the editor of the *Falmouth Post* (April 8, 1859) proposed the strengthening of the armed forces on the island as one way of dealing with the situation. He called for:

> A well organised Police Force – a standing militia composed of men in whom confidence can be reposed – and the re-occupation of barracks by military troops, to whose commanders the Magistracy can apply for assistance in every case of absolute emergency.

The proprietor of the *Falmouth Post* also proposed that leaders of the people should be spied on, that their activities be monitored and the law 'be made to fall heavily upon all who are convicted of sowing the seed of sedition' (*Falmouth Post* April 8, 1859). For the same reason, Fyfe wrote to William Hosack after the Underhill meeting in Vere, early in 1865, expressing his fears of disturbance. He urged the authorities to act before it was too late.

> There was a general excitement that led me to think there would be a disturbance; and I wrote Mr. Hosack to that effect, after the meeting in Vere, to say that I thought the law officers of the Crown ought to interfere; that things were going too far, that is, the meetings held by Mr. Gordon; and they were I thought sleeping upon a volcano (Royal Commission 1866, 901).

Raising Violence

It was hardly surprising, therefore, that within the broad context of the people's struggles for reform, members of the labouring classes resorted to individual or collective violence and other forms of protests involving the use of force to counter the uncompromising hardline positions of the ruling classes. In 1865, just prior to the Morant Bay conflict, for example, came reports of the two separate incidents of violence involving in each case, a labourer attacking his employer. The first incident occurred on the Spring Estate near Lucea in Hanover. According to the *Colonial Standard* (October 19, 1865):

> A serious assault was committed a few weeks ago, at Spring Estate, a few miles from the town of Lucea, on the person of Mr. Elijah Vosper. It appears that Mr. Vosper; the Lessee of Spring, on riding through a field, observed a lot of cane trash, and saw a labourer, Cambridge Barker, eating canes. He remonstrated with Barker who became insolent, saying that he would eat as many canes as he pleased. Mr. Vosper desired him to leave, but he refused, and an attempt being made to eject him, he stabbed Mr. Vosper with a knife which entered one of his eyes; and threatened to do the same to any person who should dare approach him.

What alarmed the *Colonial Standard* was the show of 'a most improper sympathy' for Barker by the 'peasantry' who attended the preliminary examination of the matter at the courthouse (*Colonial Standard* October 19, 1865).

The other incident took place on the Round Hill Estate, also in Hanover. The overseer of that estate, one 'Mr. Seivwright' was assaulted by Cuniffe, a labourer. Seivwright, who was considered to be in 'a dying state', miraculously survived and gave the following statement:

> About a month ago, I gave the prisoner Cuniffe the job of cleaning a pasture. He informed me last Friday, that the job was finished, and he wished to have it measured. I told him the amount due would be deducted from the rent he owed. He said I wanted to rob him, and I ordered him to leave the house, but he would not go, and I shut the door in his face to get rid of him. On the following morning while I was riding over the estate, I saw Cuniffe, and told him to go to the house for the chain. He came towards me, took hold of the bridle on the horse, lifted his macheat, and chopped through the large bone of my right arm. Seeing that he aimed another blow at my head, I attempted to dodge on the opposite side of my horse's neck, when he made a chop at my head, cut off a piece of the scalp, and laid the brains bare. He chopped my head a second time, and on my falling he wounded my hand, and inflicted three cuts on my neck – two of the last cuts penetrating from the side of my neck down to the gullet (*Colonial Standard* September 14, 1865).

These two incidents revealed the deep antagonisms between the plantocracy and the labouring classes, even though in both instances, they revealed themselves in conflicts between two individuals. Incidentally, when members of the ruling classes employed violence against members of the labouring classes, the conservative press which sided with the upper class victims of labourers' violence, sympathised with the employers of violence against blacks. One such case was reported by the *Colonial Standard* (September 14, 1865). Naval Officer, Captain Thomas Stephen kicked and killed a black boy in Port Antonio. According to the newspaper:

> On Thursday evening last, the quiet little town of Port Antonio was thrown suddenly into considerable excitement, the streets crowded by the rabble shouting vengeance on the Magistracy. On enquiry it was soon discovered that the Captain of the Brigantine 'Isabella Thompson' was in custody for kicking a boy. It appears that the Captain had been drinking rather freely during the day, and all the vagrants of the town, as he walked about the streets, hissed and teased him at a great rate, which got the Captain very much excited. At about half-past six in the evening, the Captain was at Mr. Escoffery's liquor shop, and a sickly boy, named Gilchrist, happened to be there. The boy was ordered out of the shop by Mr. Escoffery, and not moving off immediately, he was ordered off the second time. The Captain then gave him a kick.

The boy died about an hour after 'from one or more kicks' according to the inquest held on his body.

The year 1859 saw the first two serious cases of collective violence by the labouring classes against the ruling classes. The 'Toll-Gates Riots', the first of the two outbreaks commenced 'on Saturday night', February 12, 1859 at Truro, Westmoreland when labourers destroyed the toll gates. The following evening, the protestors, numbering 200–300, returned, pulled down the toll-keeper's house and wounded the toll-keeper (*Falmouth Post* February 22, 1859). By Monday the 14th, the Truro protestors were joined 'by residents in Savanna-la-Mar' who 'assembled at Manning Toll-gate near the town', and 'completely destroyed it' along with the Toll-keeper's house (*Falmouth Post* February 22, 1859). According to reports, 'they proceeded to Dunbar's River, marching to the music of a fife, horn, and tambourine – the ringleaders being disguised in female attire' (*Falmouth Post* February 22, 1859). There they destroyed all the toll-gates along with another 'on the road leading to Smithfield Wharf' as well as one 'on the leeward road' (*Falmouth Post* February 22, 1859).

The movement of the protestors was such and the sympathy it generated among the lower classes led to 'a general work stoppage...on all estates except Belleisle' when some were brought to trial (Schuler 1980, 100). During the trial on May 9, 1859 in Savanna-la-Mar, there was a 'vast assemblage in the streets' (*Falmouth Post* February 22, 1859). Among them were 'bands of armed men who went from St. James to Westmoreland to aid and abet,' what the *Falmouth Post* (February 22, 1859), called 'outrage.' Some 2,000 'ruffians', according to that newspaper, 'crowded the Court House' and 'intimidated the Judge and Jurors' (*Falmouth Post* February 22, 1859).

The toll gates revolt was blamed by conservative quarters on 'low radicalism' (*Falmouth Post* February 25, 1859). As proof of this 'low radicalism' the *Falmouth Post* (February 25, 1859) quoted the *Watchman*'s correspondent, who wrote that the protestors were 'determined to take the matter into their own hands,' that they 'went resolutely to work' and 'are resolved, no longer to endure the oppression to which they have been subjected.'

Six months after the toll gates events came the 'Trelawny Riots'. These grew out of land tenure disputes at Florence Hall Pen in Trelawny which, according to reports, led to rioting. Further trouble broke when all but one of the persons apprehended in connection with the Florence Hall Pen incident were freed by 'a large number of men and women', who set upon the police and two magistrates entrusted with taking the prisoners to the Falmouth gaol (*Falmouth Post* August 2, 1859). The crowd proceeded to attack the police station and the houses of Bourke, Justices Lindo and Nunes with 'stones and other missiles'.

The crowd retreated when Castle read the Riot Act. The rebels returned, however, and resumed stoning the police station when the police opened fire on them, killing three. Present at the police station while it was under attack were prominent members of the Trelawny planter and merchant classes – Kitchen, Castle, Salmon, Abraham, Lindo, Bliss, M.A. Nunes and Fowles. Following the shooting incident, at least two fires were started in the town. The roof of 'one of the buildings connected with the Druggist Store of Mr. Charles Delgado, was in bright flame' (*Falmouth Post* August 5, 1859). Another fire gutted 'one of the stores on the Trelawny Wharf' (*Falmouth Post* August 5, 1859). That wharf was operated by George Delisser and Son.

Over 140 persons were arrested in connection with the disturbances in the town. Most of them were charged with 'riot' and/or 'assault' (*Falmouth Post* August 19, 1859). The authorities of the parish felt it necessary to request police reinforcement from St James, St Ann and Hanover. Soldiers were also sent in to prevent further outbreaks.

These disturbances became the basis for island-wide debates. Both the upper and lower classes were drawing lessons and taking stock of these conflicts. Two main lessons were cited by the ruling classes. In the first place, some felt that the 'ring leaders' of the disturbances were out to have 'vengeance'. They wanted to make the island 'another Saint Domingo' (*Falmouth Post* August 12, 1859). These 'ring leaders', it was felt, were aiming to 'murder the White male inhabitants, whose wives [would] be employed as servants to their concubines'. The 'respectable portion of the coloured population' would also 'share the same fate' (*Falmouth Post* August 12, 1859). The second lesson drawn by members of the ruling classes was never to be restrained or lenient with black people and their backers who employed force 'to break through restraints of the law'. It was felt that the authorities were too soft on those who participated in the first 'riots' and, as a result, people were encouraged to 'riot' a second time. This view was echoed by the *Morning Journal* when it stated that:

> The riots in Trelawny, are in some measure, to be attributed to the mistaken leniency with which the parties to the late disorders in Westmoreland were treated... but no one who is acquainted with the character of the people – generally peaceable and perhaps difficult to be aroused into action, but when once stirred utterly ungovernable – will deny, that the only means to prevent the contagion of disorder spreading from one district, and at length assuming dimensions such as to render existing means of suppression abortive, is to make a signal and most forcible example of those who are the first to break through the restraints of the law (qtd in *Falmouth Post* August 12, 1859).

The conclusions drawn and the experience gained from dealing with the two disturbances became for the ruling classes, a sort of dress rehearsal for the suppression of the Morant Bay Rebellion, five years later. From among the masses, one of the most important lessons drawn was said to have been pointed out by Revd Roach at a public meeting in Kingston. He said the masses have proven 'that the People were a rising People' that 'they had the power of opposing the laws: and the late movement in Savanna-la-Mar showed what the people were' (*Falmouth Post* March 4, 1859). This lesson and the people's experience would doubtlessly become a sort of dress rehearsal for their rising in October 1865.

The growth of mass activities in Jamaica from 1858 to 1865 was certain indication of the determination of the black population to effect reform, and a similar determination by the plantocracy to oppose it. From the so-called 'New Agitation Movement' of 1858, the 'Riots' of 1859, the 'Great Revival' of 1860–61 and 'The Underhill Meetings' of 1865, thousands of black people throughout the island participated in the struggle for reform. Their actions, sometimes secular, sometimes religious, sometimes violent and forceful, sometimes moral and spiritual, were all aimed at giving real meaning to emancipation.

The year 1865 saw the most frequent mobilisation of the people around the country to protest the poor state of the colony and to press for reform. The people frequently came together in activities with distinctive political motives. Between April and September 1865, public meetings, some known as the 'Underhill Meetings', or 'Underhill Convocations' were held across the island. These meetings bore the name of Edward Underhill, a leading British Baptist official who compiled a report called the 'Underhill Letter', exposing the poverty-stricken condition of the Jamaican labouring classes to Governor Eyre. The meetings were held, among other things, in support of Underhill's Letter which the authorities tried to discredit.

Interestingly, the first set of meetings was supported by important sections of the ruling classes who saw in them a potentially important political weapon to pressure Britain into doing more to improve the economic conditions of the Jamaican planters and merchants. They also supported and played a leading role in the meetings out of disagreements with the leadership style and policy of Governor Eyre. On the basis of these two motives, it can be argued that the meetings had something in common for both the labouring classes and the upper classes. It was little wonder, therefore, that the *Falmouth Post* (May 30, 1859), promoted those meetings and encouraged the convening of others.

The wronged inhabitants of Jamaica are waking at last, and we trust it will be a successful effort to obtain Justice from the Queen and the imperial Parliament. Public meetings have been held in Kingston and Spanish Town, in Montego Bay, Lucea, and Savanna-la-Mar, in Chapelton, and Mandeville, and in all these towns Resolutions, strongly but respectfully worded, have been agreed to, setting forth the fact, of a complete paralysation of agriculture, and a lamentable decadence of commerce in all parts of the Island. They felt the sad, truthful, tale of estates being rendered un-remunerative and almost valueless by the equalisation in England of the duties of Free and Slave-manufactured sugar, they reprobate the improvident and wasteful expenditure of money by our Governor and Legislature: and they declare, that the continuance of the Cuban Slave-trade on the one hand, and the reckless financial policy pursued by the Authorities here and the People's Representatives on the other, must inevitably lead to increased poverty, destitution, and crime, and compel the withdrawal of the diminished capital which is at present in circulation. Trelawny has not yet followed the example of her sister parishes in the country of Cornwall, and we earnestly call upon its Custos to adopt the means necessary to issue an immediate demonstration by planters, merchants, and other persons who have property at stake, and who are naturally concerned in the future well-being or ruin of the colony. Public meetings can only be effective by being held in every town: and it is the duty of all classes of the population to be up and doing – to seek by legal, constitutional means, the concession of privileges to which they are honestly entitled.

However, the euphoria in these public meetings soon ended for planters and merchants. The *Falmouth Post* and those planters and merchants who supported and participated in some of these meetings, took a complete about turn when the leaders of the labouring classes asserted their positions with the backing of the masses who comprised almost the entire audience of subsequent meetings. This meant that the meetings increasingly became an instrument of race and class struggle between the plantocracy and the labouring population, just like when Myaalists took over the Great Revival in 1860 and 1861. While the planters sought to restrict the meetings to adopting resolutions denouncing the equalisation of sugar duties, which they blamed for most of the island's socio-economic ills, leaders representing the black masses denounced high taxes, the immigration policy, low wages and bad government which they blamed on the upper classes. The meeting held in Montego Bay on May 19, 1865 was a good example of the contention between the interests of the plantocracy and labour. According to the *Falmouth Post* (May 26, 1865):

> Mr. Bourke, the Senior Representative of the Parish, submitted several Resolutions that he had prepared, and stated that, in his opinion, the sufferings of the colonists have been caused by the equalisation of the Sugar Duties Act, and by enormous taxation employed in the Department of the Public Service.

However, a reverend gentleman held a different perspective and emphasis from the senior Parliamentarian, which he declared for all to hear, only to be immediately denounced by a planter.

> The Reverend Mr. Hewett (Baptist Missionary) declaimed against the support, at the public cost, the Established Church; and declared, that the labouring people had been oppressed by being required to pay for the importation of immigrants for the sole benefit to the Plantocracy. This declaration was denounced by a gentleman who is in charge of estates, and he and others engaged in the manufacture of sugar left the meeting (*Falmouth Post* May 26, 1865).

At the Hanover meeting, members of the ruling classes in attendance also felt the wrath of the labouring classes. According to a report:

> The meeting at Lucea was the most turbulent and disorderly one ever witnessed in the Court House...The first gentleman who spoke at the meeting was Mr. E. Sharpe (a planting Attorney of longstanding who had always liberally identified himself with the people's welfare); and merely for depreciating extravagance of expression regarding the alleged state of distress of the labouring classes, he was put down by a storm of hisses and vociferous cries from the people of 'No! No!! No!!! Mr. Trench, the Clerk of the Peace, next followed, but he had no sooner touched on the tender ground, than the 'audience roared like inmates of bedlam! Clenched fists were lifted above the crowd, and seemed to threaten the annihilation of any one who would dare to assert that the picture of poverty was capable of being overdrawn' (*Colonial Standard* May 21, 1865).

The fact that members of the most influential and powerful classes had to walk out of a public meeting or were shouted down in another in the full view of the labourers employed to them, was certainly an indication of the level of growth and political impact of the masses on the country. This signalled a rejection of the leadership of the plantocracy and efforts made by it to gain control and direction of the people's political assemblies.

The labouring classes and their leaders dominated and directed most of the meetings held throughout the island. Indeed, it could be said that the Underhill Meetings were essentially political assemblies of the lower classes engaged in a determined struggle against the plantocracy. This determination was made abundantly clear at the September 4, 1865 Vere meeting which was addressed by George William Gordon. A not so brief extract from the speech he was reported to have made and the response of the people to him will suffice to demonstrate the character of that meeting and others like it.[2]

> Since my arrival here, I have been advised that even from the pulpit,...the custos and the magistrates, the slaves of the heads of department, have been representing , or rather mis-representing, to the people that the Queen said they were idle and worthless. Now, the paper, the subject of this letter, speaks that the people were doing well, now, people is that so? – (Cries of No, no.) People mind to work, to render the plantations productive. Would you refuse to work? (Cries of No, no! We can't get work. Busha buy champagne wid what we work for, and play billiards at the alley billiard room, den when dem done, come da Court-house to try the poor who ask for money. Massa den [put] shops upon the estates; dat's de way wages is paid to us poor people.) Is it true you can't get anything to eat? – (Cries of Yes, yes. A voice: some get 1s.3d., 1s.6d., 9d., 6d., and in some cases 2s. per week, and some nothing at all...) Is it possible that all this I hear is true? – (Vociferous cries of Yes, yes, yes!) Now let me advise you to be good, to protect your just rights, at the same time in a lawful and correct manner...The gentlemen, you complain, do not care for you; so you must care for yourselves...the black people must be raised; they ought not to be kept down, help yourselves. When I speak of the custos, understand, I have every respect for him, but am only dealing with him as a public man; no wish whatever have I to rebuke him or any other gentleman, but justice calls for some one to speak out for the poor and oppressed people of Jamaica, and Vere particularly...I am glad to see you all come here, and behaving yourselves in defending your rights, and the rights of those poor and unfortunate ones who could not come out for want of clothing. Mr. Phillips will move the resolutions, and several of your own people will address the meeting (Royal Commission 1866, 889).

The August 12 meeting, held three weeks earlier in Morant Bay, was similar in many respects to the Vere meeting. It was chaired by George William Gordon and addressed by several persons, including John Anderson, a coloured teacher, and Samuel Clarke, a freeholder and vestry member from St David. The meeting expressed, among other things, indignation that planters were calling black people 'darned brutes' and 'darned beasts' (1,156).

The May 3, 1865 Underhill Meeting held in Kingston, like the Vere and Morant Bay meetings, was quite stormy. It was chaired by George William Gordon. Among those who addressed the meeting were the Revd Palmer, Baptist Minister, Revd Crole of Gordon's Tabernacle, Thomas Harry, shoemaker, and Emanuel Goldson, a former sergeant of police. George Fouche, a reporter of the *Sentinel*, who attended the meeting, said the substance of the gathering was:

> that the people were oppressed with the heavy burden of taxation, and it was time for them to seek for liberties; that the blacks were oppressed by the white and coloured people of the country very much; that they were kept under; that they had no situations given to them, neither in the customs, or the post-office, or any place of that kind;...that government gave them no encouragement, although they were large tax payers, and they formed the greater part of the community; that they had no advantages whatever, but it was their duty to stand up as men, and seek for their rights and privileges (554).

Fouche said the speeches were received with 'very great' applause 'especially when they were told that the Government was not to be obeyed, because it was immoral' (554). The *Sentinel* reporter noted that the audience cried 'shame, shame' at the authorities when Emanuel Goldson 'spoke of the mal-administration of justice respecting Black people.' Goldson, according to Fouche, referred to the case of Myrie who was:

> sent by Mr. Hart to prison for something like sixty days instead of fining him. He said if it had been a white or coloured person he would have [been] made [to] pay a fine, instead of sending him to the Penitentiary (554).

The meeting passed 17 or 18 resolutions.

The Underhill Meetings were attended by hundreds drawn mainly from the labouring classes. In bearing out this observation, Henry Westmorland noted that these meetings 'were attended by the lower orders almost exclusively' (854). The Montego Bay meeting was reported to have been attended by 'hundreds of the labouring population' (*Falmouth Post* May 26, 1865). The Lucea meeting 'was numerously attended.' According to a report 'a large body of the labouring population of Hanover filled the Court Room to overflowing' (*Falmouth Post* May 30, 1865). According to the reporter:

> The stalwart forms of four or five hundred (some say more, but I like to be within bounds) of the Labourers of the Parish, with a good sprinkling of crinolined and hand-kerchief-turbaned females, in itself a pleasing sight, afforded anything the corroborative testimony of the assertion that the distress, undeniably prevailing, had fixed its firmest grasp on the labouring and black populations of Hanover (*Falmouth Post* May 23, 1865).

Meanwhile, it was reported that the Kingston meeting was attended by 250 –300 people, mostly blacks, because 'there were comparatively few white or coloured people present' (Royal Commission 1866, 554). The Morant Bay assemblage was described as 'a very numerous meeting of the inhabitants of St Thomas-in-the-East' (1,156).

Apart from the large meetings that were usually held in the chief parish towns, many smaller meetings were held in villages and rural towns during that time. George William Gordon, for example, addressed one such meeting August 1, 1865 in Trelawny. That meeting, which was attended by about 150 people, was organised by Revd Thomas Lee (604). Another of these meetings took place in Stokes Hall, St Thomas-in-the-East. That meeting passed several resolutions and named a deputation, headed by John Anderson, to meet with Governor Eyre (959). Over in St Ann, George William Gordon organised several meetings (773).

The Emergence of Secular Political Organisations

To assist their struggles, the more conscious sections of the black population formed a number of organisations. These organisations included, among others, the Jamaica Reform Association, the Workingmen's Literary Society of St David, the Liberation Society and the Society of Friends.

The *Jamaica Reform Association* was probably the largest and most influential organisation of the people. It was based in Kingston and was instrumental in organising several popular meetings in the city against the Immigration Act, Election Law, etc. The *Jamaica Reform Association*, which was 'notorious' to the planters and merchants, was highly respected by hundreds of black people. Among prominent members and associates of this organisation were Alexander Sinclair, Revd R.A. Johnson, Revd Roach and George William Gordon. An insight into the influence of the Association was given by Revd Roach, who spoke at a public meeting on February 24, 1859. The *Colonial Standard* reported that:

> The Reverend Lewis Roach was glad to find the meeting attended by a very large number of the members of the 'Jamaica Reform Association.' Although the Society was despised by certain persons, its influence was deepening; and if the meeting had been convened by them there would have been hundreds present (qtd in *Falmouth Post* March 1, 1859).[3]

Revd Roach and Alexander Sinclair were detained as 'political prisoners' during martial law, while George William Gordon was executed.

The *Workingmen's Literary Society of St David* was founded in 1865 in the parish of St David by John Willis Menard. The main focus of this organisation was ideology, political education and debate. In a letter to the editor of the *Sentinel* (February 25, 1865), Samuel Wilson, one of the members of the Society, proudly wrote the following about his organisation and its leader:

> I am glad to inform the numerous readers of your very excellent paper that St. David is making a move in the right direction. Through the untiring efforts of our widely respected and talented new parishioner, J.W. Menard, Esqr. the above name Society was started on the 18th of January last, and now has a membership of sixteen. It meets once a week, and is growing in importance and interest. The last question debated was 'which is the more powerful, the Pen or the Sword?' The discussion of this subject was spirited and very entertaining. Mr. Menard, the President and founder, is a very valuable acquisition to this parish, and too much credit cannot be bestowed upon him for setting on foot this much needed work among us. These Societies form the only remaining hope for the redemption of this island from the power of ignorance.[4]

During the suppression of the Morant Bay uprising, Menard was detained and deported.

The *Liberation Society* was founded in St Ann. The leader of this Society was one Mr Rodney. The *Colonial Standard* (November 3, 1865), said the 'very appellation' of the *Liberation Society:*

> smells of conspiracy and treason, since its obvious meaning seems 'the liberation' of the island from the existing government, and since its head, Mr. Rodney appeared to be a proselyte to the Gordon-Haytien doctrine, and a supporter of the Underhill letter. Societies of this description, which aim at rebellion...must be suppressed by the strong arm of the law.

Rodney and seven members of the *Liberation Society* were arrested as 'political prisoners' in St Ann during martial law in St Thomas-in-the-East, in 1865.

The *Society of Friends* was founded in Morant Bay. Its importance to the political struggles of the people in St Thomas-in-the-East should not be underestimated. Members of this Society included George McIntosh, a black contractor; James McLaren, a deputy to Paul Bogle; Henry Clyne, William Grant, a saddler and 'Captain' of the 1865 revolt. These men were influential and respected leaders among the people of St Thomas-in-the-East. Henry Clyne, it would appear, was the leader of this Society, and McLaren the secretary. Meetings were held, if nowhere else, in a house of Mr Chisholm's' (Royal Commission 1866, 737).[5] Reports of one of the Society's meetings stated that 'between 20 and 30 people attended' (205). All the above named members of the Society, except Henry Clyne, were executed by martial law forces. Clyne was detained, flogged and forced to watch the execution of his comrades.

These organisations and others that arose were not national associations, but they marked a beginning in the people's efforts to take things into their own hands and shape their lives, and to provide organised political and ideological leadership for their struggles. The organisations profiled above were essentially secular in their formation and activities. However, there were other organisations that were religious in their formation and activities but performed very important social, political and ideological roles. Top on the list of these organisations were the Native Baptist Church, founded by Paul Bogle in Stony Gut where his chapel was located, and the Native Baptist Church organised by George William Gordon at the Parade in Kingston where his 'Tabernacle' was erected.

Feeling of Impending Catastrophe

By 1865, a feeling of an impending catastrophe began to sweep the colony. Apocalyptic rumours swept through the households of all classes and races across the island. Fear of a black uprising gripped the white and upper sections of the coloured population. Among the black population the fear of being returned to slavery was just as gripping. A marked change in the attitude of blacks towards whites began to emerge as the social and political activities of the labouring classes quickened. The change in attitude meant a serious erosion of the monumental respect that many, perhaps a majority of former enslaved Africans, held for their former owners. This type of respect was, on the one hand, the product of over 200 years of almost uninterrupted hegemony of the white race over the black race. On the other hand, it was pretence, a feigned respect in the best tradition of the African Jamaican proverb: 'Plie fuul fe kech wiz' (Play fool to catch wise/Pretend to be stupid to trap those who claimed they are the wise).

Daniel Callagan, proprietor for one estate and attorney for six or seven others in the parish of Vere, gave an insight into the loss of respect that blacks had for whites. He said that after the Vere Underhill meeting, the 'negroes' looked 'very sour and very sulky' (514). This employer of over 1,000 labourers said:

> formerly when you passed they would always say, 'How do you do, massa', but they left that off... they were very sour and very sulky, and did not care whether they worked or not, they would turn out late to try and annoy the planters (514).

From St Thomas-in-the-East, Samuel Shortridge, owner of two estates and attorney of 'six of the largest estates' in that parish, noted an almost similar state of affairs. According to him:

> For two or three months before the massacre at Morant Bay [black people] were sulky and sullen – they would not perform their usual tasks, and then

of course they did not get their usual amount of wages on pay day, and they quarrelled and kicked up a great noise, and became very restive (22).

From the parishes of Metcalfe and St Mary, Henry Westmorland, planter and member of the Executive Committee said it was reported to him that 'there was a strange feeling among the people; they did not go to work; they were very unwilling to do so' (856). In another incident, Joshua Morais, a white clerk employed to 'Messrs. Finzi and Co.' in Kingston, noted that 'some draymen' sided with black policemen involved in a dispute with white sailors on the ship *Rosario*. Morais said the draymen 'spoke very disrespectfully of white people, and said that the black people would soon get the better of the white people' (859). Morais said on several occasions he heard black men 'repeatedly say that any black man was fit to trash 10 whites' (888).

Along with the growth of disrespect that black people displayed towards the white plantocracy and its allies was a growth of fear and rumours of a black uprising. In a letter dated July 22, 1865, the Custos of St Elizabeth told Governor Eyre that there were fears of 'negro disturbances' in that parish. He believed that 'the minds of many persons in this parish are distressed by rumours of intended disturbances by the negroes...I am told the chat among the negroes is, 'Buckra has gun, negro has firestick' (857).

The Custos called upon the Governor to present 'before the people some force ready to punish, and put down' any attempt at rebellion.[6] On August 7, 1865, Rayne Smith, member of the House of Assembly representing St Elizabeth, also wrote to Edward Eyre to bring to his 'notice the conduct of the labouring population' on his estate. He noted that:

> Considerable excitement has for some time existed in this parish in consequence of rumours of a rising of the peasantry in this and some other parishes of the county to such an extent that many families fled from their homes seeking safety at Black River (858).

From St Thomas-in-the-East, planter and Inspector-General of Immigration, Wellwood Anderson, was so afraid of being hurt by the people that he travelled with a 'capped' loaded revolver. The 'evident change in the manners of the people and their address caused' him, he said, 'to carry a revolver loaded and capped whenever [he] went up into the country' (566). Meanwhile, from Hermitage on the border of Hanover and Westmoreland, William Cooke, a Magistrate serving St James, Hanover and Westmoreland, placed a guard around his house because he and his household were 'disturbed by horns or shells blowing at nights.' He said:

> The ladies of my house never retired to rest from the state of alarm they were in. Two nights they awoke me...I placed a guard round the house. They woke me up in the night two or three times (695).

Back in St Elizabeth, Archdeacon Rowe noted that by July 1865 so acute was the fear of white people of being attacked by blacks that most of them employed guards. Speaking of his family's situation, he said, 'We were almost the only family in St. Elizabeth's that did not keep guard about that period' (647).

Evidently, for a race and class of people accustomed to ruling over the black race, the undisguised display of 'disrespect' that Africans showed to Europeans, coupled with rumour and threats of black risings, must have been rather traumatic for the ruling classes.

For their part, the fear of a return to slavery must have had an equally traumatic effect on the masses of black people. The trauma, nervousness, anxiety and feeling that an impending showdown would commence between the rulers and the ruled, was a product of the intense, persistent and uncompromising struggle between those who favoured reform in the interests of the black masses and those who opposed it. The development of this tendency in the political struggle increasingly favoured a resolution involving the use of force. The call by Paul Bogle and other leaders in St Thomas-in-the-East for their people to prepare to meet the white people who were 'now cleaning up their guns for us,...for they determine to make us a slave again' (1,082), provided a classical example of how the two antagonistic social groups saw each other on the eve of the outbreak in 1865.

Notes

1. Universal Adult Suffrage was won by the black masses in 1944, following a national uprising of workers, peasants and small own-account people in 1938. In general elections that year, the people used their franchise to defeat the Jamaica Democratic Party, the party of planters and merchants in the first truly national elections to be held in Jamaica at that time.
2. Gordon's speech was reported in the County Union newspaper, September 12, 1865. The person who made the report on Gordon's speech was William Marsh, a coloured man. Before he sent the report to the newspaper, it was verified by Dr Robert Bruce, chairman of the meeting. Marsh was employed to Gordon as a 'job writing clerk' to 'prepare his bills for the Assembly'. He was detained during martial law.
3. Revd Lewis Roach was called Revd James Roach in other publications.
4. Samuel Wilson, the author of this letter, could very well have been Samuel Clarke, a close friend and political ally of Menard.

5. There were conflicting views as to whether the house was owned by Chisholm or George William Gordon.
6. At Custos John Salmon's request, Governor Eyre sent a warship, the Bulldog, with troops to Black River and Savanna-la-Mar, while the Cadmus, another naval vessel, was sent to Montego Bay.

4 'Their Very Independence is an Evil': Cane Sugar Elites Creating Inflammable Materials in Post-slavery Society

> The people are too independent, too well off here – too fickle, arbitrary, and uncertain as to when they will work and when they will not work.
>
> – A Planter

While the objective factors that gave rise to the violent confrontation in St Thomas-in-the-East were present and developing in one form or another throughout Jamaica, they appeared to have matured faster in that parish in 1865. Several factors favoured confrontation in St Thomas-in-the-East.

Firstly, the dominance of the cane sugar plantation sector over the economy of that parish was such that the own-account peasant/labouring classes had little economic alternative but to submit to the existing regime or wage a determined struggle to reform it, since little alternative in the acquisition of land or migration existed at that time.

Secondly, there was the emergence of two opposing polarised socio-economic and political camps and the simultaneous fettering of the importance and role of centre positions in the social, economic and political life of that parish.

Thirdly, there was the dominance of the spiritual, religious and political role of a more African-centred movement over the masses and the relatively weak influence of dissenting British liberal missionaries who encouraged obedience to official authority and discouraged the masses from taking things into their own hands.

Fourthly, there appeared to have emerged a higher level of organisation, agitation and consciousness among the black masses surpassing their counterparts in most parts of the island in the realisation that they needed to take things into their own hands and create alternative institutions to the ones they considered oppressive rather than wait for help from above.

Fifthly, was the development of a reliable alliance between estate labourers and own-account blacks as part of a broader and highly important alliance between blacks and sections of the coloured population against the planter/merchant alliance and colonial officials who supported them in an openly partisan way.

Sixthly, there was the emergence of a crop of activist leaders who were consistent in linking with the people, giving them guidance, hope and leadership against the anti-people activities and hawkishness of the executive, judicial, ecclesiastic and economic leadership in the St Thomas-in-the-East plantocracy.

Despite the fact that the number of sugar estates in St Thomas-in-the-East fell from 67 in 1834 to 21 in 1854 (Hall 1959, 82), the economic life of that parish was still dominated by the cane sugar plantation system. St Thomas-in-the-East ranked third in the island in the production of sugar. Only Trelawny and Westmoreland produced more sugar than St Thomas-in-the-East. But, St Thomas-in-the-East ranked first in the island in the number of hundred weight of sugar produced per estate (71). It was, therefore, one of the most important parishes in the colony in consequence of its economic position.

On account of the overwhelming dominance of sugar, the economy of St Thomas-in-the-East was less diversified than some of the other parishes. As a result, instead of having diverse economic groupings, the population of that parish was divided primarily into two main opposing social groups, planters and estate labourers. The more concentrated and dominant the sugar areas were, the more pronounced the tendency for rigid social stratification which had a stronger potential for violent confrontation in efforts by people to budge or to maintain the status quo. On this score, Justice Allan Kerr noted that the peculiar circumstances which distinguished St Thomas-in-the-East from other parishes had to do with the dominance of sugar production over the economy of that parish.

> I should say the distinguishing peculiarities of St. Thomas in the East is, that being a great sugar parish – probably a larger portion of the population are what we called 'Estate's negroes,' that is, they work for wages and not on their own account' (Royal Commission 1866, 286).

Justice Kerr also touched upon the conflicting nature of the relationship inherent in the rigid stratification system that developed in that cane parish.

> St. Thomas in the East has been conspicuous in Jamaica as a district torn by dissensions of every kind. It is almost a distress to travel through it. All the leading parties there, so far back as my recollection extends, rank upon one side or the other,...It is very much the reverse of that which should be expected of Christian men (301).

As can be seen in Kerr's statement, the conflicting relationship between blacks and whites in St Thomas-in-the-East was known for sometime throughout Jamaica. This was complicated by the lack of cohesion within the ruling classes of that parish whose behaviour was the reverse of what could be expected of Christian men. Kerr's statement contains important clues pointing to reasons for St Thomas-in-the-East becoming the epicentre of the post-slavery struggle between the aspiration of the black majority and the continued desire of the white minority to maintain the status quo.

What was said of social stratification and social relationships in St Thomas-in-the-East could be said more or less for the principal sugar producing areas across the island with respect to the black population. Harvey and Brewin noted that the sugar parish of Vere resembled 'in many of its features,' the 'river district' of St Thomas-in-the-East (1867, 30). They further noted that 'in its social and moral condition Vere is no exception to the general character of the sugar districts' (30).

The production of sugar more than the production of any other exportable tropical crop in the island, more than cattle or horse breeding, required a large consistently reliable and accessible labour force, i.e., 'estate's negroes'.

Figure 1. Sugar cane plantations still dominate the Plantain Garden River District of St Thomas. Photo by Clinton Hutton.

Their Very Independence is an Evil

The production of sugar more than the production of any other exportable tropical crops in the island, more than cattle or horse breeding, required a large consistently reliable and accessible labour force, i.e., 'estate's negroes'. This labour force, organised around backward methods and techniques of production by planters steeped in the ways and prejudices of the late slave epoch, had to be made consistently reliable and accessible. To do this, a state of dependency had to be created to subject the labourers to the requirements of the estates. To establish this regime of dependency required that the plantocracy put the severest restrictions on the freedom of the labouring classes. Hence, the plantocracy and its allies invariably reacted in a hostile manner to blacks who showed a certain degree of independence. For example, William Carr, magistrate and proprietor of Rivers Dale and New Hall estates in St Thomas-in-the-Vale said he would prefer a system where he had labourers on regular pay continuously, fed them and denied them provision grounds (and hence a path to freeholdership) because:

> I should be glad if they would be dependent on my capital;...the negroes are not like those in Barbados, they are not dependent upon estates for their livelihood...that is the great cause of our non-prosperity, the want of population; no doubt, that is the root of all the evil; their very independence is an evil (Royal Commission 1866, 508).

The parish of St Thomas-in-the-Vale had a more diverse economy. It was not a classical sugar parish like Vere or the island of Barbados and so there was a less rigid path to diversity. Despite being like St Thomas-in-the-East and Vere, Barbados's geography and extant land ownership regime and larger settler white population, had little or no own-account alternative for the black population.

From St Thomas-in-the-East, 'large landed proprietor', member of the Assembly, and Custos, Peter Espeut expressed similar views. He said: 'Continuous labour are very badly off for; I mean persons that will work on estates whenever their services are required, but it so happens they do not do it. They have their own patches to cultivate, and you very often find that they are doing that when you require them' (96).

An unnamed planter also expressed this view to W.G. Sewell, the visiting American writer in 1860. The planter said:

> [T]he people are too independent, too well off here – too fickle, arbitrary, and uncertain as to when they will work and when they will not work. They just do as they please. They work on the roads for a month and then give it up. Then they take to something else and give that up. This is the way they have treated

us. They ride upon our backs, sir. They work for us only four days in the week, and hang about their own properties or go to market on the other two. We cannot improve our estates without a full week's labor (Sewell 1861, 193–94).

Everything had to be done, therefore, to make labourers less independent, less fickle, less arbitrary and uncertain. Above all, they were to be made propertyless without the means to make their own living, since access to even the smallest patch of land, including rented land, represented hope and possibility of cultivating the ontological culture of freeholdership. Hence, the organisers of labour for sugar production became at the same time the organisers of the subjection of labour, especially denying it the means of labouring for itself on its own account. They invariably adopted a hostile intolerant position steeped in race and class chauvinism in their relationship to the black population, whose role was to be a class of menials at the perpetual service of white people.

The evidence presented by the black people of St Thomas-in-the-East to the Royal Commission 1866, clearly revealed the regime of dependency that the plantocracy created in that parish. Mary Williams, a labourer of Holland Estate, for example, had to work ten hours daily, five days weekly, weeding 25 chains of sugar cane each day for sixpence per day or two shillings and sixpence per week. Williams, however, ended up getting one shilling each week because the estate management 'take four bits for the rent' (Royal Commission 1866, 248). Williams lived in a house she rented on the estate for 'four bits' or one shilling and sixpence, 60 per cent of her weekly pay, the cost for weeding 75 chains of cane. More often than not, Mary Williams went through her working day without resting or eating. According to her, 'I only got water to drink. When we get any food to carry, [we eat] but when we do not get any we go without' (249).

In another case, Anne Wedderman, a labourer who was born on Holland Estate and 'never work anywhere else,' worked every day for the year except on Sundays and when she fell ill. She was always owed one week's wages by the estate management. Accordingly she said, 'if I work last week I should not get paid till the following Tuesday' (251).

The practice of withholding one week's wages was widespread in St Thomas-in-the-East. In this regard, Harvey and Brewin noted that:

> It is the custom in this parish to retain a week's wages in hand for [the] avowed purpose of ensuring the return of the labourer to his work. The latter asserts that if he changes to another estate, or stays to work his own ground, or remains at home from sickness, or other cause, he always loses this last week's hire (1867, 18).

Their Very Independence is an Evil

Not only was it a 'custom' to retain one week of the labourers' wages, Wedderman also revealed that management often did not abide by the contract to pay the agreed rate of remuneration. Hence, while Wedderman agreed with the estate management to pay her one shilling and sixpence for each day's work, the management soon reneged on its duty.

> [F]or the week; sometimes you just get two shillings...sometimes I work all the week and just get a shillings, and sometimes four bits, after the rent is paid. Anything he [the overseer] gave I was obliged to be satisfied with. I work from Monday chock down to Saturday, except when I sick. [I work] from before day-light in the morning. Sometimes I had to budge part of the night (Royal Commission 1866, 251).

Thus, the wage regime which gave the planters the power to deduct, reduce, withhold and abolish wages became a major instrument for the creation of a dependent labour force, especially since these planters and the state which they composed, had power over land distribution.

The use of the land became a principal means of constricting the development of the power of independence and sovereignty in the culture of formerly enslaved Africans and preserving the hegemonic power of the plantocratic elites in particular and the white land owning and merchant classes in general.

As early as August 17, 1838, 16 days after Emancipation Day, an essay titled, 'A Few Hints on the Negro Character', appeared in the *Jamaica Despatch and Kingston Chronicle*. In this essay, a clear ontological basis for the promotion and maintenance of power, authority and policy in the post-slavery state, was being articulated on the principle of race and class superiority, the episteme of pro-slavery.

> Labour appears to the African the greatest curse on earth: nor do I believe cultivation will continue unless laws are made to enforce a due obedience on the part of negroes to do their duty...; and these laws must not be administered by individuals possessing no property in the country. Such men have, and they will again, render laws [useless] by an unjust administration of them; besides, they are unacquainted with the negro character, and act towards him as if he were a black Cockney! In London.

For the *Jamaica Despatch and Kingston Chronicle*: 'The negro requires to be constantly followed up...'Driver' he must have.' Earlier in 1838, another newspaper, *The West Indian*, stated that one of its main aims was to 'put within the reach of the Labouring Population the means of acquiring such information' to make them 'honest, industrious and contented labourers.' That paper also stated, among other things:

> The honour of a servant is his fidelity, his highest virtues are submission and obedience.
>
> Be patient therefore under the reproofs of thy master, and when he rebuketh thee, answer not again; the silence of thy resignation shall not be forgotten.
>
> Be studious of his interest: be deligent in his affairs, and faithful to the trust which he reposeth in thee. Thy time and thy labour belong unto him: defraud him not thereof (*The West Indian* January 20, 1838).

This framing of the African in post-slavery as a being who, as in slavery must be constantly followed up by the whip and a racist doctrine to imprint in his/her agency a fidelity to whiteness comparable to the biblical role of the sacrificial lamb, reflected a portentousness in these newspapers that was quite common. It reflected the confidence in the former and soon to be former slaveholders who never lost their power over the state and its affairs with the abolition of slavery, for which they were handsomely compensated.

Their role was to make the post-slavery state as close as possible to the slavery state epistemologically, ontologically, culturally and psychologically. In their framing of this state and its policy 'to enforce a due obedience on the part of negroes to do their duty', Thomas Carlyle was a philosophical godsend.

In 1849, Carlyle published anonymously in *Fraser's Magazine for Town and Country of London* an essay titled, 'Occasional Discourse on the Negro Question'. This essay was expanded and reprinted in 1853 as a pamphlet with the title, 'Occasional Discourse on the Nigger Question'. It became for the plantocracy a cherished guide/manifesto for the making of the post-slavery state and society.[1] In his manifesto, Carlyle declared:

> Not a square inch of soil in those fruitful Isles, purchased by British blood, shall any Black man hold to grow pumpkins for him, except on terms that are fair towards Britain...Fair towards Britain it will be, that Quashee give work for privilege to grow pumpkins. Not a pumpkin, Quashee, not a square yard of soil, till you agree to do the State so many days of service. Annually that soil will grow you pumpkins; but annually also, without fail, shall you, for the owner thereof, do your appointed days of labour. The State has plenty of waste soil; but the State will religiously give you none of it in other terms.[2]

One of Carlyle's fiercest critics was John Bigelow, a leading advocate of free competition. Bigelow (1851) said of Carlyle in his essay:

> Such is the solution of the West Indian problem, advocated by one of the most distinguished writers and thinkers in England: a restoration of slavery. He would introduce compulsory labor, the price of which should not

be regulated by the laws of supply and demand which control the wages of whites, but by acts of parliament, or by the caprice and avarice of landowners. If this form of slavery should not be effectual, he would restore the chattel slavery which formerly prevailed. He admits that the whites do not work here, but he does not propose to make labor compulsory upon them. He would have the rate of wages for the negroes determined by an arbitrary regulation and not by the supply, as it is everywhere else. He would exclude all white labourers from the West Indies, by compelling the blacks to work at lower than the market prices. As these propositions logically assume that the organization of the black man is inferior to that of the white man – and that he is not entitled to equal rights before the law, but is to be classified with the brute creation (122–23).

In the sugar cane producing areas, it was much more difficult for the people to have access to the land for personal use. According to available evidence, St Thomas-in-the-East was probably the sugar producing area where it was most difficult for labourers to have access to the land. In their efforts to become more independent, the labouring classes found that, in their bid to acquire land, the arm of the estate was everywhere. Indeed, it was the issue of land that was at the core of the violent confrontation in Morant Bay. In this regard, Harvey and Brewin (1867) stated the following:

> It was well know that the recent disturbances were connected with a supposed claim of the Stony Gut villagers to the adjoining Middleton estate. Elsewhere several hundred negroes had combined to take up a large tract of mountain land called Smoothland, adjoining the back lands of Hordley and Amity Hall estates. They had acted under legal advice, whether good or bad, had paid hard money for the land, but found possession disputed on behalf of the estates named. Hire, the attorney for Amity Hall, went on the land with a surveyor to claim possession, and being resisted he took out summonses against fourteen men for trespass (19).

The requirements of old-style sugar production invariably led to a rigid stratification system where two opposing social groups, planters and labourers were united in the process of production and society by the coercive powers of the plantocracy and the British Colonial State. It was sugar production that gave rise to two main social blocks with interests antagonistic to each other why St Thomas-in-the-East, a mighty sugar parish, became a prime candidate for social confrontation. This rise of two antagonistic blocks in the sugar-producing areas was accompanied by great wealth/asset accumulation for the planters and great impoverishment for the labourers. While they were tied to the estates, the labourers were to become socially and materially poorer than the rest of the black population throughout the island. Baptist Missionary of St James, Revd J. Maxwell, observed that, 'As a rule those who labour on the estates are poorer than those who depend on their own home cultivation' (Underhill 'C' 1865, 62). Harvey and Brewin said much the same when they noted that 'labourers on sugar estates are generally the least advanced part of the population of Jamaica' (Harvey and Brewin 1867, 17).

Compared to freeholders and other blacks who were more independent economically, the 'estate negroes' had among their ranks the worse houses, the highest level of illiteracy and the lowest number in the black population with the right to vote. They were prime targets for some of the worst prejudices against black people. One case in point was the attack by the *Falmouth Post* (February 25, 1848) and magistrates against the *Morality of the 'People' in Hampden District*.

> "Do you come from Hampden?" this is the question, invariably asked by the sitting magistrates, at the Police Court, whenever a case of a particularly disgusting nature is brought before them. If the records in the office of the Clerk of the Peace were searched, it would be found, that there is an awful amount of crime committed, by the labourers, on Hampden, Dundee, and Bounty Hall estates, and at the village, which has been built in the neighbourhood of 'Good Will.' Scarcely a week, is allowed to pass, without the perpetration of a serious assault – the people seem to live in unchecked indulgence of gross sensual passions – adultery is an everyday occurrence.

In areas where the economy was more diversified or sugar played a subordinate role, the picture was somewhat different. Social stratification was more diverse. Hence, social intercourse, interests and objectives were more diverse and less confrontational compared to a situation where two opposing social groups dominated. In areas where a mixed economy predominated, a black population socially and materially more advanced than Africans tied to estates tended to emerge. Harvey and Brewin alluded to this when they noted that:

> Manchester is probably at present the most advanced and prosperous parish in the island, as regard the black population. Coffee is its great staple. The value of this crop for the whole island we heard computed at £300,000, of which two-thirds is grown by the small settlers. Some of the people here are fairly raising into a middle class. We found one black freeholder, once a slave, living in a house, which with its out-buildings, coffee-floor, water-tank, etc., must have cost him several hundred pounds, and what was better still it was comfortably and even elegantly furnished, with books on the table and framed prints on the walls (1867, 33).

Manchester did not possess any sugar estates at that time. In St Elizabeth where a few sugar estates were situated, the black population was less constricted and less dependent on wage labour for its livelihood. Sewell (1861) noted on his visit to that parish, in 1860, that:

> The population of St. Elizabeth parish numbers 119 persons to the square mile – a larger proportion than can be found in most of the sugar-growing parishes. But I know of no locality in Jamaica where labor for sugar-cultivation is more needed than here. The settlers have their own properties to look after, and it would be surprising indeed if they neglected them to hire themselves out as field labourers at a shilling a day (221).

In an economic crisis, combined with other factors such as drought and epidemic, social and political polarisation tended to occur more easily and with greater risks of confrontation in the sugar belt compared to areas where the economy and economic relations were more diversified. This state of affairs was not likely to be made less confrontational when the so-called 'estates negroes' saw the real possibility of a comparably better alternative in freeholdings or other own-account economic ventures. However, the relationship of tens of thousands of persons of African descent to sugar production stood in their way to material and social advancement.

It was no accident, therefore, that the three most prominent violent confrontations to have taken place in Jamaica in the early post-slavery period, 1838–65, occurred in the three top sugar producing parishes – Westmoreland, Trelawny and St Thomas-in-the-East.

The 'Morant Bay Rebellion' was the classic example of violent confrontations between blacks and whites in the society that emerged in Jamaica after the abolition of slavery. St Thomas-in-the-East was a classic cane parish. The sugar interests were responsible for hiring most of the labourers and renting lands to blacks.

But not even the strongest and most rigid of the sugar parishes could prevent some alternative forms of economic activities alongside sugar production and its satellite economy such as cattle breeding. St Thomas-in-the-East also boasted its own freeholders and other own-account Africans who were more independent of the estates. Among them was Richard Harris, formerly a labourer and resident of Cross Paths. He had seven acres of land in sugar, coffee and ground provision cultivation. Harris had 100 acres of land which he bought at £2.10s per acre. With a sense of pride and achievement Harris said, 'I hired labourers and worked myself '(Royal Commission 1866, 537). There was Richard Davidson, a shopkeeper who also reared pigs, fowls and cultivated coffee and ground provisions. When his house was burnt during the suppression, he lost '100 dollars' which he kept there. George Hamilton had his own land and shop from which he sold salt provisions. When his shop was burnt by the authorities following October 11, 1865, he lost £82 (570). Stephen Telford, a rural constable. He was self-employed, working his own land. He owned 50 acres of land (499–510), four houses and a shop (432). In the suppression that followed the October 11, 1865 armed confrontation, it was this section of the black population that lost the most.

It was primarily from this section of the black population, the own-account Africans, that Paul Bogle and other leaders of the 'Morant Bay Rebellion' were drawn. Francis Hobbs went as far as attributing the confrontation at Morant Bay solely to the agency of this section of the population. According to the British colonial army colonel: 'the class of people who are employed in this rebellion are not the poor, but a class of small landholders who are, in every sense of the word, freeholders' (1,120). Hobbs considered this class of Africans to be the freest and hence the most dangerous to the existence of the post-slavery society imagined by Thomas Carlyle. Here, even if sections of 'own-account' Africans sided with the plantocracy, black freeholdership was incompatible to white freedom and sovereignty and thus in the thought and action of the authorities, it had to be rooted out.

This class of 'own-account' Africans or 'freeholders' to use Hobbs's designation, especially that section of the black middle class which emerged in the cane sugar parishes and districts, played a role in post-slavery society that was particularly significant in its radical opposition to the former slaveholding plantocracy. This emerging black middle class was smaller and more compressed in the sugar parishes because of the greater restrictions imposed on Africans in the more immediate domain of the plantocracy.

These freeholders lived a tenuous existence between the plantocracy and the masses of estate labourers. But, despite their tenuous position, they held a place in post-slavery society that made them inflammable material with the potential of triggering the eruption of social magma among the masses of labourers. That explained to a great extent why the freeholders were so feared by the plantocracy and its allies. William Carr, the magistrate and proprietor of several estates expressed this fear in part when he said of the black population which did not depend wholly on the estate: 'their very independence is an evil' (508).

This post-slavery fear was generated by the black freeholders who were deemed to have ontologically and agentially reverted to their unsupervised primitive state of being, since freeholdership removed them from under the control and guidance of white people. Freeholdership was thus a state of unsupervised blackness whose state of existence undermined the existential viability of whiteness, while the 'estate negroes' were considered to be in their proper position under the supervision of white people. Freeholders were deemed to be inherently subversive and a bad example to Africans under the control of white people.

This view was not lost in Francis Hobbs's assessment: 'I believe the better off the negroes were, the more bitter they were against the whites' (1,129). It is true that most of the leaders associated with the Morant Bay conflict were of the social stratum of Africans of which Hobbs spoke. They included persons such as Paul Bogle, E.K., Bailey, Arthur Wellington, William Grant, John Edwards and George McIntosh. It is equally true to say that the better off some Africans were, the less bitter they were against whites. These Africans, like some from St Ann, attributed their success to the 'generosity that the white race bestowed upon the black race.'

They, therefore, supported the whites and staked their claim in the existing order and its preservation. These freeholders included four men interviewed by a correspondent for the *New York Daily Tribune* during the suppression following the events of October 11, 1865. According to one of the interviewees:

> Black people too fool! – yes wosser dan fool, dem no free man already. Buckra no make one law fe we all, teef go a me ground law no de fe me? Him nock me down, law de fe me? Neber see de day when me will trus black negro fe make law to gobern me, or protect me little and much (*New York Daily Tribune* November 17, 1865).

The position of the other three men, all freeholders from the parish of St Ann, was similar. Said another:

> I is owner of five acre of land, me hab me house, and me coffee walk – me hab me cart and horse, what going hat me fe take myself out a white people law so go trus... black negro? Dem no walk in tomorrow, knok me down, and take way my place, who me going to fe ax protection? Tan safely me breda! Go plant we coffee and coco, make dem in St. Thomas in de East keep dem fool to demself (*New York Daily Tribune* November 17, 1865).

These men were evidently supporters of the status quo or playing the fool to catch the wise. Based on evidence, they did not fit Hobbs's over-generalisation of the freeholding class as naturally radical. The statements from the St Ann freeholders disproved Hobbs's argument. They would have been regarded in African Jamaican ontology during that time as having 'black skin' and 'white heart'. It was not from this category of freeholders from whence the leadership for radical reform came.

What developed in St Thomas-in-the-East and matured faster than in the other areas was a firm alliance between the estate labourers and freeholders. In this alliance the better off own-account blacks assumed the role of leaders while the majority of estate labourers acted as the shock force in the frontline of confrontation with the plantocracy. Without this alliance, the political upheaval in Morant Bay and, indeed, the whole political and social movement in St Thomas-in-the-East would have had less chance of materialising.

The alliance between own-account blacks and the masses of dependent African labourers formed part of a wider alliance between the African masses on the one hand, and left, radical and reformist section of the coloured and white population on the other hand. This alliance was symbolised by the relationship between Paul Bogle and George William Gordon.

The material and social realisation of that alliance had to do with the willingness of men of Gordon's background and blacks with a higher social and material status to combine against the plantocracy and its established authority. This willingness to combine was a product of the objective needs of these sections to jointly combat the plantocracy.

More subjectively, the willingness to combine sprang from the fact that political legitimacy and influence for Bogle, Gordon and the masses required that they command representation in the House of Assembly, the Vestry and the Court system. It was from the own-account blacks in St Thomas-in-the-East that most of the votes for Gordon's bid to the Assembly would have been drawn and from which local government representatives would have been elected to the Vestry of that parish.

St Thomas-in-the-East had more than polarisation in social stratification. It also had political and ideological polarisation, two necessary ingredients for the emergence of social confrontation, including the use of violence. Of course, polarisation in social stratification does not automatically lead to political and ideological polarisation. Needless to say, the latter could not take place without the material basis provided by the former.

Political and ideological polarisation developed in St Thomas-in-the-East as a result of the combination of several factors. The first of these was the fact that that parish was divided into two main political religious camps, the Anglican Church, which was an arm of the Colonial state and the Native Baptist Church. These two bodies were the most influential religious groups in St Thomas-in-the-East. The centre churches, especially the English Baptist, played an insignificant role in the socio-political life of that parish compared to other parishes across the island.[3] With respect to the role and influence of the English Baptist Church in St Thomas-in-the-East, Edward B. Underhill stated:

Their Very Independence is an Evil

> In the district to which the outbreak has been confined, there are no Baptist missionaries, nor any congregations connected with them...The Baptist spoken of by Governor Eyre are Native Baptists. They originated in the preaching of an American Negro about 1783, thirty years before the Baptist Mission sent any agents to Jamaica, and with whom no union of any kind has taken place (Underhill 1971, 8).

In fact, in the whole parish of St Thomas-in-the-East, there was only one English Baptist Missionary, Henry Harris, a coloured man who resided in and operated out of Belle Castle, Portland for 13 years. His missionary work was confined to two communities, Belle Castle in Portland and Stokes Hill, St Thomas-in-the-East. He operated two schools in these communities and had a congregation averaging about 300 (Royal Commission 1866, 960–61). In addition to the Baptist Missionary, there was a Wesleyan Missionary at Bath and one near Manchioneal.

The English Baptist and other churches or centres of liberal political and social persuasions and influence among the black population were weak in St Thomas-in-the-East. Hence, the influence of the political and religious centre over the black masses as a go-between labourers and planters was quite minimal.

In Vere, Trelawny and Westmoreland, where social stratification and conditions were more or less similar to St Thomas-in-the-East, the political and religious centre was, to some extent, more influential than in St Thomas-in-the-East. In Vere, there were at least two English Baptist Missionaries, five missions and a Wesleyan church. Meanwhile, over in Trelawny, there were at least nine English Baptist Missionaries and 13 missions (Underhill 1971, 59). Among these missionaries were Revd D.J. East, W. Dendy and J.E. Henderson, three of the most influential Baptist leaders in Jamaica up to the time of the Morant Bay outbreak. In addition to the English Baptists were the Wesleyans, among others. Commenting on the influence of the political and religious centre on the masses in the number one sugar producing parish in the island, Trelawny Custos Robert Nunes said:

> I would state that the reason why our parish had been in a more quite state than many others is, that we have been more free from the influence of the interfering parties, demagogues, who in several other parishes have led the people astray. I believe our parish is pretty well managed, and a great deal of this result is to be attributed to the conduct of the dissenting ministers, who have taken a very active part in doing good there (Royal Commission 1866, 832).

Notes

1. American journalist, politician and diplomat John Bigelow, said on a visit to Jamaica at the beginning of the 1850s:

    > The complaint made by Mr. Carlyle, is the first thing a stranger hears out of the mouths of white residents on landing at Jamaica, "The wages are so high that nothing can be made off our estates without protection...." I did not meet a single planter, who did not insist it was the unnatural price of labor that was sinking them. Mr. Stanley carried off the same impression, and makes it the staple of his argument for a restoration of the old protective duties on colonial produce. See John Bigelow, Jamaica in 1850 (New York and London: 1851), 124.

2. See Thomas Carlyle, *The Nigger Question: The Negro Question*, ed. Eugene R. August (New York: Appleton-Century-Crofts, 1971), 32.
3. See the English Baptist organisational network across Jamaica in Inez Sibley, *The Baptists of Jamaica 1793 to 1965* (Kingston: The Jamaica Baptist Union 1965).

5 'Legal Redress is Shut out from One Class Altogether': Magisterial Oppression in St Thomas-in-the-East

> If a Negro was injured, he could seldom secure justice because his judges were among his oppressors.
>
> – *New York Times*

> We can't get work. Busha buy champagne wid what we work for, and play billiards at the alley billiard room, den when dem done, come da Courthouse to try the poor who ask for money.
>
> – *Sugar worker at a public meeting in Vere*

The attitude of the ruling classes to the black population was most starkly revealed in what George William Gordon called 'magisterial oppression' (Royal Commission 1866, 1,154). An examination of cases brought before the Petty Session Courts in Bath, St Thomas-in-the-East, from 1863 to 1965, revealed the sharp classist and racist nature of the trials and the depth of the polarisation between the plantocracy and the labouring classes.

Of the 661 civil and criminal cases heard in Petty Sessions in Bath, 299 or 45.2 per cent of them had to do with conflicts between planters and labourers. This represented the largest category of cases reflecting the deep polarisation between the two main contending social groups in St Thomas-in-the-East.

The court system and magisterial proceedings were highly stacked against the labouring classes. According to the law, 'in the event of any dispute between the labourers and their employers, it is a matter which the Justices of the Peace have jurisdiction.'¹ Of the 299 cases, the planters were complainants on 296 occasions and defendants only three times. For every time a labourer took a planter to court, the planter took the labourer 98.666 times (see table 5.1).

A breakdown of the cases revealed that planters took labourers to court 94 times for larceny; 84 times for misconduct as servant and 37 times for other 'offences'. All of these cases, except two, were ruled in favour of the planters, resulting in costs and penalty or imprisonment for the labourers.

TABLE 5.1. STATUS OF COMPLAINANTS AND DEFENDANTS IN CIVIL AND CRIMINAL CASES HEARD IN PETTY SESSIONS AT BATH, ST THOMAS-IN-THE-EAST, 1863–65

No. of times planters took labourers to court	296 (.447)
No. of times labourers took planters to court	3 (.004)
No. of times planters took planters to court	2 (.003)
No. of times labourers took labourers to court	206 (.311)
No. of times police/state took planters to court	1 (.001)
No. of times police/state took labourers to court	79 (.119)
No. of times planters took police/state to court	0 (.000)
No. of times labourers took police/state to court	1 (.001)
No. of times others	73 (.11)
Total no. of cases brought to court	**661 (100)**

Note: This table was constructed based on an analysis of statistics of cases published in the Royal Commission Report, 1,083–98.

Justice Allan Kerr's declaration that 'legal redress is shut out from one class altogether' (Royal Commission 1866, 286), aptly summed up the position of the court with respect to labourers and planters.

The class and, by implication, race nature of the laws convicting labourers of larceny, trespass, breach of contract and misconduct as servants can hardly be disguised. Indeed, these laws reflected the practical day to day unequal relationships between planters and labourers. The law on trespass was primarily a weapon against a people who were largely deprived of land by those who commanded most of the soil. The laws on contract and misconduct as servants were used as instruments of subjection in the main by the upper classes against the black masses since labourers were hardly in a position to employ servants and other categories of workers.

Apart from the 296 cases brought against labourers by planters, police and other agents representing the Crown brought 79 cases against labourers. Of these cases, 51 were for disorderly conduct, ten for assault, seven for larceny and six for indecent language, among others. The labourers lost all the cases heard against them by the Crown and were ordered to pay costs and penalties or were committed to gaol.

While agents representing the Crown took labourers to court on 79 occasions, they took planters only once (see table 5.1). Taken together, planters and the state took labourers to court 375 times. This represented 56.7 per cent of all civil and criminal cases heard at Bath during that time.

By comparison, the parish of St Thomas-in-the-Vale showed more social diversity in the background and calling of complainants and defendants involved in the 1,134 civil and criminal cases brought before Petty Sessions in that parish, 1863–65 (1,103). Of these cases, only 35 or three per cent involved planters compared to 308 or 46.5 per cent in Bath. A breakdown of these showed that of the 127 cases of larceny of growing produce, only 25 involved planters as complainants. Of the 68 cases of trespass, only a mere three cases involved planters.

A total of 41 appeals or 3.6 per cent of cases were filed by complainants not satisfied with the verdicts of the court against them. By comparison, only ten appeals or less than one per cent of cases heard were filed against verdicts handed down in Bath. In addition to the 1,134 civil and criminal cases heard in St Thomas-in-the-Vale, were 443 petty debt cases. Not one of those involved planters as complainants or defendants. Twelve appeals were filed against verdicts handed down by the Justices (1,103).

These statistics suggested that conflicts between planters and labourers were far less polarised in St Thomas-in-the-Vale compared to St Thomas-in-the-East. The courts in the Vale were, therefore, not openly used or perceived to be used as instruments of social and political struggle by the plantocracy against the labouring classes, as evident in St Thomas-in-the-East. There seemed to have been more flexibility in the justice system in the Vale. Hence, people tended to show more confidence in its ability to be fair and balanced in handing down justice.

The following statement by planter/magistrate William Carr in a way reflected a far less rigid justice system in St Thomas-in-the-Vale: 'I think the people have every confidence in the magistrates, although I am a magistrate myself; it is very rarely that a case in which the magistrates themselves are interested is ever brought before us' (507).

The polarisation between planters and labourers evident in St Thomas-in-the-East was absent in the Vale because sugar played a far less important role in that parish's economy. William Carr noted that out of a population of 14,000^2 in St Thomas-in-the-Vale, only about 1,400 worked on the estates in 1865 (507). By then, most sugar estates in that parish had folded. As a result, the economy became even more diversified.

An examination of the economic links of magistrates presiding over cases in St Thomas-in-the-East revealed the basis for the skewed verdicts against the labouring classes. Of the 28 Justices of the Peace on roll for that parish in 1865, 25 or 89.2 per cent were linked to estates and pens as owners, managers, lessees, and/or attorneys (see table 5.2). Of this group

TABLE 5.2. THE ECONOMIC LINKS OF JUSTICES OF THE PEACE IN ST THOMAS-IN-THE-EAST

Categories	Numbers	% of all Categories
Proprietors of Estates	5	17.8
Attorneys of Estates	5	17.8
Managers of Estates	6	21.4
Lessees of Estates/Pens	2	7.1
Proprietors of Pens	6	21.4
Store Keepers	2	7.1
Others	2	7.1
Total	**28**	**100**

Note: This table was constructed from calculations made from a study of Justices of the Peace in St Thomas-in-the-East. Documents of Justices of the Peace were published in the Royal Commission Report, 1,101.

Figure 2. Ruins of the Bath courthouse. Photo by Clinton Hutton.

Five Justices linked to eight sugar estates were complainants in 159 or 53.7 per cent of the 296 cases brought against labourers by planters. At the same time, these five Justices adjudicated in 265 or 89.5 per cent of all cases brought against labourers by planters. Among these planter-magistrates were Augustus Hire, attorney of Amity Hall Estate; William McKay, attorney of Wheelerfield Estate; James Harrison, attorney, Hordly Estate and Samuel Shortridge, attorney of Golden Grove and Serge Island estates and lessee of Holland and Rozelle estates. Hire, for example, took 51 labourers to court for breach of contract, misconduct as servant, larceny, etc.; and he adjudicated in 58 cases brought against labourers by other planter-magistrates.

There were also a few instances where a planter-magistrate, having taken a labourer to court, became adjudicator in that case. James Harrison, for example, adjudicated in five cases in which he was the complainant (see table 5.3).

TABLE 5.3. PLANTER-MAGISTRATES VS LABOURERS IN CIVIL AND CRIMINAL CASES HEARD AT BATH, ST THOMAS-IN-THE-EAST, 1863–65

Complainants	Calling/ Occupation	No. of Cases Against Labourers	% of all Cases	No. Cases Adjudicated	% of all Cases	No. Cases Where Complaints Adjudicated	% of all Cases
Augustus Hire	Attorney, Amity Hall Estate	51	17.2	32	10.8	3	1
William McKay	Attorney, Wheeler-field Estate	34	11.4	58	19.5	4	1.6
Samuel Shortridge	Attorney, Golden Grove and Serge Island Estates; Lessee, Holland and Rozelle Estates	32	10.8	28	9.4	2	.006
James Harrison	Attorney, Hordly Estate	25	8.4	106	35.8	5	1.6
Williams James	Manager, Duckenfield Estate	17	5.7	41	13.8	0	0
W.C. Groves	Lessee, Dalvey Pen	21	7	37	12.5	0	0

Note: This table was constructed based on an analysis of statistics of cases published in the Royal Commission Report, 1,083–98.

TABLE 5.4. JUDGMENTS HANDED DOWN AGAINST TAX OFFENCES IN PETTY SESSIONS AT BATH, ST THOMAS-IN-THE-EAST, 1863–65

Defendants	Tax Owed £ S D	Fine/Costs £ S D	Fine/Costs as % of Tax	Terms in Gaol if Fine/Costs not Paid
Planter	6 6 8	- 8 -	.063	30 days
Planter	8 15 -	5 16 -	.662	30 days
Planter	5 5 4	1 18 4	.36	10 days
Planter	14 6 -	5 16 -	.405	30 days
Planter	3 15 -	4 3 -	1.106	30 days
Labourer	- 15 -	- 15 -	1.033	10 days
Labourer	- 11 -	- 19 -	1.727	30 days
Labourer	1 - -	1 8 -	1.4	30 days
Labourer	- 16 -	1 4 -	1.5	30 days
Labourer	- 14 6	- 12 6	.43	10 days

Note: This table was constructed based on an analysis of statistics of cases published in the Royal Commission, 1,101.

The use of the court as a weapon of class and racial oppression was not only confined to the civil and criminal cases. Members of the ruling classes taken to Bath Petty Sessions for tax violation under the 'Registration Duty' paid less penalty/costs in relation to the amount of tax they owed to the state compared to blacks found guilty of the same offence. The biased judgment of the magistrates in favour of the plantocracy was unmistakable.

In the Court's rulings, the tendency was to impose fines and costs below the taxes planters owed while imposing fines and costs above the taxes owed by labourers. Where the fines and costs were not paid, the tendency was to impose similar gaol terms for both planters and labourers (see table 5.4). The Justices who presided over these cases were the same core of planter-magistrates drawn from eight sugar estates.

Domestic Conflicts among the Masses

In the midst of 'magisterial oppression' were serious conflicts among the masses in St Thomas-in-the-East. While planters were prepared to take their peers to court only on two occasions, and labourers 296 times, labourers were not able or willing to take planters to court, save for three occasions.

Legal Redress is Shut out from One Class Altogether

They were nevertheless prepared to take their counterparts to court 206 times or 31.1 per cent of all cases heard at Bath Petty Sessions, 1863–65. Indeed, in the first nine months of 1865, the number of cases of labourers as complainants and defendants superseded the total number of cases of 1863 and accounted for 93.2 per cent of those in 1864.

A breakdown of these cases revealed that abuse/assault constituted the main area of conflict or of settling conflicts among the labouring class. In 1863, this category constituted 74.6 per cent of cases; 1864, 71.6 per cent and up to September 1865, 62.3 per cent. Overall, abuse/assault amounted to 143 or 69.4 per cent of cases involving labourers as complainants and defendants. While labourers were willing to abuse and physically assault each other, six out of every ten conflicts heard in the courts, they seemed incapable or unwilling to do the same to planters who abused, assaulted and oppressed them.

The second most important category of conflicts related to larceny, especially of agricultural products. Overall, larceny accounted for 31 (or 15 per cent) of the cases. Trespass accounted for only 14 (or 6.7 per cent) of the cases involving labourers as complainants and defendants (see table 5.5). One possible reason for this relatively low area of conflict may have had to do with the fact that most black people did not own their own land and had to depend on the estates for land to rent or lease. On the other hand, cases of trespass brought against labourers by planters amounted to 17.5 per cent of the cases involving planters and labourers.

Cases were rarely dismissed in the Bath Petty Sessions. Most defendants, 650 or 98.3 per cent either had to pay fines and costs or were committed to prison. Almost all civil and criminal cases heard in Bath were resolved in favour of the complainants whether they were planters or labourers, white, brown or black, male or female. In this respect, complainants were treated equally.

Of course, this equal treatment meant that planters were able to use the court as an instrument to subject labourers to their will; earn money by collecting costs that labourers had to pay over to them and to assist the state to earn money from fines that defendants, deemed guilty more often than not, had to pay to the court. This equal treatment of complainants also meant that labourers were able to use the court to earn money by collecting costs that other labourer-defendants found guilty of offences had to pay over to them and to assist the state to earn money from fines imposed on 'guilty' labourer-defendants.

TABLE 5.5. LABOURERS VS LABOURERS, CIVIL AND CRIMINAL CASES HEARD IN PETTY SESSIONS AT BATH, ST THOMAS-IN-THE-EAST, 1863–65

Categories	1863	1864	1865	Total
Abuses/Assaults	47	53	43	143
Larceny	8	13	10	31
Trespass	4	3	7	14
Others	4	5	9	18
Totals	63	74	69	206

Note: This table was constructed based on an analysis of cases published in the Royal Commission Report, 108–98.

With a complainant almost a guaranteed winner in a case against a defendant and hence a likely winner of 'cash', it was no wonder that magistrate George Lyons, member of the Assembly, said, 'The black people are very fond of the lower Court' (Royal Commission 1866, 808). Similarly, magistrate John Kitchen, Clerk of the Trelawny Vestry said the black people 'seem to be too fond of going to court. They are very fond of [the] law' (568).

One of the primary reasons for this 'fond of [the] law' had to do with the fact that a Black complainant could earn more money in one day in the court than he would earn in a week working on the estate. More than that, approximately 85 per cent of the costs and fines levied against defendants found guilty could rent from one to ten acres of land for one year.

Going to court for complainants was, in a way, a status symbol for many black people who saw their participation as involving themselves with officialdom, 'civilization' and higher society. Their participation was also encouraged by the state though its officials.[3]

Despite the real or perceived benefits of the system of justice, labourers lost confidence in it because they lost confidence in the ability of their employers/Justices to be impartial in administering justice. Of the 296 cases brought against labourers by planters in Bath, only on six occasions did defendants appeal the verdict against them. In this respect, Justice Kerr noted that there was 'hardly any' appeals to the court, either on the part of the labourers or on the part of the employers with respect to contracts between the two (286). This was not surprising, for, on the one hand, the employers had no need to appeal, since the court usually ruled in their favour, while on the other hand, the system was so biased against the employees that it did not make sense for them to appeal.

Kerr noted that, 'If a man wishes to appeal...he must travel all the way to Kingston, a distance of 60 miles, before he can get a man to draw up his papers.' The two lawyers responsible for handling cases in St Thomas-in-the-East lived in Kingston. Kerr described the lawyers' fee as 'a large expense'. In addition, the complainant had to pay a fee to the Clerk of the Peace and 'has to procure a surety, which surety may live 10 miles off'. Kerr noted that the complainant and his surety 'have to attend before a magistrate, who may live 15 miles off'. The complainant then 'has to serve notice on the other side, and to serve endless grounds of appeal' (287). A labourer-complainant had to face magistrates manoeuvring and manipulation of the court to frustrate his/her efforts at appeals.[4] Then there was the uncertainty of whether justice would be done in practice even if the court ruled in favour of the complainant.[5]

Perhaps the most important reason that prevented labourers from taking planters to court or appealing against them was the fact that they were dependent on the estates for employment, house spot and provision ground. If labourers took their employers to court, that would jeopardise these. Hence, John Kitchen, magistrate and attorney for several estates in Trelawny said he did 'not think a man would be likely to employ another who had sued him' (568). For similar reasons, the labourers of Vere did not take their employers to court. According to Baptist Missionary Angus Duckett:

> The people do complain generally all the time I have been in Vere, it has been a constant complaint, that they have never received justice in the petty Courts, so much so that they would either suffer any wrong than take a planter or employer into Court... they said sometimes one oversee would sit and hear the case for him (884).

While at the local level there were 'hardly any appeals' filed at Petty Sessions in St Thomas-in-the-East, when a high court official from outside visited that parish, the number of appeals made by labourers was rather high. From 'hardly any appeals' locally, Justice Kerr said:

> I paid four visits altogether to the parish of St. Thomas-in-the-East, with an interval of upwards of a year between each, and the number of appeals in that parish was greater than in any other parish of Jamaica (286).

The People's Court

Loss of confidence in the system of justice by the black masses was higher in the sugar parishes. It was in these parishes that conflicts between employers and employees were at their highest. It was in these parishes that the highest number of planters, attorneys, lessees and overseers who were magistrates could be found. Large scale sugar production was, therefore, the basis for sustained 'magisterial oppression'. St Thomas-in-the-East seemed to rank first in the island in the level of 'magisterial oppression' and the people's response to it.

The loss of confidence in the system of justice soon led to disaffection and opposition. In St Thomas-in-the-East, this disaffection turned into an active organised opposition. This organised opposition to the legal system took the form of the creation of a parallel, or people's court in the early 1860s. The people set up their own court because they lost confidence in the formal court system and there was also a need for the masses to come to grips with the acute levels of conflict and indiscipline that set them against each other.

The people's court system, its structure, officer core, terms of reference, among other things, were worked out and decided on at several meetings. A meeting held at Letter Hill on July 11, 1863, for example, decided on the appointment of W.C. Minknot to the office of 'State General'. The meeting also looked at the question of who should qualify to be barristers and lawyers, as well as proposed fees for officers and set court dates for hearing cases. According to the minutes of that meeting, those in attendance took the following decisions:

> Move by Mr. James Steen and was unanimously carried that Mr. W.C. Minknot be appointed State General. Move by Mr. Daniel Bailey Secondd. By Mr. W. Bowie that the Qualyfication of Barristers and Lawyers be a Surtificate From the Judge and he Receiving a Fee, of One Pound.

> Move by Mr. Lake, Secondd. By D. Bailey that the Fees of the Peace office for each Process be a £1...Move by Mr. Mathew Ford, Secondd. By Mr. W. Mcknob that two Petty Sessions be held one on the 18th and one on the 25th inst:, each Courts do Commence at, 6, o clock in the afternoon, and that the Court of Arispagus be held on the 4th of August 1863. Resolve that the Courts be held at the Above name place (1,160–61).

That meeting also addressed the question of the conduct of persons in and around the venue designated 'courthouse' and the penalty to be imposed should the code of conduct be violated: 'Resolvd. That all Person or Persons who shall wilfully Misshebave themselves in the Vecinity of the Court the same shall be Commited for, trial and if wont Submit be disbands as Unsivilise' (1,161).

The meeting further looked at the question of fees for officers of the courts as well as the imposition of fines if they failed in their obligations. The meeting also elected Paul Bogle as a Justice of the Peace and indicated that trial would be by jury (1,161).

Legal Redress is Shut out from One Class Altogether

Another meeting, attended by 13 men at Letter Hill on August 4, 1863, elected other officers to the court. Among these officers were policemen of different ranks, secretary and treasurer, etc., Geo. B. Clarke was elected to be a 'Judge'; William Bogle, 'Clerk of the Peace'; Jas. Tobin, 'Crier'; William Bowie, 'Prevance Marshall General'; D. Bailey, 'Inspector'; William Tobin, 'Sargent'; Mathew Ford, 'Privett'; William Bogle, 'Secritary' and Mr. Lake, 'Treasurer'.

Officials of the people's court issued written or printed summonses to people whom it was felt violated the laws and discipline in the various communities throughout St Thomas-in-the-East. In a letter dated January 4, 1866 from William Miller to the Custos of St Thomas-in-the-East, the Serge Island and Blue Mountain Valley estates planter noted the following:

> They (the Negroes) held Courts of their own in the interior district of Manchioneal, and punished offenses by way of money fine. And the same procedure, up to the time of the late rebellion, has been carried on in the Blue Mountain Valley, at a Village called 'Huntley'. I have a summons now, that was taken from one of my Africans since the rebellion, and signed, 'John G. Lamont' J.P., this man is a field labourer on Serge Island Estate (1,161).

The summons retrieved from the indentured African labourer by Miller read in part:

> To James Millin of the Parish of St. Thomas-in-the-East, labourer, did made use to one Richard Grant of the parish on the 25 day of Feby 1865, abusive and Columnious Languages, tending to Provoke a breach of the peace,...These are therefore to command you the said James Millin In Her magistics name to be and appear on Saturday the 4 day of March at the Court House Huntley Village Before such Justices of the peace, as shall then be there, to answer to the said Charge, and to be further dealt with according to Law (1,161).

As can be seen from the above, the language and titles, along with other symbols of the colonial authority were employed in the various documents emanating from the people's courts.

Of course, there were objective impediments hampering the operations of the people's courts. The people's justices and other officers of these informal sittings could only try people who were willing to submit to their jurisdiction, because they saw the need for it, or were forced to accept it. Whatever their shortcomings, the people's courts were a primary indicator of the significant rise in the race and class consciousness of the labouring masses in St Thomas-in-the-East. The consciousness reflected in the setting up of the courts was, in a way, a rejection of the ideology of the ruling classes, reflected in the views of one of those black labourers from St Ann, who said in 1865:

> Black people too fool! – yes wosser dan fool, dem no free man already. Buckra no make one law fe we all, teef go a me ground law no da fe me? Him nock me down, law de fe me? Neber see de day when me will trus black negro fe make law to gobern me, or protect me little and much(*New York Daily Tribune* November 17, 1965).

The rise in the race and class consciousness of important sections of the black population in St Thomas-in-the-East who obviously 'trus black negro fe make law to gobern' them was a factor in the people's rising in that parish.

The organised opposition to the proceedings and decisions taken by the formal court system was not only reflected in the creation of an alternative court system. People were rallied and organised to attend the official courts in support of persons felt to be unjustly charged. Indeed, it was as a result of the mobilisation of scores of people from several communities in St Thomas-in-the-East to attend an October 7, 1865 Morant Bay court hearing in solidarity with a man charged with trespassing that provided the spark for the Morant war.

Anti-Slavery Society Revived

In most parts of the island, while the fear of a return to slavery found expression primarily through spontaneous gossip and rumours, speculation, public speeches and newspaper reports, in St Thomas-in-the-East it found organised expression in the revival of the Anti-Slavery Society in 1863. Rising beyond the necessity of gossip, rumours, speculation and speeches, the black people of St Thomas-in-the-East turned to organisation to assist them to resist any real or imagined attempts to turn them back to slavery. According to Revd Richard Warren, a Native Baptist minister in that parish, 1963, a 'document' to 'revive the anti-slavery society' was circulated for the people to sign (Royal Commission 1866, 1,067). The Native Baptist preacher said, 'a good many members [of my congregation] put their names to it, (1,067). Meetings of the Society were held in a house in Morant Bay. Warren said the house was 'hired' by George William Gordon for the purpose of housing meetings of the revived Anti-Slavery Society as well as for other meetings. He said among those who attended the meeting to revive the Anti-Slavery Society were 'A number of voters, tax-payers' (1,067). Most of the principal persons in the organisation and deliberations of the Society 'were citizens round about Morant Bay' (1,067). Among those who took part in the revival of the Anti-Slavery Society were Paul Bogle, his son, William Bogle, Henry Clyne, James Bowie, William Chisholm, George William Gordon and Richard Warren.

Legal Redress is Shut out from One Class Altogether

The meetings had a chairman in the person of Henry Clyne. Members were required to pay subscriptions or dues of 3d. or 6d. A committee was set up and an agent in the person of William Chisholm was appointed. His chief duties it would appear were of fundraiser and correspondent to the London based Anti-Slavery Society. Revd Warren said the Anti-Slavery Society 'was reorganised for the purpose of raising a fund to keep up a correspondence with the home Society' in London (1,067). The St Thomas-in-the-East Society raised 'a small sum...and forwarded [it] on' to the parent society in London (1,068). Subscriptions from members were also used 'for the purpose to pay the expenses of the house during the evening-lights, and so on' (1,068). The support for the revival of the Anti-Slavery Society was very broad. 'Most in the parish' signed or put their mark on the document agreeing to its revival.

Thus, there were several important differences between key sections of the African-Jamaican people of St Thomas-in-the-East and many of those in other parishes. They developed a higher level of consistent political activism and were more class and race conscious. They also developed a greater collective affinity to their African world views and cultural ethos and a strong sense of organised/collective self-help in dealing with the socio-economic and political problems in the parish. The people of St Thomas-in-the-East had a broad-based political leadership that was conscious, organised and determined in their efforts to rally the masses against plantocratic injustice and oppression and to seek help from sources they felt would be sympathetic to their cause.

Social and political upheavals do not usually happen just because of bad conditions or the severity of oppression, injustice and exploitation. Indeed, if this were so, there would have been rioting in Vere and other parishes with similar socio-economic conditions as St Thomas-in-the-East. Although objective condition ultimately constitutes the primary basis for social confrontation, it is unlikely to generate this kind of social behaviour by itself. Objective reality requires a subjective determination by the affected to do something about their condition as well as a corresponding willingness by the authorities to prevent them from doing so if social confrontation were to materialise. It was the growth and development of this subjective factor, evident, among other things, in the establishment of an alternative court and militia by Bogle's core people and the willingness of the plantocrats to turn that parish state machinery into an effective repressive apparatus that made the difference between St Thomas-in-the-East and other parishes.

Notes

1. In the sugar producing regions, since the majority of Justices were estate operators, this provision invariably meant that the employers of masses of labourers were adjudicators in conflicts between employers and labourers.
2. The 1861 census put the population of St Thomas-in-the-Vale....at 14,000.
3. Attorney-General Heslop noted that a letter from a certain parish stated that: 'There is still a large attendance here at the Saturday Courts. This spirit of litigation is favoured by the Clerk of the Peace for the sake of the fees, which sometimes for warrants and cross-warrants amount to pounds, and after all perhaps the case is dismissed with costs.' Cited in Thomas Harvey and William Brewin, Jamaica in 1866 (London 1867), 17.
4. This refers to the evidence of the constant putting off of cases or frequent absences of magistrates from appeal cases involving labourer complainants against planter defendants. This had the effect of frustrating complainants who constantly turned up for cases without having a hearing (Royal Commission 1866, 301).
5. One indication of this uncertainty came from evidence given to the Royal Commission by Alexander Scott. Scott, a labourer, sued Augustus Hire for eight pounds nine shillings that he owed him. After paying the necessary fees, including four pounds for a lawyer's service, Scott obtained a verdict against the Amity Hall attorney. However, three years after that, Scott had still not obtained his money from Hire.

6 'Colour for Colour, Skin for Skin': The Intellectual Foundations and Leadership of the 'Morant Bay Rebellion'

> [C]ivilization in its highest order is not the result of an innate superiority of any portion of the human race.
> — *John Willis Menard*

> Jamaica is not ruined. The ruin of the slave-owner has been taken for the ruin of Jamaica.
> — *John Willis Menard*

> Not as long as I live shall the white man trample me under foot.
> — *Samuel Clarke*

The abolition of slavery saw a significant increase in the social and political consciousness of the former enslaved population. Several factors were responsible for this. In the first place, emancipation meant that black people were considerably freer to meet, socialise, form associations, converse and live with each other across estates, parishes and counties in ways that were not possible under slavery. This newfound social intercourse which became a primary reason for the noteworthy rise in the consciousness of the people also meant that persons of African descent were in a better position to engage ancestral episteme, ontology and culture in recreating their existential pathways in post-slavery. A good example of this was the Great Revival of the early 1860s which modernised older forms of African Jamaican spirituality, begetting Zion and Poko Revival with a trans-parish/national appeal.

Secondly, the abolition of slavery saw a tremendous rise in the amount of African Jamaicans who could read and write when compared to their status under slavery. Then, it was illegal and taboo to teach Africans to read and write, or for Africans to engage in self-education. Emancipation ended that prohibition, and created a regime in which blacks were technically free to pool their resources and establish their own schools, and among other things, to attend institutions of learning founded, organised and operated mostly by the Church.

According to the 1861 census, 60,724 people could read, of which 50,726 could both read and write, while 33,521 children were more or less attending school.[1] These totals came from a population of over 400,000 and therefore were appallingly low.

However, there can be no doubt that emancipation, unlike slavery, allowed the Church and missionaries immeasurably more freedom to move around the island and to establish a form of school system as well as to train black instructors and operate schools for black children. The dissenting churches which were so reviled and physically attacked by the slaveholding classes, often with the approval of the colonial authorities, had to be relied on in post-slavery, even grudgingly, to play the leading role in the social control of the black masses. Their role was to lead the making of a system of white control based on cultural colonial servitude in the absence of chattel servitude.

It was this post-slavery atmosphere that also allowed some blacks to establish their own schools and to educate themselves on their own account, and to influence the direction of the emerging dominant system of education. The ability to read and write allowed blacks to make use of written ideas which influenced their thought processes and the way they conversed with both those who could and could not read. The black St Ann baker, that former enslaved man who 'obtained various kinds of employment, and put himself to school' after emancipation, gave us an idea of the impact of reading on his consciousness when he told Edward Underhill that he was 'now able...to read the newspapers, and know what is going on in the island and in the world' (Underhill 1970, 278).

Thirdly, the growth in the number and circulation of newspapers/advertisers sheets also contributed to the rise in consciousness of the black masses. Several newspapers were established in the post-slavery period 1838–65. They included *The Sentinel* (1864), whose proprietor was Robert A. Johnson; *The Jamaica Guardian* (1860), with proprietor George Henderson; *The Tribune and Public Advertiser* (1859), founder/editor, Isaac Lawton; *The Watchman and People's Free Press* (1852), whose proprietor was Isaac Vaz; *The County Union* (1850), proprietor and editor, Sidney Levien; *The Colonial Standard* (1849), founder George Levy; *The Trelawny* (1849), founder J.O. Clerk, and *The Morning Journal* (1838), founded by Edward Jordan and Robert Osborn. Fully one-half of these post-emancipation newspapers were owned by Jews and one-quarter owned by coloureds. For the first time black people were generally free to subscribe to newspapers, contribute letters to them and publicly read and discuss articles published in the press. Most of these newspapers (in excess of 75 per cent) were established after emancipation and, therefore, were products of the greater freedom engendered by the abolition of slavery.

Fourthly, the formation of organisations, societies, churches, and associations after slavery had a direct or indirect bearing on the growth and development of the consciousness/awareness of the black masses. Organisations and societies such as the *St. David's Liberal, Recording, and Election Association* (formed 1849), *Hanover Society of Industry* (founded 1855), the *Colonial Literary and Reading Society* (established 1849), the *St Ann's Literary and Reading Society* (founded 1856), the *Freeman Chapel Provident Society* (founded 1856), contributed to the rise in consciousness of the people. Then there were the *Workingmen's Literary Society of St David* (founded 1865), the *Liberation Society of St Ann* (established 1865), and the various churches/religious societies, which contributed in a more direct way to the development of the people's consciousness/awareness.

Fifthly, the granting to people of African descent limited political rights, including the elective franchise and the freedom to organise mass meetings and to canvass and campaign, had a positive impact on the growth of their consciousness.[2] Mass consciousness grew rapidly as well because the very existence of wage labour, contracts, the inclusion of blacks in acquiring property and political representation, paying tax and their subjection to new laws, among other features of post-slavery society became key reference points for formerly enslaved Africans to privately or publicly voice their opinion.

Mass consciousness developed out of a spontaneous response of the masses to their immediate circumstances. This naturally spontaneous, unschooled/layman's way of interpreting events and phenomena did not mean that there was no permanence in the features of mass consciousness. Indeed, mass consciousness, this produce of common experience, provided a main basis for the development of a Jamaican psychology, personality and linguistic ethos after slavery. However, while mass consciousness developed more rapidly across the island after 1838, there was an aspect of the people's consciousness that developed more slowly, more systematically, more methodically, more scholastically and more deliberately and analytically. This form of consciousness could be referred to as ideology. It was the product of persons deliberately formulating and articulating ideas of a political nature about the nature and purpose of people in the making of free, sovereign, just, viable, existential space.

Mass consciousness and ideological consciousness were dialectically interconnected. The growth of ideological consciousness was relatively slower than mass consciousness and was attributable to the slower development and culturing of race, class and nationalist consciousness among the black masses.

There were black Jamaicans who wanted fundamental reform or change to post-slavery society. Some of these Jamaicans spent part of their time purposefully reading, listening, reflecting, formulating and distributing ideas, often contradicting the views of the plantocracy and the authorities on fundamental issues in Jamaican society and the world. These persons emerged primarily from among own-account blacks who were more often than not the main leaders of the people's struggles. They included, among others, Henry Clyne, Samuel Clarke, Paul Bogle, George William Gordon, George McIntosh, William Grant, James McLaren, James Dacres, William Bowie, Moses Bogle and John Anderson. When compared to the majority of the population, these men represented part of the post-emancipation success story. The black masses looked to them for leadership because, among other things, they represented the embodiment of the social being which African Jamaicans were aspiring to be at that time.

Francisco Cutanda the Spanish critic, argued in 1860 that 'the statements or actions of degraded slaves' or 'the conduct of freedmen or mulattoes' were not 'worth writing down' since these were of no 'interest' and no value to 'the public' (i.e., white people). This was a commonly held position in European epistemology and political discourses. My approach to the mapping of the world view of the former enslaved, is to invert the position of Cutanda et al.

What did the thoughts and actions of people of African descent desiring change in post-slavery society tell us about the world view of own-account Africans in particular, and the black masses in general and the ideological foundations of the Morant Bay war? The approach here is to codify and categorise aspects of the philosophy of the thoughts and actions (praxis) of a selection of persons of African descent regarding the social, political, economic, cultural and ontological direction of post-slavery society.

John Willis Menard, the 'Talented New Parishioner'

One of the most prominent ideologists influencing the people's movement in and around St Thomas-in-the-East was John Willis Menard, (also spelt Minard and Maynard). Menard, 'a coloured American' (Eyre 1971, 50), was referred to in a letter to the *Sentinel* February 25, 1865) by one of his comrades as 'our widely respected and talented new parishioner' who came to reside in St David. The parish of St David bordered St Thomas-in-the-

East to the West. Menard first came to Jamaica in 1863. He stopped in Jamaica on his way back from British Honduras (Belize) to the US. Menard had gone on a mission on behalf of the Lincoln Administration to check out the viability of resettling African Americans in that British colony after emancipation. While passing through Jamaica, the 25-year-old Menard met a 17 year old Jamaican woman, Elizabeth. They fell in love and eventually got married.

John Willis Menard returned to Jamaica about the beginning of 1865 and settled in the parish of St David. The south eastern geographic belt of Jamaica linking Kingston, Port Royal, St David and St Thomas-in-the-East, held the significant

Figure 3. John Willis Menard – Edith Menard – 'John Willis Menard' – Negro History Bulletin 23–No.3 (1964). Restored by Clinton Hutton.

presence of the alliance and joint social, political and economic endeavour of some of the island's most active and committed radical black and brown freeholding political leaders.

They included George William Gordon and Paul Bogle, to whom Menard was almost certainly introduced, and Samuel Clarke, in whose St David's house, the 'new parishioner' stayed with his pregnant Jamaican wife. Menard's return to Jamaica might be in part connected to the fact that his wife was a Jamaican. Perhaps a more pressing reason, however, had to do with the African American resettlement scheme pursued by the Abraham Lincoln Presidency, which Menard was sent to explore in British Honduras in 1863.

This scheme appeared to have collapsed and Menard found himself in Jamaica with what seemed to be uncertainty on his part about the position of Africans in the US. Already, while he was on his trip to British Honduras, the Draft Riots which resulted in the lynching of African Americans erupted in

New York and the 13th Amendment to the American Constitution outlawing slavery throughout the US happened on February 1, 1865 while he was in Jamaica.

African Americans were attracted to the British West Indies where slavery was abolished a generation before it took place in the US. This fact might have made these islands more attractive to blacks still in bondage. Indeed, before emancipation in the US, African Americans would commemorate the August 1 Emancipation Day Anniversary celebrated in the British Caribbean, where slavery had ended in 1838. The racial climate was also less hostile, especially to fair skinned Africans like Menard. The British West Indian colonies also provided an easier gateway for blacks wanting to travel to England to link up with British anti-slavery activists or to petition the British government which, at that time, generally favoured an end to trafficking and slavery.

Several North American blacks found their way to Jamaica and made various contributions to the life of the colony. Prominent among them were two of the world's most outstanding black Abolitionists, Henry Highland Garnet (who would become a friend and comrade of Menard), and Samuel Ringgold Ward (Ripley 1985, 227, 407–411, 421).

While in St David, Menard, not yet 27 years old, founded the *Workingmen's Literary Society of St David*, January 18, 1865. By February 25, that society boasted 16 members (*Sentinel* February 25, 1865). The association was essentially a debating society/study group. Topics dealing with issues facing the people were debated. Some of these topics were of a highly political and philosophical nature. A principal goal of the Society was 'the redemption of this island from the power of ignorance' (*Sentinel* February 25, 1865). Among the questions debated at the Society's meetings were:

> Whether republican or kingly government was best adapted for the good of mankind; whether fire or water was the greater element; the pen or the sword the more able instrument.

> Alexander the Great or Peter was the greatest warrior, or did most for the good of mankind (Eyre 1971, 50).

The name of the Society, 'Workingmen's Literary', seemed to reflect Menard's association with or knowledge of the emerging working class and possibly social democratic movement in the US. 'J.W. Menard, Esqr.' as the president and founder of the St David based society, was addressed by one of his colleagues, appeared to have been highly appreciated and respected by his Jamaican comrades. He was very knowledgeable in history and world affairs, and was an excellent essayist.

Back in the US, one source described Menard as 'a scholar and a good writer.'[3] John Willis Menard was born April 3, 1838, in Kaskaskia, Illinois. He was sent to school in Sparta...after having spent 18 years of his life as a farmer (Menard 1964, 53). By age 23, 'he entered Iberia College in Ohio' (53).

Apart from organising discussions and debates in the *Workingmen's Literary Society*, Menard was a reader and contributor to the press. Two newspapers to which he contributed letters were the *Watchman* and the *Sentinel*.[4] His letters to the press reflected in part the considered thinking of Menard, the radical black/coloured Jamaican progressives and a main political and philosophical reason for founding the *Workingmen's Literary Society*.

On January 16, 1865, Menard, or J.W.M. as he usually signed his letters, wrote a letter on 'Popular Education' to the *Sentinel* (January 19, 1865). In that letter, which was published three days later, he argued for adequate schooling and education for the masses of the people as the basis for social cohesion, economic development, happiness and prosperity. This view sharply contradicted the views of the plantocratic forces and their allies who argued that blacks could not be educated in any serious way because of their supposedly innate inferior intellectual capacity which marked them out to be menials. Menard asserted that:

> The happiness and prosperity of a nation depends – not on its mineral wealth, largeness of population, but mainly upon the intelligence of the great mass of its people; without the latter, the former will forever sleep undisturbed in the dark domains of blissful ignorance.

The key principle for Menard in this statement was that national development was contingent on the agency of the masses of the people. In this profound statement, education and training, the agential trigger for the awakening of the creative, imaginative and intellectual power of the masses must be pursued with urgent, unflinching vigour and commitment.

The 27-year-old Menard believed deeply in the policy viability of his ideas on popular education for development in post-slavery Jamaican society. This belief was rooted in his conviction and knowledge of his own recent pedagogical experience back in Ohio. This experience seemed to have created in him, the model of what the Jamaican masses could be if educated and trained in the way he advocated in his letters to the press.

He was only able to read at 18 years, but by age 23, he became a student at Iberia College, the basis for the unfurling for him of a vista of possibilities. His achievements, his social and professional status, even within the context of a suffocating landscape of prejudice, was not only impressive, but appeared to have significantly contributed to Menard's philosophy of education as well as his conviction of its successful policy application in the development of post-slavery society.

By January 27, 1965, a contributor's letter under the pseudonym 'Honesty' appeared in the *Sentinel* supporting Menard's view on popular education. According to the writer:

> In the *Sentinel* of the 19th inst. appeared a very characteristic letter, on the subject of Popular Education, signed J.W.M. the letter abounds in charges against the present system of Popular Education in Jamaica, which I regard in very many respects, as proper and truthful. It is a fact, that the present system is defective in all its parts and, therefore, defective in its results.

Honesty's response to Menard's letter represented in essence a similar trend of thought evident in the views of some of the leaders who were involved in the Morant Bay courthouse assault in October 1865.

On January 30, 1865, J.W.M. had another of his letters published in the *Sentinel*. This letter, which was titled 'Popular Education: No. 2', vigorously contended with the white racist notion that only people from temperate climate found in places like England and France were capable of 'a full development of the reasoning faculty'. Demonstrating his knowledge of world development, Menard used historical facts to reject one of the central arguments developed in modern European epistemology to justify placing blacks and other Non-Europeans in slavery and other forms of colonial bondage. According to Menard:

> It has been said by some who boast of their physiological and phrenological research that extreme climate is unfavourable to the spread of civilization – that 'a full development of the reasoning faculty can only take place where physical circumstances conspire – that the human race is indebted to the climate of England and France for the intellect of Newton and Laplace.' This argument may be admissible in modern times, but the experience of history teaches that it could not be held true with regard to the ancient world, whose civilization was nurtured under the benign influences of a tropical sun. An investigation of the physical circumstances, would, most surely, settle the fact, that civilization, in its highest order is not the result of an innate superiority of any portion of the human race.

Here, Menard employed one of the key component sources of African diaspora episteme to combat the racist theory of knowledge and being, which posited that the African capacity to conceptualise and to know, was inherently flawed, and thus fixed in nature, rendering his thought and actions devoid of the creative ingredients of civilisation. He was therefore capable of worth, only under the guidance and certitude of the European.

Menard's rejection of this racist episteme and his application of black consciousness as a category of knowing in philosophy were not unique to him. Indeed, black consciousness was a mode of perception, a lens and a tool of analysis in the fashioning of a system of knowledge on which, to an important degree, the ideological and political activism of blacks rested, and had broad application in African diaspora epistemology in the Americas, since the struggles to end slavery.

Menard, who believed that the pen was more powerful than the sword, felt that, by depriving blacks access to education, the whites were blocking Africans' advancement and fettering the development of Jamaican civilisation. He argued that lack of education led blacks into believing/internalising white racist stereotypes about Africans. Menard thus concluded that education had to play the leading role in the liberation and empowerment of the African or anybody so deprived.

> In Jamaica, I am afraid, the greater portion of the people have been made to believe that they are not susceptible of attaining high degree of civilization, that its higher avenues are open to the "superiority of the family." This belief has so lulled them that they look upon the fine arts and sciences as unattainable – great impossibilities! This belief forms another formidable barrier to the spread of education in this beautiful island. Then, the expected new administrative reform should be organised as to rescue the rising generation before this dangerous belief germinates in the young mind (*Sentinel* January 30, 1865).

As can be seen here, Menard was not just campaigning and arguing for popular education, but popular education embracing a philosophy antithetical to prejudice.

At a time when the churches were obviously playing the leading role in organising, funding, and making elementary education available to sections of the black population, Menard argued that 'government alone' possessed the capability to fund and organise the education of the masses on a scale necessary to lay the basis for this 'much needed reformation'. Besides, he intimated that most parents were not educated enough to provide the necessary support for their children's education. This was a compelling reason for the government to establish popular education to include adult education. He felt also that it was to government's benefit to conduct 'this great humane work' (making education available) since it was easier to rule an educated man than 'a barbarian', and since government rooted on the education of the governed would provide a foundation that was 'firmer and more lasting'.

> The greater portion of the parents of the rising generation [is] not sufficiently educated to lay the basis of this much needed reformation; therefore, Government alone must be its protector. If Government does its duty in this great humane work, it will only help to strengthen its own life – building its foundation on a firmer and more lasting basis; for it is easier to rule a fully civilized man (comparatively speaking) than a barbarian (*Sentinel* January 30, 1865).

Education was thus regarded as a critical instrument in the building of the nation state in consequence of its agential and identity constructing function, possessing the capability to engender an ontology of useful, peaceful citizenship.

The founding president of the *Workingmen's Literary Society of St David* who blamed areas of the temperate regions for denying tropical peoples the right to attaining a high order of civilization, said it was the people's duty to correct that state of affairs. It was imperative that the people unite to see to the realisation of a system of popular education based on 'philanthropic principles' and racial equality in order 'to break the blighting fetters of ignorance from all shades and hues.'

> But to return 'as children of the sun, and as susceptibility of attaining a higher order of civilization has been denied us by many of the temperate regions, it is our duty to correct, and if possible, controvert this impression which seems to be gaining strength in the world. Popular education, then, should be our first step. What I mean by popular education, is a system based on Philanthropic principles – a system that seeks the advancement of the arts and sciences among all men, that seeks to break the blighting fetters of ignorance from all shades and hues – from the white as well as the black,... – a system at war with sectarianism – one that diffuses knowledge equally among the varied branches of the great human family (*Sentinel* January 30, 1865).

Menard's answer to racism was racial equality from which emanated 'a system at war with sectarianism' and diffused 'knowledge equally among the varied branches of the great human family'. Menard's anti-racist views were not only hostile to ideological plantocracy, but conflicted with some of the prejudices expressed in white abolitionists' thought, since his philosophy rejected the notion of the superiority of one race over the other.

John Menard, who held that education constituted the motive force of civilisation, argued that the road to honour, dignity, economic development and modernity was only possible through education. Jamaica, he said, had the necessary natural resources to make its people self-sufficient rather than to 'wait to be fed with manna from abroad'. This socio-economic regime however, was only viable if the system 'seeks the advancement of the arts and sciences among all men' and makes 'labor honourable in all its branches'. If not, the island would remain underdeveloped, uncivilised and hopelessly relying on foreign expert and goods. How to build the agential capacity for freedom and free society was Menard's mission and it is worth citing him at length in the poetic language of his conviction.

> [W]e should have every nerve strung, and every energy aroused in the noble work of bringing this neglected country to a high standard of modern convenience, invention and civilization: we should lay aside all paltry prejudice, and go to work in earnest – making labor honourable in all its branches.
>
> We must be educated. The rising generation of the half million of people inhabiting this island must be trained in all the varied branches of mechanical, commercial and agricultural industry – in the arts and sciences, in jurisprudence, in morals, in religion, in political economy and in all the noble pathways which lead to manly honor and dignity. Unless this great work is accomplished, the unexplored wealth which has so long been sleeping in the mountains of this island, waiting, apparently, for imported genius to be developed will still rest undisturbed beneath the sweet, sad chorus of the weeping hills. For the resources of any country are developed in proportion to the engineering skill of its people. Jamaica has almost all the materials which are requisite in the formation of a great nation. First – she has territory. Second – she has population. Third – she has resources for self-maintenance. All she wants now is the proper cultivation of native genius – native mechanical skill. She must learn to stand alone, and not wait to be fed with manna from abroad. The Jamaica press has not entirely done its duty in this direction; it has been handling the subject with kid gloves. This crying necessity should be thundered from every pulpit, from every editorial sanctum, and from the halls of legislation. The facts should no longer be disguised, for they tell loudly against us as free men (*Sentinel* January 30, 1865).

What is clear is that John Willis Menard was not just unfurling a post-slavery narrative brimming with important ingredients for recreating the island, following on the abolition of slavery. In Menard's subversive insights, if Jamaica were to be more humane, more civilised, more educated and trained, freer, just and equal, the masses of black people would have to constitute the motive force of development and authority. And he expected/hoped and encouraged the press, church and legislature, out of self-interest, to champion this self-evident principle for development in the island.

The assumptions on which Menard made his case for the agency of the black masses to be central to the making and development of post-slavery society were, to a great extent, the opposite from those of the colonial authorities and the alliance of foreign (mostly British) and local (Jamaican) elites. This difference was epistemological, ontological, cultural and political. An examination of colonial documents on education, for example, clearly showed the difference when compared to the ideas of Menard, George William Gordon and Samuel Clarke on the same issue.

Hence, the 'Report of Sterling to the British Government, 11 May 1835', in considering the Imperial Government scheme for the 'Negro Education Grant' for emancipated Africans, said:

> The certain result of the new situation [emancipation], when the minds of the people are at all in movement, will be a consciousness of their own independent value as rational beings without reference to the purposes for which they may be profitable to others. There is a danger that the cheapness of land compared to labour, the fertility of the soil, and the warm climate, may reduce them to a thoughtless inactivity (Gordon 1963, 21).

Thus, from the beginning of the end of slavery, the powers that be were clear (i.e., Carlylean) that the spirit of independence must never be allowed to germinate in the identity and agency of post-slavery blackness.

Menard's call for the 'rising generation' to be trained in 'all the varied branches of mechanical, commercial and agricultural industry – in the arts and sciences', was profoundly revolutionary because it rejected the white racist notion that Africans were intellectually inferior to Europeans, could not grapple with complex ideas respecting the arts and sciences and thus could only benefit from an education which trained them to be better manual labourers. His call demonstrated in his ideas a strong sense of nationalism. How else could the training he advocated take place without developing national institutions? And how would this be even possible if agency did not reside in the black majority? What would be the use of this training if the island's economy was controlled by men who had no desire to live in Jamaica and whose existential position on the island was antithetical to black freedom and sovereignty?

Menard's call not only radically contradicted the position of the ruling ideology, for, in order for it to be implemented, Jamaica must increasingly become a nation culturally and politically. His call for this British colony to 'learn to stand alone, and not wait to be fed with manna from abroad', his call for the 'proper cultivation of native genius – native mechanical skill' to exploit the island's natural resources, was primarily a call to develop a more modern, enlightened, self-reliant Jamaican nation with modern convenience rooted in the agency of former enslaved Africans as its principal motive force. Sometimes Menard's Black Nationalist stand was quite explicit. For example, documents said to have been seized from Menard by the Jamaican authorities during the suppression of the masses, revealed, among other things, his Black Nationalist ethos: 'I am for black nationalities. The prosperity and happiness of our race and their posterity lay in a separation from the white race (US Government 1868, 115). After his Jamaican sojourn was cut short by the Jamaican authorities, Menard advised blacks in the US to 'look at a white man as a mere common human being, and not as a ruler or superior'. Moreover, he asserted that 'most of the [white] Republicans, Radicals or Abolitionists, who are the well-wishers of the black man, only sympathize with him in his servile condition' (Rankin 1974, 434).

Menard's nationalism must be seen within the context of antebellum America and his Jamaican experience – the impulses that motivated this 'aristocrat of color' to lead a US government mission to Belize to investigate and report on the feasibility of establishing a colony for African Americans in 1863, moved him to passionately argue for 'a system at war with sectarianism' in Jamaica, in 1865, and impelled him to contest election to the US Congress in 1868. His nationalism could or should not be thus reduced merely to a separationist ethos as Lord Stanley of the British Foreign Office implied in 1866, and Gad Heuman uncritically repeated in 1994 (Heuman 1994, 158).

In 1866, Stanley had a clear political motive for his one-sided assessment of Menard's politics and philosophy. He was obviously intent on preventing the development of a possible row between Britain and the US over the treatment of John Willis Menard by the Jamaican authorities during the suppression of 1865.

Kingston (Jamaica)-based US Consul Gregg, who, at the time of the outbreak in Morant Bay, was reported to have requested US military assistance for the British colony, reported weeks afterwards to the State Department, that American citizen, John Willis Menard, was mistreated by the Jamaican authorities. According to Charles Adams, US diplomat in London, Gregg reported that Menard,

> a resident in the parish of St. David's, in that island, was, on or about the 27th of October, 1865, without warrant or complaint under oath, seized by order of the authorities, in a district not under martial law, was conveyed by force into a portion of the country of Surry, then under martial law, and was there put in close confinement, no charges being exhibited against him, until the 4th of November, when he was banished from the island, by virtue of a simple order issued by the governor.

> The consul, after investigating the circumstances attending this case, reports that he can find no evidence of any offence committed by Mr. Menard, nor any reasonable ground for suspecting him to have been implicated in illegal transactions or designs of any kind. So peremptory was the order that Mr. Menard was compelled to leave behind him a wife in destitute circumstances, who was soon afterwards delivered of a child, but whom he was not permitted to visit (US Government 1868, 114).

That child was Willis Menard, John's son.

The response of the British Foreign Office to the State Department inquiry into the matter was to try to isolate and discredit Menard by using documents said to be found on him, to show that he spoke of his 'deep hatred for the ruling class' of America and, by implication, of Jamaica, where 'The overseer of Albion estate has inaugurated a most hellish system of oppression and imposition in this parish' (115).

Rather than answering the legal and human rights issue raised by the State Department, the first response of the Foreign Office was to sue for racial solidarity with its American counterpart, because, if Menard the Black Nationalist and separatist were a danger to the white ruling classes in Jamaica, he was of necessity also a danger to the white ruling classes in the US. However, Menard was no ordinary African American. He belonged to a prominent middle-class coloured family known on Capitol Hill and Washington, DC, generally. He was employed to a clerkship in the Department of the Interior, Washington, DC. He was the first black to 'hold such a position in Washington' (Menard 1964, 53). He was also appointed by the US government to investigate the feasibility of establishing a black American colony in Belize. Moreover, he was a member of the ruling Republican Party at a time when radical reconstruction was about to take off in the US.

The appearance of another of Menard's letters in the *Sentinel* (February 22, 1865) further revealed the strong nationalist tendency in his ideological position. To him, the elimination of the consequences of slavery and the utilisation of the best achievements of humankind through openness to the outside world were prerequisites for national development. In this letter, Menard argued that the development of the Jamaican nation was being fettered by her 'primeval selfishness' or refusal to utilise the achievements of enlightened nations and her 'ancient conservatism', the product of slavery.

> [W]ith all the noble national examples of modern time set before her...she is still groping her way amid the darkness of her primeval selfishness, and ancient conservatism. Like Japan, she would shut herself from the world –

from mankind, from the arts and sciences, civilization, progress, invention – in a word from earth and heaven!

This letter differed from previous ones in its focus on Menard's thought on economic issues. His economic perspective radically opposed the plantation outlook. In a strong defence of a more enlightened, nationally focused, self-reliant Jamaican economy, Menard blamed the island's 'primeval selfishness' and 'ancient conservatism', the products of its slavery past, for allowing 'foreign speculators' a free hand to 'plunder' the island's 'best resources' and repatriating the capital accumulated from those ventures. In his opposition to that state of affairs, he called for the colony's 'life struggles' to be 'speedily put forth' to right the historical injustice done to the land and the former enslaved population.

> Since the 'balmy day' of slavery, Jamaica seems to have dragged through life like an emaciated victim unable to walk in life. Her commerce, her trade, her agriculture and industry seem to have departed hand-in-hand with slavery! Apparently, freedom seems to have brought her ruin! Jamaicans have proven to be their own enemies – enemies to their country, its progress and commerce, its industry and independence. They have permitted foreign speculators to invade their country and plunder its best resources, to hoard millions of money and then depart in peace to revel in princely luxury across the waters, leaving them (the Jamaicans) hirelings and agents on paltry commissions! Foreign speculators and slavery have basely consigned this island to a pit from which it cannot easily risen, unless its life-struggles are speedily put forth. But Jamaica is not ruined. The ruin of the slave owner has been taken for the ruin of Jamaica (*Sentinel* February 22, 1865).

What is damming here was Menard's assessment of the position of the Jamaican elites who did everything to undermine the social and economic viability of the black masses, but 'permitted foreign speculators to invade their country and plunder its best resources' and 'hoard millions of money' and 'leaving them hirelings and agents on paltry commissions'. The psychology, episteme and modus operandi Menard described in the ontology of the Jamaican elites remained relevant, well beyond post-coloniality. Here, Menard provided another reason for the black masses with an emerging middle class in the van, to lead the post-slavery reconstruction of Jamaican society.

The estates, the principal units of the plantation economy, and the major source of foreign domination in Jamaica, did not escape Menard's economic focus. Those estates, which he saw as constituting the basis of the brutal oppression of the black masses, must be dealt with (according to him) to put an end to that regime and develop the island's economy. While Menard did not outline any specific theory respecting the type of economy he would like to see develop in post-slavery society, he was blunt in his criticisms of the role of the estates in Jamaica and predicted that they 'shall soon be purged.'

> These beautiful and extensive estates shall soon be purged. The chains and whips, and sighs of the desponding bondman, and the tears of his anguish and blood drops of his heart, and life are still upon them. When they shall be purified, and the walls of their dungeons with the last remnant of oppression shall crumble and decay, they shall be made to yield as of old, their rich and golden harvest (*Sentinel* February 22, 1865).

What methods were to be employed to purify these estates and what the ownership structure would look like, the President of the *Workingmen's Literary Society* did not say. Whatever the type of economy that was to emerge, however, 'study' and 'observation of the means which have contributed to the progress of other nations', 'honest industry and free labor' must be employed to play central roles in the development of that economy. Accordingly, Menard wrote:

> All that is now wanting for the perfect development of the innumerable resources which are commanded by the people of this island, in that direction to their enterprise which might be afforded by study, and observation of the means which have contributed to the progress of other nations; and when that point is obtained, she will resume the position in wealth and enterprise which she once filled, with this difference, however, that whereas her first prosperity grew out of injustice, and wrong – her last will arise from honest industry and free labor (*Sentinel* February 22, 1865).

At the time of the Morant Bay conflict, Menard was said to be employed, or was once employed, to the Albion Estate in St David (Royal Commission 1866, 386). There he worked in or with the 'Irrigation Land Gang' (387). He was a close friend and associate of Samuel Clarke, 'a vestryman and politician of St David (Eyre 1971, 191). Menard was expelled from Jamaica because of his association and friendship with Samuel Clarke and the political movement especially in St David and St Thomas-in-the-East. He was also expelled because of his work in the *Workingmen's Literary Society*, and for the views he expressed in letters published in the press.

Back in the US, he settled in New Orleans where he joined the reconstruction effort. In 1868, he was elected to the US Congress representing the Second Congressional District of Louisiana. He polled 5,107 votes to his rival, fellow Republican Caleb Hunt, a white man, who received 2,833 votes. Menard was the first person of African descent to have been elected to the US Congress. However, he was never seated because the Congress adopted Congressman James Garfield's motion that 'it was too early to admit a Negro to the U.S. Congress' (Menard 1964, 53).

Samuel Clarke: 'One of the Most Indefatigable Advocates'

Before Paul Bogle was known to the political landscape, there was Samuel Clarke, a radical black political leader and power broker in the parish bordering St Thomas-in-the-East, St David. Clarke was probably born a slave and was probably in his mid to late 30s or somewhere in his 40s at the time of the Morant Bay outbreak. In 1866, St David's Custos, William P. Georges, said he knew Clarke 'as a boy 30 years ago' (Royal Commission 1866, 892). Clarke was a carpenter by trade (1,149). He also cultivated sugar cane and manufactured sugar and rum using the facilities of the Custos. Georges, however, withdrew the use of his facilities from Clarke around 1862 (892).

Samuel Clarke was referred to as 'a sort of lawyer' by the Custos because he usually assisted many of his black parishioners in matters regarding the courts. He was certain to be one of the members of the *Workingmen's Literary Society of St David*. He was the principal leader of the black masses of that parish and beyond and played a central role supporting Menard, and introducing him to the people of St David, and likely, St Thomas-in-the-East. According to reports, these two men were seen together on several occasions.⁵ When suppressionist forces, led by Captain Astwood of the Kingston Volunteer Troop, went to Samuel Clarke's house on orders to arrest him, they found Menard at the black Vestryman's residence, but he (Clarke) was in Kingston. In his report to Major General O'Connor, Astwood said:

> I next visited the residence of Sam Clarke, breaking open any lock-fast places, but found no papers, and but one suspicious party, a friend of his, by name Maynard, from whom I elicited oath with a pistol to his head, that Clarke had left for Kingston on Sabbath last, and was believed still to be there.... We examined Maynard,...in the presence of Justices Smith and McLean, who turned out to be Secretary to a Debating Society, and general scribbler to the newspapers; but as in the opinion of the Justices, nothing certain could be proven, he was admonished an dismissed, with a warning; that his actions were watched (*Colonial Standard* October 20, 1865).

Later, the October 31, 1865 issue of the *Gleaner* reported that J.W. Menard 'was yesterday captured and taken to Up-Park Camp for safe custody'. Obviously, the authorities went back on their decision to just admonish and dismiss the President of the *Workingmen's Literary Society*.

While I have not come across any record to throw light on a systematically argued ideological position of Samuel Clarke, it seemed likely that his outlook coincided with Menard's and the *Workingmen's Literary Society of St David*. He was a contributor (of letters) to the *Watchman*, but the preserved remnants and whole copies of that newspaper at the National Library of Jamaica do not seem to bear any letter identified as his. However, an indication of his ideological position can be gleaned from reports about his behaviour and social and political activities. See Swithin Wilmot's essay 'The Politics of Samuel Clarke: Black Political Martyr in Jamaica 1851–1865' in the *Jamaica Historical Review* XIX: 17–29 for a good account of the political leadership, journey and demise of Samuel Clarke. With respect to Samuel Clarke's political activism, Charles McLean, Clerk of the Vestry for St David, gave a statement in which he said the following about Clarke:

> Political agitation was always kept up in St. David by Samuel Clarke, and this man invariably taught the people to be insolent and rude to their employers; he attended the courts and caused great mischief by his always rude and overbearing conduct; the people at all times resorted for him for advice and instruction, and of late he was greatly aided and abetted by J.W. Menard, a coloured American. This latter had a debating society in the parish,....
>
> These two men, Clarke and Menard, aided by others, wrote scurrilous and abusive letters at all times in the *Watchman* newspapers, tending to bring the authorities into disrespect (Eyre 1971, 50).

Clarke was hostile to the plantocracy and those black people who supported that class. He and 'his party' were said to have organised to exclude a black local government representative from the Vestry because he was 'too much buckra'. Measures were also said to be taken by Clarke and his colleagues to remove schoolmasters from their posts for similar reasons. According to Samuel Ringgold Ward, once a highly respected and renowned African American abolitionist who ended up living in Jamaica and actively sided with the plantocracy against Bogle and black progressives:

> [I]n June, [1865] I think, a vestry meeting was held there, and a man was excluded from the vestry because he was said to be 'too much buckra.' He was a very decent old man, named Dewany; he was a black vestryman, but they all joined to put him out;... he did not go with them in their radical measures. Samuel Clarke and some others were for disturbing things, and seeking to get the control of everything into their own hands. For years past whatever side the magistracy took, they would take the opposite side; a constant 'confusion' as the Baptist call it, between Sam Clarke and his party and the Hon. Mr. Georges and the magistrates. Because he [Dewany] took

the side of the gentry; that was what was alleged against him, that he was too much buckra. After that they wanted to have all the schoolmasters turned out, and they asked me to take one of the schools. I, of course, declined; then they said they must have a man of the name of Minard, an American, put into one of the schools, and a person turned out for that purpose (Royal Commission 1866, 556).

Clarke's attempt[s] to get Samuel Ward to side with his party against 'buckra' did not seem to have been successful. Indeed, Ward, who, along with Henry Highland Garnet, was explicitly criticised by Garrisonian Abolitionist Parker Pillsbury 'for abandoning the movement and accepting land or positions in Jamaica' (Ripley 1985, 421), sided with the plantocracy and the British colonial authorities while Garnet sided with the masses from his home in western Jamaica before he went back to the US prior to the outbreak in Morant Bay.

Samuel Ringgold Ward noted that Samuel Clarke was 'a bold, cheerful man at all times' (Royal Commission 1866, 558). From all accounts, he was a proud, self-assured black man, who, for some, did not know his place. He did not feel himself less capable or inferior to whites or upper-class coloureds. Indeed, he was quite outspoken and blunt in his rejection of the subservient/self-hating way in which Europeans and upper-class coloureds expected black people to conduct themselves.[6]

The St David Vestryman who was reported to have told boys at a school in Alehouse Bay to 'learn well,' because in short the island will 'belong to 'we,' as there are very few white and coloured people in the island, and we will be the ruler of it' (Eyre 1971, 202),[7] had an outlook with a strong basis in race consciousness. This consciousness allowed him to conclude that the conditions of blacks resulted from the oppression of Africans by Europeans and not as a consequence of their natural station vis-à-vis whites as plantation ideologists advocated. Hence, Clarke felt that if blacks were to right the wrong done to them, they would have to take things into their own hands and 'throw off the yoke and seek…liberty.' George Fouche's account of Clarke's address to the May 3, 1865 'Underhill meeting' in Kingston gave an indication of the ideological/political direction of the black Vestryman. Fouche, who at that time was working as a 'reporter for the *Sentinel*,' said Samuel Clarke, next to whom he sat at that meeting, told his audience that:

> The white man looked down upon the Negro as nothing better than a beast, but you cannot keep down Negroes, and although you won't give us education we will show them that we shall yet have a position in the country. As for that flogging bill it must be put down….We must cry against it. It was only intended for the black man not for the white or colored man…Not as long as

> I live shall the white man trample me under foot...Isn't this oppression? Isn't it time for the negro to throw off the yoke and seek your liberty (230)?

Clarke was also a main participant of the June 1865 'Underhill meeting' in St David as well as the August meeting held that same year in Morant Bay. At the Morant Bay meeting, the St David Vestryman seconded the 11 resolutions that were passed (Royal Commission 1866, 1,156).

Clarke, Menard and other members of the black political movement in St David had close social and political contact with some influential black political leaders in Kingston and St Thomas-in-the-East.[8] In Kingston, members of the St David party (especially Clarke) were in contact with and shared the same political platform with William Kelly Smith,[9] editor of the *Watchman*; Emanuel Joseph Goldson,[10] former sergeant of police; Robert Miller, shoemaker; Revd James Roach,[11] and Alexander Miller, 'Vendue storekeeper and.. Commission agent' (345).

Some of these men were associated with the *Jamaica Reform Association*. Most of them were detained as 'political prisoners' during martial law. When Samuel Clarke surrendered to martial law forces that were seeking to detain him, he was staying at the home of Alexander Miller in Kingston. Miller was also detained.

Clarke and his comrades in St David had what appeared to be close social and political ties with Paul Bogle and his party in St Thomas-in-the-East. Attorney General Alexander Heslop's statement to the Royal Commission that he knew that 'there is a very intimate connexion, especially between the political agitators' of St David and St Thomas-in-the-East represented a fairly accurate account of one side of the coin (327). As far as the other side of the coin was concerned, it could be said that an 'intimate connection' also existed between the 'political agitators' of St David and St Thomas-in-the-East whose views represented the position of the ruling classes. There were regular social and political contacts between the people representing different interests in both parishes. William Georges, for example, was the Custos of St David as well as a member of the Assembly representing St Thomas-in-the-East. He was ex-officio member of the Vestries of both parishes and served as magistrate in St David and St Thomas-in-the-East. Because of his political and state duties he travelled regularly between the two parishes.

In another example, Samuel Ringgold Ward, who expressed opposition to George William Gordon because he 'was going about holding meetings' which had the effect of unsettling 'the peasantry, and to interfere with the relation of master and employee, and lord and tenant' (555), agreed with Stephen Cooke, Clerk of the Peace for St Thomas-in-the-East, Henry Mais and Colonel A.G. Fyfe, that the only way to 'counteract' that 'evil influence', was to hold 'counter-meetings, teaching the people loyalty and good order' (555). To this end, Ward, who 'occasionally travelled to preach in St Thomas-in-the-East' said he 'wrote a letter to Baron Ketelholdt', the Custos of that parish, 'asking him for the use' of the Morant Bay courthouse 'to hold a meeting' to address the 'peasantry' (555).

Permission was granted and the meeting was held on September 9, 1865 on 'the court day' and 'market day'. Samuel Ward, the main speaker, 'had the magistracy and the people together', and 'addressed both' (555).

By contrast, when a request was made in July that same year to the Custos for the use of that same courthouse to hold a public meeting, it was denied because that intended meeting was associated with Gordon, Bogle and the Underhill Letter. That meeting was held on August 12, under a 'guinep' tree in Morant Bay. It was hardly surprising, therefore, when George McIntosh led a 'noisy opposition' to disrupt the officially sanctioned meeting, and, according to one source cited by Ward, 'he tried to marshal men to injure me' (556).

Obviously, the state officials and planters in St Thomas-in-the-East and St David gave encouragement and assisted Samuel Ward to convene meetings across St Thomas-in-the-East to counter the influence of George William Gordon and Paul Bogle on the black population. However, things began to 'get hot' for this black man, as he did not show at a meeting he planned for September 16, 1865 at Font Hill because, according to him, 'I was led to believe if I had gone I should have been in trouble there' (556).

While Ward was conducting meetings in St Thomas-in-the-East, members of Bogle's party were having meetings in St David. On September 2, 1865, for example, James McLaren, one of Bogle's closest political associates and deputies, addressed a meeting in Alehouse where he was reported to have said 'the people wanted lands, and if the owners did not allow them to have lands there would be blood' (556).

Samuel Clarke was no stranger to St Thomas-in-the-East. Before he became a local government representative in St David, he was elected to the St Thomas-in-the-East Vestry. Clarke was, therefore, quite familiar with the people of that parish as he was familiar with black leaders intimately linked to the violent clash in Morant Bay. His visits to St Thomas-in-the-East were quite frequent. Indeed, he never ceased doing political work in that parish. He was an integral part of the leadership of the grass root political movement in St Thomas-in-the-East.

Along with Paul Bogle, George William Gordon, George Clarke, and Henry Lawrence, Samuel Clarke was a leading organiser and campaigner to get

George William Gordon elected to the Assembly. On this issue, John Ashley Lord, Inspector of Police, said he often saw George William Gordon with 'Paul Bogle, Samuel Clarke, Mr. Lawrence, and George Clarke taking active part at the elections' (Eyre 1971, 158). The police inspector said at 'the last election at Morant Bay for members', Samuel Clarke warned him that 'blood would flow in the streets like water' (158).

According to Lord, Clarke used that expression 'because I would not allow Gordon's party to hold a flag on rods of four feet length for the magistrates to creep under; they placed it on the lower steps at the entrance to the courthouse, and I removed it, as I saw it was a marked insult to Her Majesty's Commission held by these gentlemen' (158).

Apart from his strong political ties to St Thomas-in-the-East, Samuel Clarke also had family connections in that parish. George Clarke, mentioned above, was Samuel Clarke's brother. He was the son-in-law of Paul Bogle. George Bassett Clarke married Bogle's daughter, Elizabeth, in about 1861. The couple lived in Stony Gut, that same small community in which Bogle, its leading citizen, also resided with his family. George Clarke, who was the father of the couple's two children, said he left Stony Gut in July 1865 to 'live out at Spring Garden a mile off' because he and Bogle 'could not agree' (Royal Commission 1866, 130). Whether Clarke was saying he left Stony Gut because of disagreements with his father-in-law or in a bid to save his skin from the suppressionists' noose, we might never know, but one thing was evident, both men worked together up to August 1865 as political allies.[12]

George Clarke, who also had a sister living in St David, was, like his brother Samuel, a carpenter by trade (130). He worked for the navy and farmed 'modestly' as well (130). Like his brother Samuel Clarke, George Clarke was also a Vestryman. He represented constituents in St Thomas-in-the-East (130).

George Clarke was detained by martial law forces and was very lucky not to have been executed. He was discharged from lack of evidence against him, but was told by Inspector Ramsey not to be seen in the Vestry, at public meetings or in Morant Bay (130). His brother fared worse. He was whipped on November 2, 1865 and executed the following day after he was found guilty of treason (1,148). George Clarke was forced to watch his brother being whipped and executed.

This father of nine children was executed, not because he participated in the outbreak, but for political views he was alleged to have expressed prior to the Morant Bay outbreak. According to the military court, 'Samuel Clarke was charged with treason and with having said the Queen's proclamation was a "Damned red lie,"... and with having said that if the people had not their grievances redressed there must be a fight and bloodshed for it' (1,149).

Paul Bogle the 'General'

Paul Bogle was the leading figure and inspiration behind the hundreds of people who clashed with the militia, state officials and members of the plantocracy in Morant Bay, October 11, 1865. He was the man to whom many blacks (probably a majority) looked for leadership in St Thomas-in-the-East. He was said to be about 45 years old (*Colonial Standard* October 28, 1865). He was probably born into slavery about 1820, presumably in St Thomas-in-the-East. Bogle, 'a man of some substance,'[13] was better off socially and materially compared to the majority of his parishioners. He was a baker by trade (Royal Commission 1866, 693) and a freeholder owning land and engaging in farming (Eyre 1971, 50). He owned horses and was said to have had money in the bank (*Colonial Standard* December 23, 1865). As a taxpayer and proprietor, the leader of the Morant Bay war represented a very tiny portion of the population of St Thomas-in-the-East who met the legislative requirements to vote in state elections.

Paul Bogle was a married man (Royal Commission 1866, 33) (*Colonial Standard* November 6, 1865) and had at least two children, Elizabeth and William.[14] He had an older brother, Moses Bogle, a baker by trade and one of his most trusted deputies.[15] Bogle, it was rumoured, had several 'concubines' (Eyre 1971, 92), all of whom, as well as most of his family, were very active in the struggle against oppression.

Paul Bogle was said to 'be well known to the residents and other persons acquainted with the parish, and has always hitherto borne the best character for civility, quietness, and good conduct' (*Colonial Standard* October 16, 1865). Not only was he 'well known' to the residents of St Thomas-in-the-East, he was their spiritual and political leader. He was respected by many and,

Figure 4. This photograph is believed to be of Paul Bogle. Courtesy of the National Library of Jamaica. Restoration and Art by Ainsley Kerr.

perhaps, some even feared him. Bogle was a symbol of authority among the people and in their struggle against the plantocracy. This authority, respect and fear found expression in the description of him being 'a kind of Jamaica King' (Royal Commission 1866, 1,037), and 'lord'.[16]

Paul Bogle was an exceedingly religious man. He was the leading Native Baptist preacher in St Thomas-in-the-East. The St Thomas-in-the-East Native Baptists comprised the largest organised group of worshippers in Jamaica led by black men not sanctioned by, or operating under, the supervision and authority of European missionaries or missionary societies. The history of the formation of religious organisations in Jamaica showed that whenever black religious groups emerged and developed as independent or autonomous entities, black churches or religious/spiritual orders tended to embrace aspects of African ancestral orders and rituals to shape their diasporic existential circumstances. Perhaps a better way to frame it is to say that the making of faith, spirituality and religion among Africans and their descendants in Jamaica, was conceptually and methodically rooted in the weaving or gathering of nations of African spirits, cosmologies, aesthetics and rituals as the basis for interpreting, appropriating and incorporating other forms – European, Native American and Asian – into a diasporic expression of their presence.

What was true of Paul Bogle's Native Baptist Church of St Thomas-in-the-East was to varying degrees true of Alexander Bedward's Jamaica Native Baptist Free Church in August Town,[17] Leonard Howell's Rastafarianism (Chevannes 1971, 53–65) (Barrett 1977, 80–89), and Claudius 'Cyrus' Henry's International Peace Makers Association (Chevannes 1971, 100–129). These black religious groups developed a theology advocating some if not all of the following: self-reliance and community/communal solidarity in social, cultural and economic relations; black consciousness as a world view and racial solidarity; spiritual or physical repatriation to the ancestral homeland and the rejection of white cultural and religious beliefs as superior to the Africans'.

Bogle's religion, like Bedward, Howell and Henry's, was a philosophical, psychological, cultural and political expression of resistance to colonialism and racism as part of the process of fashioning an alternative mode of existence. His religion was the expression of the own-account, poor, destitute and oppressed black majority who were located at the bottom of post-emancipation society. Joseph Owens felt that this expression was, 'in many instances,' used as 'an ideological, cultural, social, psychological basis for a revolutionary trust' (Owens 1976, 5). For his part, noted Anthropologist Barry Chevannes intimated that the native religion became useful as a starting point for political activity and for resistance to the culture of the white man, whose superiority, it must be remembered, was felt not only in his military strength and control but also, like that of the ancient Jews, in a more powerful god (1971, 100–129).

There was no denying that Bogle's Native Baptist Church had a 'revolutionary trust,' that it 'became useful as a starting point for political activity and for resistance to the culture of the white man.' Bogle's chapel in Stony Gut was a principal meeting place where social, political and economic issues were raised, discussed and acted upon. It was within this chapel that publications of the *British Anti-slavery Society* were circulated and copies of the *Watchman* newspaper sold. Bogle's meeting house was the base from which hundreds were administered the ancestral centred oath, to 'cleave to the black' and 'cleave from the whites' in their impending confrontation with the plantocracy and that part of the state under its control. It was within the walls of this chapel that the black masses received their last briefing/instruction/charge in Stony Gut from Paul Bogle before they marched to Morant Bay, on October 11, 1865, as it was to this building they repaired later to prayer, assessment of the day's events and to plan further responses to the ruling classes.

Since Bogle's views were not recorded in the press or in colonial documents and most of his comrades were executed with him, there is little to go by in putting together systematically, the tenets of his world view without breaching the realm of pure speculation. Save for engaging philosophically, knowable social, political and cultural activities of Paul Bogle and persons closely associated with him, there is little to go by in delineating and articulating in any systematic way, his philosophical and ideological position. It is, however, safe to say that Bogle's outlook and agency were rooted in an open-ended ancestral mode of thinking, knowing and doing, and were located in the social, cultural, cosmological, political and philosophical terrain or universe of progressive black freeholdership.

What appeared to be some of the clearest indications of Deacon Paul Bogle's ideological justification for the 'Morant Bay Rebellion' were found in passages of 'Psalms of David, with the Supplementary Hymns by the Rev Isaac Watts, D.D.' (*Gleaner* October 21, 1865).

On the day Bogle was executed a *Gleaner* 'Special Correspondent' who was present, removed from the Deacon's pocket, his hymn book. According to a report: 'This Arch Traitor's Hymn Book!! Taken from his pocket by our Special Correspondent is to be seen at the Stationery Establishment of Messrs. M. De Cordova, McDougall & Co, 62, Harbour Street' (*Gleaner* October 27, 1865).

According to the 'Special Correspondent' for the *Gleaner*, the Psalms and hymns marked were:

> 3rd, Verses 1, 5, 8; 11th; 50th 'the last Judgement;... 115th, 2nd version; 121st, 2nd version; 139, 3rd version and 143rd. Hymns: 44th, 46th, 136th, 140th. Book 2nd: 4th, 57th, 89th, 97th, 107th. Book 3rd: 23rd (*Gleaner* November 3, 1865).

An examination of the Psalms and Hymns marked in Bogle's book, were themes of hope, fortitude and perseverance; composure and dignity; justice and the inevitable triumph of right over wrong, good over evil, happiness over sorrow by judgement on the oppressor. In this text, therefore, were reasons to justify the hopes, dreams and aspirations of the people and their struggles to secure a life that was just, free and fruitful and a determination, if needs be, to use force (judgement) to achieve black people's goals in post-slavery society.

As they marched down from Stony Gut to Morant Bay on that fateful Wednesday afternoon, they stopped under a huge cotton tree just before they entered the town. Then, perhaps, most Jamaicans of African descent would have easily recognised the symbological, cosmological and agential meaning of this stop: conferencing with the ancestors. Here, Bogle was likely to have had his Christian text, the 'Psalms of David with the Supplementary Hymns by the Revd Isaacs Watts, D.D.'

In this text, among the messages underlined as 'The Last Judgement,' reads like the Warner/Revivalist/Myaalist text of the 'vision' of judgement penned as a placard by 'A Son of Africa' and stuck upon a wharf gate in the town of Lucea about June in 1865.[18] 'The Last Judgement' said in part:

> The Lord, the Sovereign, sends his summons forth,
> Calls the south nations, and awakes the north;
> From east to west the sounding orders spread,
> Through distant worlds and regions of the dead;
> No more shall atheists mock his long delay;
> His vengeance sleeps no more; behold the day!
> Silent I waited with long-suffering love,
> But didst thou hope that I should ne'er reprove?
> And cherish such an impious thought within,
> That God the righteous would indulge thy sin?
> Behold my terrors now, my thunders roll,
> And thy own crimes allright thy guilty soul
> (Watts 1718, 29).

Bogle's use of the Psalmist/Hymnalist text and likely the Bible for political/ideological objectives was not new. Indeed, this practice became one of the main traditions of black abolitionism, a tradition developed during black people's struggles against slavery but never lost its relevance in post-emancipation struggles. Black abolitionists like Samuel Sharpe,[19] Daniel A. Payne, Henry Highland Garnet,[20] and Olaudah Equiano (Gustavus Vassa)[21] represented that black abolitionist tradition in the diaspora which Bogle so ably embraced in his leadership of the post-slavery struggles of the people of St Thomas-in-the-East.

Daniel Payne's speech at Fordsboro, New York, 1839 on the occasion of 'his ordination by the Francean Synod of the Lutheran Church', demonstrated what a powerful ideological tool the Bible and Christianity had become in the hands of oppressed blacks. Payne argued that slavery 'subverts the moral government of God' by showing how that system violated specific commandments given to the people by the 'Creator' to live righteously.[22] The refashioning of Christianity by enslaved Africans into an instrument of freedom and political struggle, constituted a major source of what would later become known as Liberation Theology. One of the most important streams of Liberation Theology was Ethiopianism, which played a central role in shaping and developing the philosophy and opinions of Marcus Garvey and the Universal Negro Improvement Association (UNIA) and the Rastafari movement which followed in the wake of the UNIA. Traces of Ethiopianism were visible in the political and ideological terrain of the 1850s and 1860s and in the Bedwardite movement that emerged in the last decade of the nineteenth century.

Paul Bogle was acutely aware of the need for black solidarity. He was aware that if serious reforms in favour of the masses were to be realised, African Jamaicans would have to stand with each other 'Colour for colour, skin for skin,' and that black people would have to rule Jamaica. To this end, Bogle placed a lot of emphasis on the broadest mobilisation of the black masses and the cultivation of alliances among different black groups. Bogle placed his ultimate hope for success in the struggle against the plantocracy on the alliance between the Maroons and the rest of the black population.

The importance of the solidarity of skin and colour and the alliance between the Maroons and the rest of the black population found expression in a letter, seeking to rally the people of St Thomas-in-the-East to take a determined stand against what was seen as the resolve by the white people to use military means to make them slaves again. That letter, apparently written six days after the outbreak, was signed by Paul Bogle, B. Clarke, J.G. McLaren, P. Cameron and E.K. Bailey.

Mr. Graham and other gentlemen. It is now time for us to help ourselves skin for skin. The iron bar is broken in this parish. The white people send a proclamation to the governor to make war against us which we all must put our shoulders to the wheels and pull together. The Maroons sent the proclamation to us to meet them at Hayfield at once without delay; that they might put us on the way how to act. Every one of you must leave your house, take your guns; who don't have guns take your cutlasses down at once, come over to Stoney Gut that we might march over to meet the Maroons at once without delay. Blow your shells – roal your drums – house to house take out every man – march them down to Stoney Gut. Any that you find in the way take them down with their arms. War is at my black skin – war is at hand from today to tomorrow. Every black man must turn out at once, for the oppression is too great. The white people are now cleaning up their guns for us, which we must prepare too – chear men chear in heart. We looking for you a part of the night or before day break (*Jamaica Tribune* October 23, 1865).

Bogle regarded the Maroons as 'our back' and 'will not do anything to hurt them' (Royal Commission 1866, 32). There seemed to be two main reasons for his attachment of such importance to winning the support of the Maroons. In the first place, the Maroons had for generations been living an autonomous existence in several settlements across the island, because of their legendary exploits in guerrilla warfare against the British soldiers, which resulted in the British granting them self-government and territory. It was this sense of history, the fighting tradition of the Maroons and their defence of territory from British encroachment that Bogle might have wished to enlist to 'back' the struggles of his people.

The second likely reason for the serious attention given to winning the Maroons to the side of the people might be related to another side of Maroon history and tradition that Bogle and others dreaded the Maroons invoking; viz acting in concert with the ruling classes to suppress the aspirations of the masses.[23]

In return for their freedom from the British, the Maroons pledged not to attack the estates and white settlements on the island or harbour runaway enslaved Africans but to apprehend and turn them over to the powers that be. When Sam Sharpe and some 20,000 enslaved Africans sought their freedom in 1831–32, the Maroons became part of the machinery that suppressed what was in effect the biggest anti-slavery insurrection in Jamaica's history (Hart 1985, 269–70, 309–310, 313–14).

With what must be an obvious realisation of the revolutionary and mercenary roles of the Maroons in Jamaica's history, Bogle made special efforts to win the support of the neighbouring Maroons leaders or at least to neutralise them. In one of his attempts to win Maroon support, Bogle, Bailey, Bowie and three others, went to see James Sterling, 'Major' of the Hayfield Maroons about four weeks before the clash at Morant Bay. Speaking about his meeting with Bogle, Sterling said:

> I came and found him quite late at my house. I said, "You should not come to my house, because I and you are not acquainted." I saw him once at Morant Bay, he said to me that he did not come for any harm, but he hear I had a meeting house, and he came to have a little meeting with us... he said they were labouring very hard and can't get any... pay; scarcely any estate will pay them; the pay was very small; then I told him, "Why you are free men; if you can't get good wages it is just as cheap for you to sit down at your house, till the planter want you, and they will send for you, and no doubt will give you good wages." He say, "Yes, but part of them [labourers] refuse, and the other will go and work for little or nothing, and on Saturday when they go up for their pay they kick them off the steps." I said, "Well, it is as cheap for you to sit at home" (Royal Commission 1866, 1,031).

The argument continued in this way until Bogle said, 'Well sir, we had better go and have a little prayers' (1,031). They 'had a little prayers for about two hours, singing and praying' (1,031). He did not win the support or sympathy of the Hayfield Maroon chief even though Bogle and his comrades spent the entire night with Sterling and 'went home on the morning of Saturday about 6 o'clock' (1,031).

Whether Bogle's rallying call to his people, 'The Maroons sent the proclamation to us to meet them at Hayfield at once without delay; that they might put us on the way how to act,' reflected a change in the position of Sterling et al., or a recognition by the rebel leader that the resolve of his people to continue the Morant Bay war would be best served if they were told that the Maroons were their 'back', I cannot say. However, history has recorded once more that the Maroons did not side with their colour in the 1865 confrontation. Indeed, they played a central role in the suppression of the people and in the destruction of their leaders, because, according to John Mendes, Hayfield Maroon captain, 'the Crown and the Maroons got an understanding one with another' and 'if when I go and hear that the Crown is against you [rebels], believe me when the Crown send an order we will come back and we don't let even your cocoa-nut to grow' (1,044).

Paul Bogle did not fare better than Samuel Sharpe, the great Jamaican anti-slavery revolutionary leader who sent his emissary, Peter Douglas, to secure from Accompong Maroon chief, Colonel White a pledge that the Maroons would not act against the rebellious blacks (Hart 1985, 269–70). This was not to be and some of the same Maroons who hunted enslaved blacks in western Jamaica in 1831–32 also hunted former enslaved Africans and their children in eastern Jamaica, in 1865. And they were led by the same military/planter representative of the colonial state who led them in 1831–32, Colonel Alexander Gordon Fyfe.[24]

The movement of people headed by Paul Bogle was in all likelihood the largest organised group of black people anywhere in Jamaica at that time despite racist stereotypes that Africans were incapable of organisation. Leading Roman Catholic priest, Revd Joseph S. Woollett's assertion, 'I do not believe they [the blacks] can combine; combination and organization are things they are not capable of, but they can be well prepared [i.e., others can put them up to it]' (Royal Commission 1866, 549), represented a typical example of these racist notions.

However, those black people who were said to have lacked the qualities for 'combination and organization' had their own symbol of organisation and combination, a flag, 'white with a red cross and a piece of black crape sewed on' (*Gleaner* November 22, 1865). Those people were in fact being organised on a community basis because, according to a report attributed to Paul Bogle, 'We want all the different places; we must have 50 men and a captain each' (Royal Commission 1866, 1,039). Each district or community was to be organised around a captain, headman or chief who would be the principal link between the community and Stony Gut the headquarters of the movement where Bogle lived.

The organisation of each community around 50 men and one captain appeared to be one of the main organisational principles of Bogle's movement. George Craddock, one of the main leaders thereof who 'spoke to the people' and 'said that one captain had 50, and another had 50' (22) would suggest that there was agreement, at least among some of the leaders respecting the form of this organisational regime.

It was within the context of this organisation that hundreds of men were drilled in military-like fashion. Later, these men and women would march down to Morant Bay 'four abreast' to confront the ruling classes and their armed detachment of volunteers (202).[25]

Estimates of the size of the crowd varied, sometimes sharply, even for people who were present at the Bay on that fateful Wednesday afternoon. St David Custos, William Payne Georges, said he 'saw about 500 or 600 people approaching the Court-house' (3), while Dr John Stoddart Gerard said he 'should think between 300 and 400 persons' were present (7). Meanwhile, Baron Alfred Kettleholdt, son-in-law to the late Custos of St Thomas-in-the-East said 'about 400 or 500 negroes came against the Court-house' (5). For his part, Stephen Cooke, Clerk of the Peace and 1st Lieutenant of the No.

2 Rifle Volunteers of St Thomas-in-the-East said he estimated about '1,200 rebels in the square opposite to the Court-house' (Eyre 1971, 138).

It was indeed this organisation that put on several meetings across the parish and mobilised hundreds of people to hear from their leaders and plan future activities. One of those meetings was held at Church Corner in Morant Bay on Tuesday, October 3, 1865. That meeting, which was said to 'be for the benefit of all the blacks', lasted about two hours, and was attended by 'plenty of people' (Royal Commission 1866, 1,039). Among those present were some young men from Nutts River who Bogle sent to call because he 'wanted to see all the youngsters in Nutts River' (1,039). Paul Bogle was the main speaker at that meeting. He was reported by George Thomas, a participant, to have called on the men present to 'join the Volunteer the same as the White man' (1,039).

This call seemed plausible because after the deputation led by Paul Bogle to see the Governor was refused an audience, Bogle appeared to have given up on peaceful methods in the struggle to secure a better life. His call on his men to join the Volunteer units in St Thomas-in-the-East could very well have been part of a conscious effort to make preparations to take the struggle to its armed phase. Whether this idea was suggested to Bogle by Edward K. Bailey, one of his deputies and a Sergeant of the Volunteers, we may never know.

The Leadership Core of Paul Bogle's Movement

The organisational regime of Paul Bogle's movement was the product of persons such as James McLaren, Edward K. Bailey, John Edwards, John Anderson, James Bowie, William Grant, Arthur Wellington, George McIntosh, Henry Clyne, Moses Bogle and William Bogle.

James McLaren turned 22 years old in 1865 (246). He was Paul Bogle's secretary (*Gleaner* October 21, 1865) and one of his closest captains. This man, the son of John McLaren, coffee farmer, and owner of a chapel (Royal Commission 1866, 246), was one of the youngest of all the captains. The fact that he was the recording secretary for several major public meetings in the parish;[26] a main speaker at public and private meetings; a recorder of the names of new recruits to the movement (133) and one of those administering the swearing (taking of oath) of allegiance to the organisation by new recruits, suggested that this young man was held in high esteem by Bogle and many of his black parishioners.

Along with Paul Bogle, George B. Clarke and Henry Clyne, among others, James McLaren was chosen by the August 12, 1865 Morant Bay Underhill

Convention to be part of a deputation to Governor Eyre to air the grievances of the people and seek redress (1,157). That meeting also appointed him to a committee 'to prepare a petition to the House of Lords and Commons of England embodying the sentiments' of the resolutions passed by the Convention (1,157).

McLaren, who was often seen in the company of Paul Bogle, was obviously one of the top leaders of the movement. This young man, who could read and write because his father 'put him to school when we was a little bit of a boy' (246), was heard by Henry Clyne to have said at the moment prior to his execution 'that he was going to be executed merely because he could write' (735).[27]

McLaren was seriously committed to the struggles of the people. Consequently, he was reported to have told his audience at a September 1865 meeting some of the reasons for his commitment and activism.

> Why cause me to hold this meeting; myself was born free, but my mother and father was slaved; but now I am still a slave by working from days to days. I cannot get money to feed my family, and I working at Coley estate for 35 chains for 1s., and after five days' working I get 2s.6d. for my family. Is that able to sustain a house full of family?" and the people said, "No." Then he said, "Well, the best we can do is to come together, and send in a petition to the Government; and if they will give up the outside land to we, we shall work with cane, and cotton, and coffee like the white. But the white people say we are lazy and won't work. He said when they rented a piece of land from the white people they had to send a man with a chain and measure an acre, and to pay heavy taxes for a horse, and he said, "you cannot keep two horses because of the taxes," but if the outside land was given up to them to work, they should pay the taxes to the Queen, and if the land was given up to them they did not want anything from the white people, they would try to make their own living themselves; but they would not give them the land to work, neither give them any money; how then were they to live?" And when he said that he said to the people without they came together and go down to Morant Bay in lump, to let the white people see there was plenty black in the island,... and cry out that they don't mean to pay any more ground rent again; [because]... the outside land was given to them a long time and the white people kept it to themselves (165).

McLaren's reported speech could be considered to be radical in two main respects. Firstly, his expressed desire to see black people independent of the whites, i.e., to 'try to make their own living themselves', ran counter to the prevailing ideological position of the plantocracy and important sections of the more liberal-minded white community who felt that economic independence would cause African Jamaicans to lose 'contact with the whites' and 'remove' them 'beyond their supervision and control, and out of the sight and influence of any examples of intelligence and industry superior to their own'.[28]

Secondly, his call on blacks not to pay 'any more ground rent again' was a declaration to wage political struggles to secure the 'outside land' without pay in order to 'make their own living themselves'. These two views, along with McLaren's insistence that he was 'still a slave by working from days to days' were fundamental elements in the definition of freedom in the ideology of the 'Morant Bay Rebellion' and radical black thought on the reconstruction of post-slavery society. In McLaren's approach to justify the struggle for freedom, justice, rights, etc., one can detect a conceptual and methodological complex often used in the political ontology of Jamaican popular music after independence in 1962. In this approach, the extent of freedom, justice and sovereignty was measured (and is still measured) by the extent to which it was believed that conditions bred and shaped by slavery or akin to slavery continue to exist. The Wailers' 'Slave Driver' (*Catch A Fire*), is a good example: 'Every time I hear the crack of the whip/My blood runs cold/I remember on the slave ship/ How they brutalised my very soul/ Today they say we are free/Only to be chained to poverty....'

McLaren was hanged on October 24, 1865 in Morant Bay for 'mutiny and rebellion' (1,136). Henry Clyne who witnessed his execution, said McLaren 'call a man, begging him to go [to] someone who owed him 7s.6d. and get it and give it to his wife' (735). His show of concern for the welfare of his wife was his last act before his life was taken away from him.

Unlike most of the other leaders of the movement, this young captain was 'a labourer employed to the Coley estate'. He was secretary of the *Society of Friends*, a political organisation founded in Morant Bay. During his trial, McLaren refuted the argument that George William Gordon was the mastermind behind the 'Morant Bay Rebellion' (619).

E.K. Bailey was a [Native] Baptist preacher (*Gleaner* October 20, 1865). He was one of the secretaries of the movement. He 'resided opposite the police station in Morant Bay. Bailey 'was an upholsterer' (Royal Commission 1866, 219) and operated a grocery shop in Morant Bay (220). This man was one of the most influential leaders of the movement. He was one of the five men (including Paul Bogle) who wrote the letter six days after the outbreak, calling on the people of St Thomas-in-the-East to rise up against their oppressors because 'the iron bar is now broken in this parish.[29] E.K. was probably one of the chief strategists of the Morant Bay war. Edward K. Bailey 'was sergeant of the Volunteers' (131),[30] the official state-organised militia. He was also a constable. He probably enlisted with the *Morant Bay Corps* and would have had some training in the use of the rifle.

On the morning of the day of the outbreak, Bailey might have played a central role in getting Bogle to eventually lead his people down to Morant Bay. According to Henry Theophilus Bogle, Paul Bogle, his uncle, was turning back after a man on a mule told him and his marching people not to 'go to the Bay or you'll get yourself killed, the Volunteers is in the Bay.' Henry Bogle said his uncle pressed on to the Bay after he 'got a letter from Bailey the Volunteer, saying they should come, and he went' (23).[31]

Bailey was detained by the Maroons (*Gleaner* October 20, 1865), and charged by the military authorities with 'desertion as volunteer' (Royal Commission 1866, 1,135). He was shot and killed by a sentry while allegedly trying to escape from a detention centre in Morant Bay (1,135).

John Edwards was a teacher. He 'was a schoolmaster of a school belonging to the Wesleyans at Rocky Point' (482). He was a captain of the movement and, along with a 'Captain Smith' was said to be 'the Captain of the troops [rebels] about 400 men' who took over Bath after the battle at Morant Bay (482). Edwards was executed in Morant Bay for 'rebellion,' on October 20, 1865 (1,135).

John Anderson was a coloured man; he was a teacher employed to the Wesleyans. He developed a close relationship with the labouring masses whose children he taught. He heard 'continual complaints' from parents who showed him the '3d. and 6d. a day' they were paid (959). He said 'I met them with tears in their eyes, and they say, "Teacher, look here, Monday we come out to work and this is all we receive"' (959). Anderson's closeness to the people was also reflected in the fact that his 'wife was one of the labouring class, and she tells me what she suffered' (960). This teacher, who said he knew many people in St Thomas-in-the-East, became a spokesman on their behalf. He spoke at several public meetings in the parish and took resolutions passed at a Stokes Hall meeting he addressed, to the August 12 Underhill meeting at Morant Bay. At that meeting, Anderson, along with Paul Bogle, Henry Clyne, R. Deveny, William Reefe, Joseph Anderson, William Grant and C.R. Walker, was appointed to a committee to study the effects of unemployment, reduced and low wages and labour relations, to obtain 'detailed and correct information on these subjects for transmission to Dr Underhill and the Secretary of State for the Colonies' (1,156). He was detained during the suppression and received 50 lashes for allegedly delivering a speech at Morant Bay accusing Chisholm, the planter, of only paying '3d., 6d. or 9d. to the labourers' (959).

James Bowie (Buie) 'an old Spaniard,' (23),[32] 'assumed the rank of Captain General, and the others were nominated Captain' (*Gleaner* October 20, 1865). If the *Gleaner* report was correct, James Bowie, a Cuban, would rank second to Paul Bogle, the 'General' (Royal Commission 1866, 457). Henry Bogle, who referred to 'Old Bowie' as 'one of the captains' (23), said the 'old Spaniard' said that 'in his country [Cuba] they killed whites' (23). James Bowie, who was the father of another activist of the movement, Captain William Bowie (a neighbour of Paul Bogle), was one of the trial judges of persons detained by Bogle's men and taken to Stony Gut.[33] There his symbol of authority was a sword. James Bowie was hanged on October 24, 1865 at Morant Bay for 'rebellion' (1,136). Accordingly *The New-York Daily Times* noted:

> The 'Captain-General' of the rebel forces was also tried and condemned on the same day [as the Bogle brothers]. He was a man we should suppose bordering on sixty-five years of age, short, thin and remarkable in his appearance from the gray beard which he wore (November 17, 1865).

William Grant 'an old coloured man' (*Gleaner* October 20, 1865) was a saddler. He had a shop close to the Morant Bay police station (Royal Commission 1966, 735). There it was alleged he held 'secret meetings' (1,148). He was one of the captains of the Bogle movement. The *Gleaner* (October 20, 1865) described Grant as 'one of those well known vagabonds termed "village politicians" and whom the country will gratefully part with for the good of those who wish it well.' Grant was said to be a 'founder' of 'a society of Friends', the political organisation in Morant Bay headed by Henry Clyne. Admission to or membership of this Society was gained by the possession of 'a blue card' said to be 'printed by Wm. Grant, funder' (Royal Commission 1966, 1,148). Among the members of this Society were George McIntosh and James McLaren. William Grant was hanged on October 24, 1865 at Morant Bay for 'rebellion' (1,136).

Arthur Wellington, reputed to be an Obeahman, was one of the leaders of the movement and political ally of Paul Bogle who 'raised him to a captain' (163). He was one of those men who helped to administer the taking of oaths to recruits who joined the movement in Coley (1,126). Obeah, like the Native Baptist religion, played an important psycho-cultural and political role in the rising of the black masses of St Thomas-in-the-East. What Bogle was able to do with the Native Baptist religion on a wide scale, Wellington was also able to do with Obeah. It was Francis Hobbs's view that:

> 'Obeism' and the deepest religious fanaticism had much to do with this rebellion, especially in Somerset, when Arthur Wellington bewitched them

[blacks], he had immense power, and was much dreaded, and persuaded the people they could not be wounded or killed by the buckra (1,129).[34]

Obeah was probably a main influencing factor used by George Craddock, a leader of the movement, who, after administering the oath to recruits, told them 'not tell to anybody' because if they did their 'belly would swell' (22). Wellington was the best known and most influential Obeahman in the movement, but he was certainly not the only one to join the rising people or to have perished because of the alleged practice of obeah. Wellington, a swayer (lumber man), freeholder (109), and 'captain to Somerset' was shot and beheaded and his head placed on public display.[35] Other alleged Obeahmen to have been executed by the suppressionist forces were: Charles Walker, for rebellion (1,137), George Williams, for 'rebellion and plunder' (1,136), John Grant, for 'sedition and murder' (1,139), and John Bartly, 'for making images' (979).

George McIntosh was a building contractor and employer of labour. He was awarded several contracts to carry out work for the local government authorities in Morant Bay. He was a highly respected and influential man in St Thomas-in-the-East and was said to be one of George William Gordon's secretaries (*Gleaner* October 21, 1865) or 'one of his leading men' (Royal Commission 1866, 1,148). McIntosh was a leading member of the *Society of Friends*, that political organisation that met regularly in Morant Bay. He was a leading speaker at meetings of this Society and was chosen by the August 12 Underhill Convention to sit on a committee with Henry Clyne, George B. Clarke, Paul Bogle and Thomas Nicholson 'to take all necessary steps...in defence of the right and privileges of the electors' (1,157). He was also chosen by that meeting to be part of the delegation which would go to Spanish Town to seek a meeting with Governor Eyre. George McIntosh was hanged on October 21, 1865 at Morant Bay for 'Complicity and rebellion' (1,135).

Henry Clyne was an 'old slave' during the late epoch. He was the respected and popular chairman of several public meetings in Morant Bay. He was one of the top leaders of the *Society of Friends* and chairman of its meetings. This 'very old man' was one of the main forces behind the move to revive the *Anti-slavery Society* in St Thomas-in-the-East. Indeed, he was the chairman of the reconvened *Anti-slavery Society* (1,068).

Clyne, who called the August 12 Morant Bay Underhill Convention to order and explained 'the objects' of the meeting to his audience, was the mover of the 12 resolutions passed at that meeting – although he was unable to chair it because he had a 'sick stomach'. This 'old man' who resided at

Friendship Pen 'since the abolition of slavery' (735), was chosen to sit on all four committees established by the Convention to carry out 'the objects' embodied in the resolutions. He was one of two persons to be appointed to all the committees. The other person so appointed was George Clarke (Vestryman). The 'people' who 'came from afar, from different places' (734), to attend the Underhill meeting must have thought highly of Clyne to put him on all four committees.

While much cannot be said about his ideas, it is clear that from the kind of activities he was involved in, this 'old man' was one of the leading ideas persons of the Bogle movement. The leading positions he held in the *Society of Friends*, his efforts to revive the *Anti-slavery Society* in that parish, among other things, suggested that Clyne was a highly respected black leader and opinion maker of St Thomas-in-the-East. During the suppression he was arrested, whipped and forced to witness the execution of some of his comrades and leading personalities in the movement (734–37).

Moses Bogle, the brother of Paul Bogle, was one of the leading figures in the movement. A baker by trade, he had a son named Henry Bogle. Moses Bogle played a leading role in the battle at the Bay on that epoch-making October afternoon. He commanded the body of marchers from Stony Gut until they reached Spring Gardens when 'some took the east way and some the north' because 'Moses said that his brother Paul say they must divide there' and 'some walk the Church Corner way, and some Stanton Road way' (202). Moses Bogle led the column that walked the Church Corner way while his brother led the Stanton Road column. It was Moses Bogle, according to one report, who first entered Morant Bay at the head of his column brandishing a pistol (Jamaica Information Service 'C.' 1965, 16). Moses Bogle, who gave William Onslow the final appeal letter from the movement's leader to take to Governor Eyre,[36] was executed along with Paul Bogle and James Bowie on October 24, 1865 for 'rebellion' (Royal Commission 1866, 1,136).

According *The New-York Daily Times* (November 17, 1865): 'MOSES BOGLE was what is generally termed a yellow negro, taller and stouter than PAUL with large heavy whiskers.' Moses Bogle was captured by a 'brown man named BOTHWELL' who severely wounded Bogle on his 'right arm'. Bothwell was also severely wounded by Moses Bogle in his bid to capture Bogle.

Other leaders of the movement included William Bogle; age about 25 years,[37] recording secretary of the August 12, 1865 Morant Bay Underhill Convention, one of the movement's main organisers and one of his father's chief emissaries. There was David Richard, 'schoolmaster from Torrington,' he assisted the leaders to formulate and write letters (23). There was Archie

Bailey, captain; Henry Lawrence, manager of George William Gordon's properties in St Thomas-in-the-East; George Craddock, captain and a leading spokesman at public meetings, and William Chisholm, among others.

Thus, the leaders of the Morant Bay Rebellion, the people who surrounded Bogle and constituted the core of the movement's organisation, were primarily own-account freehold farmers, shopkeepers/petty traders, school teachers (masters), preachers and skilled tradesmen. These men represented social and economic groups in the island which Douglas Hall felt important enough to merit about 40 pages of his book *Free Jamaica 1838–1865*, even though he felt Bogle did 'not merit recognition as a leader or lieutenant of organised rebellion' (1959, 253) and the people were lacking in 'any new social, political or economic philosophies' (250).

Hall did not say on what basis he asserted that the people were lacking in any new social, political and economic philosophies. He was wrong. In the first place, it was a commonly held view among the black masses in general and the freeholders in particular, that they were not really free and sovereign if they were poor and did not have free access to land. Their slogan in this respect: 'Liberty of person, Liberty of land', denoted the political economy of freedom and sovereignty. This view was new and progressive, a stark contrast to the neo-slavery, Carlylean philosophy of the plantocracy.

Persons like James McLaren, considered themselves to be still in slavery, since they were still mired in pre-1838 poverty, which remained a fundamental part of their ontological state in post-slavery, because liberty of the person was proceeding without liberty of the land. The battle then for the equalisation of liberty of the person with liberty of the land was a fundamental task and was personified by persons such as Samuel Clarke, Paul Bogle, George Craddock and James McLaren. In this struggle to equalise liberty of the person with liberty of the land (property), there was a clear tendency among the freeholders that black people should own Jamaica, that is to say, they earned it. And in back people's struggle for education, they were not thinking that its purpose was to make them a better labouring class in the service of white people. Rather, education in the view of persons like Samuel Clarke, George William Gordon, and John Willis Menard, should be used to develop the capacity of the black majority to take charge of the country. Education should be a tool for liberation, freedom, sovereignty, community and the unlocking/realising of the economic potential of the island.

The fierce political economic struggles waged by persons such as Samuel Clarke, Paul Bogle and George William Gordon were always centred around achieving the widest representation in the parliament and local government bodies based on the highest number of persons with the right to vote.

These were three of the areas in which the position of the progressive freeholding class in the van of the black majority, proved Douglas Hall wrong, and on which the plantocracy and its allies would unleash a reign of terror to prevent.

Notes

1. See B[arry] W. Higman, ed., *The Jamaican Censuses of 1844 and 1861*. A new Edition derived from the manuscript and printed schedules in the Jamaica Archives. Social History Project (Department of History, University of the West Indies, Mona, 1980), 20.
2. See Swithin Wilmot, 'Baptist Missionaries and Jamaica Politics, 1838–54,' in *A Selection of Papers Presented at the Twelfth Conference of the Association of Caribbean Historians 1980*, ed. K.O. Laurence (UWI, St Augustine: Association of Caribbean Historians 1986); Swithin Wilmot, 'Political Development in Jamaica in the Post Emancipation Period, 1838–1854,' PhD Thesis, Oxford University, 1977; Gad J. Heuman, *Between Black and White: Race, Politics and the Free Coloureds in Jamaica, 1792–1865* (Westport, CT: Greenwood Press, 1981), Chapter 9.
3. Quoted in David C. Rankin 'The Origins of Black Leadership in New Orleans During Reconstruction,' *The Journal of Southern History* 40 (1974): 426.
4. Although only remnants and a few good copies of *The Watchman* are preserved in the National Library of Jamaica, Kingston, Charles McLean, Clerk of the Vestry for the parish of St David did mention Menard's 'scurrilous and abusive letters' in *The Watchman*. Cited in Governor [Edward] Eyre, *Papers Laid Before The Royal Commission of Inquiry* (Shannon: Irish University Press 1971), 50.
5. On one of these occasions, the Custos of St David reported that Clarke, in the company of Menard, told him in August 1865, that Queen Victoria's proclamation in response to the petitioners of St Ann was a 'damned red lie'. The Custos said he 'saw Clarke and a man called Menard talking. He waited until I was about 10 yards from the proclamation when he walked up to it, and in the presence of all, said, "That is a lie, a damned red lie," and that neither the Queen [n]or Mr. Cardwell had ever seen the petition of St. Annes.' See Great Britain, *Report of the Jamaica Royal Commission, 1866, Part II: Minutes of Evidence and Appendix* (Shannon: Irish University Press 1966), 1,149.
6. According to Samuel Ringgold Ward, Clarke belonged to a class of black men 'who owned their 10, 15 or 100 acres of land' and 'went about on horses, such as some English gentlemen would like to gallop with.' Cited in Great Britain, *Report of the Jamaica Royal Commission, 1866, Part II: Minutes of Evidence and Appendix* (Shannon: Irish University Press 1966), 556.
7. According to Joseph Alvarenga, Clerk to the church and operation of the school where Samuel Clarke 'addressed the boys in the school.'

8. In this respect, the black political movement in St David was like a bridge between Kingston and St Thomas-in-the-East.
9. William Kelly Smith was the editor of the *Watchman*, a newspaper to which he was 'connected' 'for several years'. Smith, who knew Samuel Clarke very well, also conducted public lectures. He was an election campaigner and one of the key figures at public meetings. He was secretary of the Kingston Underhill meeting.
10. Emmanuel Joseph Goldson was a sergeant of police for 11 years and four months. He was dismissed from the force for insubordination in 1862. He served as the city inspector of Kingston for eight months and acting lessee for another 12 months. He tendered a bid of £1,000 for the market, but was out bidded by £1,066 in 1865. He was detained on October 19, 1865 for sedition. See Great Britain, *Report of the Jamaica Royal Commission, 1866, Part II: Minutes of Evidence and Appendix* (Shannon: Irish University Press 1966), 309.
11. Revd James Roach was a popular Kingston preacher. He was a leading member of the *Jamaica Reform Association* and was detained as a political prisoner during martial law.
12. George Clarke, Paul Bogle et al. were responsible for establishing a people's court system in St Thomas-in-the-East around the beginning of the 1860s. Both men also campaigned for Gordon's election to the Assembly, among other things.
13. This is according to Sidney Levien in a booklet, 'Chronicle of the Rebellion of 1865,' published shortly after 1865. The Chronicle was reprinted in the *Gleaner*, April and May 1964.
14. Elizabeth Bogle was detained (*Gleaner* October 19, 1865) and a military detachment under Lt Oxley, who held her 'children as hostages', had 'Bogle's daughter with us as a guide, with a rope round her neck. Mrs George B. Clarke, I think is her name; she was offered 100L: and the safety of her husband, if she would tell where her father Paul Bogle was' (Royal Commission 1866, 364). See reports on William Bogle in Great Britain, *Report of the Jamaica Royal Commission, 1866, Part II: Minutes of Evidence and Appendix* (Shannon: Irish University Press 1966), 229–30. Another report suggested the existence of another son of Paul Bogle. According to Thomas York, he had seen 'William Bogle and the other brother, who works Mr Marshelleck's log-wood dray, at the meetings' (Eyre 1971, 47).
15. Moses Bogle led the first group of people to enter Morant Bay on October 11, 1865.
16. One of Bogle's 'warriors' who took a prisoner to him October 15, 1865, addressed his leader thus: 'My Lord, there is a man I have brought to you' (Royal Commission 1866, 156).
17. See Alston [Barry] Chevannes 'Jamaican Lower Class Religion: Struggles against Oppression,' MSc Thesis, University of the West Indies, 1971.

18. See chapters seven and eight for more.
19. See Richard Hart, *Slaves Who Abolished Slavery, Vol. 2: Blacks in Rebellion* (Kingston: Institute of Social and Economic Research, University of the West Indies, 1985).
20. See Phillip S. Foner, ed., *The Voice of Black America: Major Speeches by Negroes in the United States, 1797–1971* (NewYork: Simon and Schuster, 1972).
21. See Alaudah Equiano, 'The Interesting Narrative of the Life of Olaudah Equiano or Gustavus Vassa, the African.' In *The Classic Slave Narratives*, ed. Henry Louis Gates, Jr. (New York: A Mentor Book, 1987).
22. Daniel Payne said:

    Thus saith the Lord, "Thou shalt not commit adultery." But does the man who owns a hundred females obey the law? Does he nullify it and compel the helpless women to disobey God? ...Thus saith the Lord, "Remember the Sabbath day, to keep it holy." Does not slavery nullify this law, and compel the slave to work on the Sabbath? Thus said the Lord, "Obey they father and mother." Can the slave children obey this command of God? Does not slavery command the children to obey the master and let him alone? Thus saith the Son of God, "What God hath joined together let no man put asunder." Does not slavery nullify this law, by breaking the sacred bonds of wedlock, and separating the husband and wife forever? (Foner 1972, 69–70).

23. See Mavis C. Campbell, *The Maroons of Jamaica 1655–1796: A History of Resistance, Collaboration & Betrayal*, (Tenton, New Jersey: Africa World Press, Inc., 1990).
24. Apart from the Accompong Maroons, it was reported that 107 Maroons from eastern Jamaica under the command of Captain Fyfe were sent to western Jamaica to assist in the suppression of the anti-slavery insurrection (Hart 1985, 309–10). Thirty-three years later, 'No less than 500 Maroons...arrived at Port Antonio [and placed] themselves under the command of their captain, the Hon A.G. Fyfe, declaring that they would die in the service of the Government' (*Jamaica Tribune* October 18, 1865).
25. Women were not permitted to march with men. They 'were all at the side'.
26. He took Minutes at the October 3, 1865 public meeting at Church Corner, Morant Bay.
27. Another version was given by Sligo Campbell, a policeman present at McLaren's execution. According to Campbell: 'What I heard him say was, that he could read and write, and he was [to be] killed because Mr Gordon called him out and [he] wrote [at] a meeting, and all must take warning by him' (Royal Commission, 630).
28. Quoted from a letter by A. Lindo, prominent resident of Falmouth, Trelawny, written to the *London Times* 'refuting' certain arguments of Dr Underhill about 'wrongs' he said the plantocracy committed against the labouring classes (*Colonial Standard* February 1, 1866).

29. William Cathcraft Gabey who knew and did business with E.K. Bailey suggested that the letter and the five signatures thereon were in Bailey's handwriting because he was familiar with E.K.'s style of writing (Royal Commission, 219–20). Gabey became familiar with Bailey's handwriting because Bailey used 'to supply the labourers' working for Charles Price, with 'a little saltfish and a little rum...during the week' and he used to 'send in the accounts' to Gabey so he 'might stop it out of the pay of the men' (Royal Commission, 220).
30. According to reports, about four other men belonging to the volunteer or police force, were involved in the rebellion or refused to be involved in its suppression. Samuel Bayley, for example, was hanged in Manchioneal after he was charged and found guilty as 'A constable joining [the] rebels' (Royal Commission, 1,141). For his part, Stephen Cameron shared the same fate at Morant Bay on October 23, 1865 for 'Rebellion and breaking to the Queen as constable' (Royal Commission, 1,136). Cameron, 'head constable for the last five years', was 'captain' (for Nutts River) in Bogle's movement (Royal Commission, 434).
31. Other reports confirmed that Paul Bogle turned back or was turning back to Stony Gut after he got two warnings that the Volunteers were out in force at Morant Bay. He finally made up his mind to go to the Bay because: one 'man called Thomas' urged Bogle not to take 'advice from buckra's side' and not go to the Bay (Royal Commission, 202). He feared that if he did not go, the men would not be willing to stay with him (Royal Commission, 202). E.K. Bailey, who was at Morant Bay, sent a letter to Paul Bogle urging him to come down to the Bay. Consequently, he commenced the journey down to Morant Bay.
32. He was called a Spaniard because he was originally from Cuba, the Spanish colony, 90 miles north of Jamaica and spoke Spanish.
33. Rural constable, John Williams told the Royal Commission that he was detained on October 12, 1865 by rebels and taken to Stony Gut. At Stony Gut 'They left me to James Buie (Bowie) to try me. He was at a table like massa (meaning the Commissioners), with a sword in his hand' (Royal Commission, 166).
34. In responding to whether an Obeahman could be wounded, black schoolmaster, Mathew Joseph said: 'Many of the common people have great confidence in Obeah; they believe them to be almighty, that they can do anything' (Royal Commission, 109).
35. The decision to execute Wellington in the way it was done was a conscious political decision to prove that the deep belief the people had in the supernatural qualities of the Obeah man was unfounded. According to Colonel Hobbs: 'that was the reason I executed him in the manner I did, he set himself up to be invulnerable to bullet shot, and I wanted to show them that no amount of incantation could prevent him from being shot (Royal Commission 1866, 764).
36. According to Onslow, a labourer from Stanton, Moses Bogle 'called me and gave me the letter, and said I must take it to Spanish Town and give it to the Governor. He gave me four and sixpence to pay expense and the train' (Royal Commission, 134). That letter was written on October 10, 1865 after five of

six constables who tried to detain Paul Bogle were themselves held captive at Stony Gut on Bogle's orders. The letter reached Spanish Town on Wednesday, October 11, 1865 at about 10:00 a.m. Edward Jordan, Secretary to Governor Eyre, acknowledged receipt of the letter at about 12:00 noon.

37. John Burnett, a black junior sergeant of police, St Thomas-in-the-East, estimated that William Bogle 'must be about 25' years old (Royal Commission, 229).

7 'You Are No Longer Slaves, But Free Men':
George William Gordon: The Brown Link Ideology and Politics

> God has destinied that the wrongs of Africa should be vindicated in these lands...There is a vein in the hearts of coloured and black men which non[e] can touch but coloured men.
>
> – Robert Osborn

The Paul Bogle movement of St Thomas-in-the-East was linked to the emergence of a process in which a tendency favouring far reaching reforms of post-emancipation society was taking shape across the island. George William Gordon was central to this process and the movement in St Thomas-in-the-East represented its most concentrated and organised mass expression. Gordon's campaign, his social and business contacts across the island, his representation of the aspiration of the black masses was turning him into a national leader, making the politics of reform a national phenomenon.

Gordon had his political base in St Thomas-in-the-East and some of the principal leaders of Bogle's movement, including the top leader himself, were his chief political organisers in that parish. Indeed, Paul Bogle was central to the building and preservation of Gordon's political base. He introduced Gordon to sections of the St Thomas-in-the-East masses and some of their leaders. Bogle was Gordon's chief electoral organiser and campaigner.

Without Paul Bogle's support and agreement, George William Gordon might not have been so successful politically in St Thomas-in-the-East, despite his wealth and humanist qualities as a leader. As a result, Gordon became exceedingly popular with the black labouring classes of that parish. It was Edward Jordon's belief, for example, that 'in St Thomas-in-the-East', the people 'had unlimited confidence in Mr Gordon' (Royal Commission 1866, 829). For his part, Revd Duncan Campbell, who acted as rector of St Thomas-in-the-East between November 19 and December 31, 1865, felt that George William Gordon had 'immense influence' among the people. According to Campbell, 'his name was a house-hold name' in St Thomas-in-the-East (842).

Paul Bogle and George William Gordon were allies. Indeed, Henry Bogle was of the view that his uncle and Gordon 'were like brothers', and 'Mr Gordon was often in my uncle's house, and my uncle used to go to Spring with him' (23). For his part, Gordon said Bogle was his 'political friend' (Jamaica Committee 1866, 51). So much so that one report stated that the Native Baptist leader accompanied George William Gordon to Underhill Conventions across the island.[1] When

Figure 5. George William Gordon. Photo by Duperly Brothers in *Harper's Weekly*.

and under what circumstances both men met is not certain. However, Gordon acquired large tracts of land in St Thomas-in-the-East in the 1840s (Hart n.d., 15); and both men were exchanging letters at least by the early 1860s (Royal Commission 1866, 1,150). These letters were usually of a religious, political and social nature.

On December 11, 1861, for example, Gordon wrote to Bogle to tell him of his upcoming baptism; 'I am to be baptised on Xmas, this day 2 wks. Remember me on that day' (1,150). Meanwhile, Paul Bogle, James Bowie, and George B. Clarke wrote to Gordon on July 25, 1862. That letter expressed their heartfelt appreciation to George William Gordon, whom they felt was being harassed by the authorities for siding with their cause.

> All hearts burnt to hear the way you are treated for our cause. But in suffering there are conciliation for there is a rest to provide for those who toil and bear persecution for truth sake in heaven (1,150).

In a move designed to publicly express thanks and support to Gordon, the authors of the letter extended an invitation to him to visit them in Stony Gut so that, among other things, that community could 'entertain' and 'arrange' with him. Apparently, George William Gordon had never visited Stony Gut prior to the issuance of that invitation.

> We want to see you at our village, which is exceedingly small, but sufficient to entertain you, for we have plans to arrange with you. Come up we beseech you as quick as possible, so that we may arrange how the baptism is to go on at Spring before the ending of this month, so that we may get up a meeting to meet you, if coming notice Mr. Warrin with best wiches (1,150).

In another letter written to Gordon on the same date as the one cited above, Paul Bogle told his 'political friend' of the decisions of a meeting respecting the plans they 'might adopt...to recover' Gordon's 'place that is lost in the political world' (1,150). That meeting was held at the *Liberal School Society* meeting house at Stony Gut.

> We hope you and [your] family are as well as we are at present. At a meeting held at the Liberal School Society meetings house at the above named place [Stony Gut] to take into consideration what plans we might adopt for to recover your place that is lost in the political world, but in the religious one we are assured your progress is great; may God grant it so. Among other plans we resolve to have an hundred tax payers put on, independent of freeholders, and those who will or can pay without borrowing from us. So we send to ask you as responsible persons to lend us £150 to lend to those that will form the tax payers, to be paid back to us the responsible parties (1,150).

The letter further stated that the £150 loan was also required 'to pay for registration' for persons to vote (1,150). In yet another letter to George William Gordon, Paul Bogle concentrated on political issues as he did in the one cited above.

> My compliment to you, hope you is well today, as I am not, from fetiguements of yesterday, I felt a severe pain in my stomach so I am not able to come down, you will be please to remember the horse that you did promise to give me to ride out on business. And you must provide something for me to vote upon for the year coming, for all my beast dead, I have also my title here which I will send down to you that you may get it record as quick as possible, for I expect to have William [my son] upon the list of voters for next year.
>
> You must try and see well to this, and we expect to have a meeting at Bogle [Moses] house at Cottage Penn next Tuesday, and your attendants will required (1,151).

This letter was written July 12, 1865.

The following letter from Gordon to Bogle revealed that, in addition to the social, political and religious relations between these men, there was also a business relationship as well.

> I have received your letter of the 24th instant. I have given Bailey the £5. Don't fail to let the sugar come forward. You have had lately from me £5 and £4 and the orders £3 and £1, making in all £13. Can wax and honey be got in your quarter?
>
> So Mr. Marshelleck was going to sue you for the £1.4s.0d. freight.
>
> I now enclose a bank cheque for £1.4s.0d., which Mr. Marshelleck will no doubt take. Remit to Mr. Levy and it will be all right.
>
> I have written to Clarke and you will hear all. Let him send the paper back by Tuesday's post.
>
> Things are bad in Jamaica, and will require a great deal of purging. Best wishes (1,150).

George William Gordon, like Paul Bogle, was an exceedingly religious man. Duncan Fletcher, Gordon's friend and biographer, said of his religious outlook:

> Mr. Gordon's Christian sentiments were very broad and catholic. In a religious sense he was a cosmopolitan. All sections claimed and enjoyed his good offices. He looked more to the piety and usefulness of ministers and people than to their creed or form of Church government...Mr. Gordon most conscientiously came to the conclusion that immersion was the scriptural mode of baptism, consequently he was publicly baptised in that way by the Rev. Mr. Phillippo, of Spanish Town; but he did not formally join the Baptist denomination (Fletcher 1867, 54).

Gordon's non-sectarian, non-denominational, non-partisan and open-minded view of Christianity was to his credit because that approach was to become a liberating force for him. That approach was to eventually lead him to embrace Native Baptism, the theology of the 'unwashed' who, according to leaders of the English churches, took themselves out of the civilising influence of the whites and were thus reverting to barbarism. The closer he moved to the people the more radical he became, and the more radical Gordon became, the more he embraced the Native Baptist religion.

Gordon became a revivalist at heart. Walter Adolphe Roberts said, 'He delighted in revivalistic methods' (Roberts 1952, 31). He played an important role in the great religious revival that gripped the island at the beginning of the 1860s (Curtin 1955). He was also instrumental in establishing a Native Baptist Missionary society with his own pastors, deacons, chapels, missionary stations and sub-stations. The headquarters of that society was the 'Tabernacle' in Kingston.

Richard Warren, a black American Baptist Minister and Abolitionist 'seeking a rest here', was one of Gordon's main ministers (Fletcher 1867,

51). He sometimes preached at the 'Tabernacle' (Royal Commission 1866, 1,069), but was mainly responsible for the society's work in St Thomas-in-the-East where he resided. Warren had operated a chapel in Morant Bay where Paul Bogle and his brother Moses attended regularly on Sundays, at least until 1864 when Bogle opened his own chapel in Stony Gut (158).

Warren was the guest speaker/preacher at the opening of Bogle's chapel. 'He was the minister of the day that claimed the pulpit' (158). Apart from claiming the pulpit on that day, Warren thereafter preached several times at Bogle's chapel (1,067). Warren, a leading Native Baptist (more in the black American tradition), was a respected member of the black political movement in St Thomas-in-the-East and a principal figure in the move to revive the *Anti-slavery Society of Morant Bay* (1,067).

Richard Warren's interest in reviving the *Anti-slavery Society of Morant Bay* was not unconnected from his own position as a formerly enslaved man and his resistance to it. He was enslaved in the US before he escaped to Canada. Then, as part of his struggle to end slavery he wrote and published an account of his life entitled, the *Narrative of the Life and Suffering of Rev. Richard Warren (A Fugitive Slave)*. It was published in 1851. It was perhaps the belief among many black people by 1865, that slavery was about to be restored in Jamaica, that motivated Warren and others to revive the *Anti-slavery Society of Morant Bay* to reflect the consciousness and political activism of people in St Thomas-in-the-East.

Revd J.H. Crole was also closely associated with Gordon's missionary society. He was the chief minister at the 'Tabernacle'. Crole was detained in 1865 under martial law as a political prisoner (1,157). He was one of Kingston's main advocates for rights and justice for the black masses.

In order to carry out the work of his Native Baptist Missionary Society, Gordon, along with Warren, Crole and others, began to ordain his own deacons. Paul Bogle was ordained in the 'Tabernacle,' in Kingston, on March 5, 1865. A letter certifying his ordination was given to Bogle by George William Gordon himself (1,150).

In 1862, Gordon opened a mission in Bath and another in Spring, St Thomas-in-the-East (Fletcher 1867, 51). He also had 'the St Andrew's Mission,' which 'is doing well' (51). Gordon's work in servicing his missions and their substations were quite hectic. Duncan Fletcher, who accompanied him on one of his regular missionary rounds, described Gordon's activities:

> We started on horse back, after attending an early prayer-meeting, and had nearly twenty miles to ride to the station at which I was engaged to preach... We galloped our horses on, at almost Jehu speed, from station to station,

alighting at some of them for a few minutes while Mr. Gordon inspected his Sabbath-schools, etc; and after several abrupt but kind inquiries as to attendance and other matters, he would address a few words of approbation to some, encouragement or perhaps reproof to others, and then we rode off to another and another station, till at length dear Mr. Gordon's attendants kept on "the even tenor of their way," and allowed him to center over his by-paths alone, through rivers and rocks and mud and jungle, to his sub-stations (48–49).

In addition to his mission stations and substations, Fletcher said Gordon 'had his Bethesda pools to visit where impotent folks, halt, withered, aged, sick, bereaved, destitute, dying ones were anxiously awaiting his angelic visits to trouble the waters of charity, patience, resignation, and comfort' (49–50). Although Revd Fletcher's description romanticised the missionary activities of a late friend he eagerly wanted to show to the world as saintly and incapable of organising armed rebellion, it revealed a basic truth: George William Gordon, a member of the coloured elite, was an exceptionally kind and caring man who was deeply motivated by his religious beliefs, a strong sense of justice and love for the black masses.

Gordon's missionary society was probably the same organisation known as the *Native Baptist Communion* of which, according to Warren, Gordon was the secretary (Royal Commission 1866, 1,068). Richard Warren, whose name appeared on Bogle's baptismal certificate, was probably the president or chairman of the *Native Baptist Communion* (perhaps for areas in the county of Surrey). Gordon's missionary commitment led him and his deputies to develop a programme of religious and secular education for the people in some of the communities where mission stations and substations were situated.

As part of this programme he distributed Bibles, hymn books and school books to the people as well as assigning them teachers. To develop that enterprise, Gordon sought assistance from friendly religious societies in Britain. In a letter to Duncan Fletcher, written May 23, 1862, Gordon stated some of his society's needs. 'We need an assistant-teacher, Bibles, tracts, hymn-books, and school-books' (Fletcher 1867, 51).

Gordon's religious activities were dialectically connected with his political activities as his religious beliefs were interwoven with his political beliefs. Along the highways and byways of his missionary work he came face to face with the stark realities of post-emancipation poverty and destitution which fired his radical tendencies.

George William Gordon, who was born in the teen years of the nineteenth century to a wealthy Scottish planter and an enslaved woman, belonged to a group of Jamaicans termed coloureds or browns. They were Afri-Europeans who emerged historically in the Diaspora primarily as the result of sexual intercourse by coercion, engineered by conquering white men against women of the subjected and enslaved black race. Depending on the degree of African and European in them, coloureds were categorised as Sambo, Mulatto, Quadroon and Mustee (Henriques 1974, 95).

Originally born into slavery, coloured Jamaicans gained their total freedom four years before the proclamation of black emancipation and about eight years before real freedom came for the majority of the enslaved Africans.[2] Coloured people had an advantageous position, vis-á-vis, blacks in the colony. The justification for that advantageous position had its roots in white racist thought, which asserted that the 'attributes' (some) coloured people inherited from Europeans, put them closer to the Caucasian respecting the so-called physiological and phrenological features of civilised man. As a result, brown people were allowed greater opportunities to succeed than their black relatives in slavery and post-slavery society.

Sheila Duncker noted that access to the means of production, including owning slaves, was made easier for coloured people compared to black people, although the 'greater part of the free coloured class was propertyless' (Duncker 1956, 101, 107). Duncker noted also that 'money or education... were advantages common to many free coloured people' (Duncker 94).[3]

Several coloureds got the opportunity to study abroad or to become students in some of the better local schools such as the Wolmers Free School (66, 132, 156–69).[4] Among those coloured men of English education were Richard Hill, the anti-slavery campaigner and internationally renowned naturalist who graduated from a British university (Rogers 1972, 258–61). John Campbell, the Montego Bay retailer, was 'extremely well educated in England (Hueman 1981, 58). Alexander Heslop, a barrister and Attorney General of Jamaica, was educated at Oxford University, England (77), while Samuel Constantine Burke, lawyer and legislator, was educated at Harrow and Cambridge in England (63).

Duncker noted that in the public and private sectors coloured males found employment as clerks and some of them became 'excellent accountants' (Duncker 1956, 112). By 1837, it was observed that 'there is hardly a respectable house among the white merchants in which some important office, oftentimes the head clerk, is not filled by a person of colour' (112).

Among the merchant class itself, there were coloured men who were 'dealers in dry goods, crockery and glassware, ironmongers, booksellers, druggists, grocers and general importers' (112). Colonial governments also gave support and 'encouragement' to men of colour who were tradesmen.

As a result, 'the greater part of the public work has for many years been done by them' (111). At the same time, coloureds such as John Anderson and William Grant, who were ontologically closer to or were a part of the social, material and aesthetic culture of the black majority, were intimately connected to the people's socio-economic and political goals and formed part of the leadership core of the struggle to realise them.

Gordon, like the other successful coloureds of whom Duncker spoke, benefited from his position in plantation society. With the assistance from the European side of his family and race, he began to acquire and invest in real estate, merchandise and life assurance, while still a young man.[5] Soon, Gordon became a very big land owner, owning land in many parishes across the island.

As a result of their more privileged position in plantation society, many coloured Jamaicans felt themselves superior to blacks. Their belief in the white racist notions of civilised people had a strong hold on their psycho-cultural and ontological evolution.

When slavery ended, the 'aristocracy of the skin' found a new pedestal in post-emancipation society. The coloured population, and especially its leading sections, bore a part of the responsibility for hoisting bigotry on that pedestal.

When Anthony Trollope visited Jamaica in 1858, he observed coloured people's 'delight to talk contemptuously of niggers', calling them 'dirty niggers, and nasty niggers, and mere niggers' (Trollope 1860, 88). Racist prejudice against Africans were also expressed when blacks sought to enter areas regarded as the natural preserve of coloured and white men. When Edward Vickars made it known his intention to seek a seat in the island's legislature by contesting national elections, he was 'totally supported by the Kingston black voters, and equally resolutely opposed by the coloured and white voters, among them, Edward Jordon and Robert Osborn, the senior coloured representatives of the Assembly, and both on the grounds of Vickars's colour' (Wilmot 1977, 306).

Vickars, a Kingston landlord and former slave owner, was one of the few blacks wealthy enough to meet the legal requirements to qualify him to run for a seat in the Assembly. However, despite the determined efforts by the philosophers of the skin to turn him back, Vickars went on to win a seat to represent St Catherine in 1847 (305–311).

While blacks' access to the House of Assembly was extremely limited because the requirements for entry were so much above their means,[6] many African Jamaicans, relatively speaking, were elected to the local government bodies, the Vestries, where the requirements for entry were more affordable to them. However, not even at this level of government did many whites and coloureds feel was the proper place for black people to be. They thus advocated measures such as the abolition of local government elections or local government itself to keep blacks in their place.

Attorney General of Jamaica at the time of the Morant Bay War, Alexander Heslop, formerly a parliamentarian, wanted the abolition of local government elections because, in the same racist language of whiteness, 'it produces excitement among an excitable people...and does mischief.' He said there was, perhaps, hardly one institution the continuance of which he 'would so much deprecate in the island as that of the parochial vestries, for this reason, it is the training school for the demagogue' (Royal Commission 1866, 331).[7]

So much was the antagonism between the coloureds and blacks, that Alexander Heslop, expressing the feeling of the browns, said the black man was 'Much more against the coloured man than the white man' (332). However, the feeling on the other side was mutual since the Africans felt that the coloureds were more oppressive and more racist than the Europeans (Heuman 1981, 72) (Duncker 1856, 200–201). That is to say, not being fully white, coloureds had to cultivate and perform social and cultural whiteness to such a degree, as to make the distinction between black and coloured like that between black and white in the mythological universe of coloured metaphysics.

However, despite the alliance between coloureds and whites, despite their sharing a common ancestry, the Europeans historically relate to the browns in a racist way (Henriques 1974, 95, 104) (Duncker 1856, 131–32, 193–94). The primary basis of that racism was the African in the coloured which the European saw as the epitome of barbarism and savagery. The second most important basis for the European racism against the coloured had to do with the brown man's post-emancipation successes in education, government, and the economy, which made him a real threat and possible alternative to the white man's power in colonial society, especially since the white population was decreasing while the coloured and black populations were increasing. While some of the most offensive features of institutional and political racism against coloureds ended in 1830, bigotry as a social movement against browns continued unabated in post-emancipation society, notwithstanding the politics of compromise between the coloureds and whites to protect the state from black majority rule (Heuman 1981, 75–77).

In spite of this compromise however, and in spite of the feeling of superiority that coloureds displayed towards blacks, both groups needed a strategic alliance to overcome white power. In their struggles to expand the rights of the subjected people in post-slavery society, the black masses needed the representation of the coloureds. As a result of their superior economic position, their blood relations with the whites, browns found it easier to access capital, get an English education, develop links with liberal progressive British parliamentarians, intellectuals, anti-slavery and ecclesiastic leaders, and enlist their support against colonial and plantocratic policies which restricted the ability of Jamaicans to expand their freedom.

In their efforts to expand and consolidate their social, economic and political power, the coloureds needed the solidarity of the black Jamaicans. They needed the votes of those with the franchise but also the support of the non-voting masses to defeat the whites who exercised control and power over the Assembly and the non-elected Executive Committee. By so doing, they hoped to gather enough forces inside and outside the legislature and executive to win support for legislations and policies aimed at developing Jamaica and its former enslaved people.

Bills such as the one introduced by Robert Osborn in 1850 to establish schools across the island or the one introduced by Alexander Heslop to sanction the creation of professional schools in the island for the training of doctors and lawyers (148) were soundly defeated in the planter dominated parliament. Yet, the essence of these defeated bills represented the direction in which the colony had to go if the aspirations of the masses of the formerly enslaved, coloured and black, were to be met.

The development of a Jamaican interest required the unity of coloureds and blacks and their ultimate victory over the absentee/colonial interest. Post-emancipation requirements found political expression in the speeches made by coloured and black men in the Assembly, public meetings and in articles published in the press. On December 31, 1858 for example, Robert Osborn told members of the House of Assembly that:

> The Government of this country will within twenty years, be left to the Brown and Black men. The Hon. Member for Metcalfe will by that time be gone. The Honourable gentleman, Mr. Speaker, is only fighting a shadow; for it is in the course of God's Providence that the change to which I allude should occur, and there is no altering it. God has destined that the wrongs of Africa should be vindicated in these lands (*Colonial Standard* January 13, 1866).

Later, 1860–61, Osborn returned to that theme. He reminded the Assembly that according to his computation, 'there was a coloured and black population of 371,657. AND THEY ARE THE PEOPLE OF THE COUNTRY and not the miserable minorities of ten or fifteen thousand whites' (*Colonial Standard*

January 13, 1866). He warned that 'if the country is going to be governed by a party', namely, the *Country Party*, coloured men would mobilise the black men to oppose such a regime. Accordingly he said, 'There is a vein in the hearts of coloured and black men which non (sic) can touch but coloured men' (*Colonial Standard* January 13, 1866).

Thus, while recognising the common ancestral link between blacks and coloureds, Osborn insisted, as most of his class would have done, that only brown men could lead the Jamaican masses to develop a Jamaican interest. Apparently, black men could not touch the vein that linked the hearts of brown and black men because their black skin did not qualify them to do so. This remark by Osborn represented an important aspect of the ontology and agency of acquired white prejudice in the metaphysical and political culture of coloured people.

At the same time, many blacks pragmatically embraced coloured leaders because brown people were in a better social and economic position to fulfil the requirements for election to the colonial parliament, the House of Assembly, and thus becoming lawmakers. Blacks clearly had a preference for coloured lawmakers over the white ones, in light of history and its relation to the existing state of affairs.

Moreover, white people were more at ease with coloured people because of familial, blood and social relationships, which placed them socially, aesthetically and culturally closer to Europeans, who used coloureds as a buffer between the black savages as a means of protection during slavery and after. Of course, black people also had familial blood and social relationship with coloured people and sought to use it to their political advantage.

Blacks were much more feared than coloureds by white people. With all of this and the practical link and knowledge that some coloureds possessed in the world controlled by white people, coloureds were in a better position to represent blacks in that world, even as blacks were constantly building their sovereign capacity and strength.

George William Gordon, like Robert Osborn, was part of the political leadership of that post-emancipation black–coloured alliance which sought to vindicate the wrongs of Africa in the island. Unlike Osborn and other members of that leadership however, Gordon was closest to the black masses, and most consistent in representing and articulating their position. In this regard, the *New York Tribune* (December 26, 1865) was on to a fundamental truth when it noted that Gordon's crime for those who wanted him dead 'was that his course of political action was calculated to open the eyes of the black people as they have never yet been opened to the true character of that system of legislation by which their rights have been trifled with, their interests sacrificed, their progress retarded' (qtd in Stewart 1995, 20).

Politically and culturally, George William Gordon represented the most radical wing of the middle and upper sections of the coloured population. Additionally, he had the broadest contact among the Jamaican people.

The breadth and pattern of his acquisition of lands meant that in order for Gordon to reach them by land, he had to travel through almost every parish in the island. This meant that he, more than most, if not all politicians, was in a position to meet a wider cross section of the Jamaican people, establish social, political and religious contact with them, and develop a national perspective on the condition of the people in post-emancipation society. Hence his business, like his missionary work, helped in advancing his political work among large masses of people and influential individuals across the island.

In time, George William Gordon became the most popular leader and the only truly national figure in post-emancipation society. The reality of his social, religious, business and political connections across the island gave a national character to his political activities.

By the last half of the 1850s, George William Gordon rose to become the most passionate advocate of the cause of the black masses. Despite his upbringing and association with white colonial society and the so-called 'refined' portion of the coloured population, Gordon became an exception in his class in consistently siding with the labouring masses.[8]

Gordon evolved from being a conservative in his early parliamentary years when he was trusted 'to have been regularly appointed to committees of the House on matters of finance' (Hart n.d., 26), or made a Justice of the Peace in several parishes, to become 'the notorious demagogue and stump orator' (*Jamaica Tribune* October 13, 1865), who was expelled from the parliament to which he was elected, and purged from the Vestry and the Magistracy. By the time Governor Darling's tenure came to an end, George William Gordon was already a committed democrat and radical reformer. The arrival of Edward Eyre, who was to become the colony's next Governor, quickened the pace of the polarisation that was already overtaking the society.[9]

The George William Gordon who first entered the House of Assembly in 1844 was, in many respects, different from the Gordon who re-entered the parliament in 1863. This time, with the backing of Bogle and his people, he came to represent 'the Negro'.

> I come here as the avowed representative of the people. I come here strictly in the capacity of the Negro, and if you permit me to claim that position, you will not withhold from me those rights, of which we have for years been deprived.

> In St. Thomas-in-the-East, people are desirous of coming down here in a body to demand redress, but I have told them that that would not do, because they would not be heard at the Bar.... The old aristocratic feeling is passing away, and those who rule must rule in a manner to suit the wants and wishes of the people (*Colonial Standard* January 13, 1866).

Gordon did not stop there; he told his fellow legislators what most of them, probably with deep apprehension, must have given some thought to.

> You must make up your minds to the future, for coming events cast their shadows before. If you look at the Census you will find 360,000 black inhabitants, about 81,000 coloured, and 13,000 whites. You will also find that the white population is diminishing, while the others are increasing, and the consequence is, that in course of time the black people must get their proper position in the country (*Colonial Standard* January 13, 1866).

Gordon used the House of Assembly to expose and attack the anti-people policies of those in government upholding the 'aristocratic feeling' in the colony even while he proposed bills in defence of the people. He was a resolute campaigner against corruption in the state which brought down the wrath of some powerful men, including Governor Eyre, on him.[10]

One of those incidents of corruption, the case 'Gordon versus Ketelholdt',[11] brought in his response, one key element of Gordon's ideological position. Gordon believed that government had a duty to uphold the law of the country and if government failed to do so by breaking or ignoring the law, the people reserved the right to rebel against that government. In a letter to the editor of the *Sentinel*, published April 27, 1865, Gordon chided Attorney General Heslop for giving Governor Eyre:

> wrong advice...to provide for Baron Ketelholdt out of the Public Treasury the means of defending his illegal proceedings, and thereby making the Government a party, supporting an act of infringement against the law, and the rights of the Constituency of the island, by striving to confound the Jury and letting them believe that Mr. Justice Cargill could proceed to adjudicate under a law which had been repealed.

With this, Gordon, who was a political ally of Ketelholdt in his earlier political life, asked, 'Who is safe in Jamaica? What may we expect?' Then he warned:

> When Charles the 1st of England refused to abide by the laws to which he had become a party – by his sanction – a revolution ensured and he was beheaded!

> When the Sovereign of the French disregarded the popular elective rights there was a revolution, and he had to abdicate and fly from the kingdom!

If in Jamaica our laws are to be disregarded, by those who are bound to conserve them, and a Judge may hold proceedings and adjudicate under repealed laws, the execution enforced, and all this is not only upheld but encouraged by the government, how long may good order be expected to continue? (*Sentinel* April 27, 1865)

Gordon was obviously aware of political upheavals in Europe's history and theories explaining them, including John Locke's. There was no doubting that Gordon's view of Eyre matched Locke's notion of tyranny, viz:

As usurpation is the Exercise of Power, which another hath a right to, tyranny is the exercise of Power beyond Right, which no Body can have a Right to. And this is making use of the Power any one has in his hands; not for the good of those, who are under it, but for his own private separate Advantage. When the Governor, however intitled, makes not Law, but his Will, the Rule; and his Commands and Actions are not directed to the preservation of the Properties of his People, but the satisfaction of his own Ambition, Revenge, Covetousness, or any other irregular Passion (Locke 1960, 446).

Such tyranny Locke concluded, put itself 'into a state of war with the people, who are thereupon absolved from any farther Obedience' (460).

As far as Gordon was concerned, Jamaica had become a Herodic state in which Governor Eyre was in a state of war with the Jamaican people. Consequently, Gordon was tending to the view that the people should be absolved from any further obedience to the Governor. Thus, the radical St Thomas-in-the-East Member of Parliament protested to the Speaker of the Assembly at his attempts to:

Suppress public opinion, to pen up the expression of indignation; but I tell you that it will soon burst forth like a flood, and sweep everything before it. There must be a limit to everything: a limit to oppression – a limit to transgression – and a limit to illegality! These proceedings remind me of the time of Herod....

I do not think that any Governor has ever acted so before. While he justifies himself in one case, he used the police force to accomplish another illegality... If the Governor is to go on in this way, what can you expect from the populace?

Another member: - Insurrection (Laughter)

Mr. Gordon:- Ah! That will be the result. When all over laws are put at defiance, the populace will break out from discontent, and the Governor will be unable to allay their feelings...When a Governor becomes a dictator, when he becomes despotic, it is time for the people to dethrone him.... I have never seen an animal more voracious for cruelty and power than the present Governor of Jamaica.

> Mr. Speaker: - Order! Order! Such language cannot be allowed...
>
> Mr. Gordon: - I say that if the law is to be disregarded it will lead to anarchy and bloodshed...If we are to be governed by such a Governor much longer, the people will have to fly to arms and become self-governing (qtd in Semmel 1976, 40–41).

George William Gordon's ideological position was decidedly biased in favour of the poor, the black masses and the Jamaican interest. Hence, his assessment of an issue or phenomenon was based on the extent to which he felt it would hurt or benefit the black masses and Jamaica's interest. This method of thought was of course based on certain assumptions. Firstly, Gordon felt that it was inevitable that the black masses would one day, in the not too distant future, rule Jamaica (*Colonial Standard* January 13, 1866). Secondly, he felt that 'the voice of the people is the voice of God' (Parliamentary Debates Vol. IX 1863, 37), which must be obeyed by politicians, governors, and planters. Thirdly, he believed in the equality of all persons and that the masses were 'men and brethren' like anyone else (Parliamentary Debates Vol. VIII 1863, 228), thus, 'if we do not hearken to the cries of the poor and needy, we will surely fall for ever' (Parliamentary Debates Vol. IX, 29). Fourthly, he believed in national development and a more nationally oriented economy. Hence, while Gordon was a passionate opponent of immigration, he took the case of immigrant Asians who were to be found on the streets of Kingston and other towns in destitution to parliament:

> The Coolies you brought to this land are dying on the roadsides from destitution... and when I write to say that these people are in destitution, and are dying from want, I am told that my report is not true...Their treatment is a disgrace to the country, and Heaven is crying out against those wretched men who turn a deaf ear to the supplications of these unfortunates. My blood boils within me when I think of the misery of the coolies; and I believe that the country is suffering in consequence of the hardness of heart of those who are entrusted with power (29).

Gordon was decidedly opposed to 'those who are entrusted with power' over immigration and the policy direction of the colony, the planter class; those with the 'old aristocratic feeling,' who 'are always crying out – "give, give, give" and are never happy' (Parliamentary Debates Vol. VIII, 228). He warned against the island being 'sacrificed for these gentlemen' (228).

George William Gordon was the most consistent opponent in the post-emancipation parliament of the unity of church and state. Accordingly, he said:

> I hold as a cardinal principle that the state has no right to support religion. Every sect is bound to support its own churches, and that religion cannot be pure and wholesome which is not free from all taint of state aid.

Apart from the purely religious reason given for opposing the unity of church and state, Gordon abhorred the fact that 'something like £50,000 a year' or 'one-fifth of the taxation of the country' (240) was granted to the Anglican Church by the state to pay men who were 'indulging in vice, immorality, luxury, and voluptuousness' (Parliamentary Debates Vol. IX, 95–96). Although Gordon viewed the Established Church as an institution of state power and oppression which had to be forced out of that position and that Anglican ministers were planters at heart in practice, he was against any union between church and state even if such church were a dissenter.

Hence, he introduced a bill in the House of Assembly 'to prohibit grants to religious denominations'[12] because it was a 'reproach and disgrace' for the dissenters who 'did their duty during the dark days of slavery' to ask the parliament for financial support (Parliamentary Debates Vol. VIII, 210). He said if the dissenting churches were to be given grants by government they 'will become as corrupt as the state church is' (210). He thus argued for the separation of church and state as was the case in Canada and Australia (210).

Like J.W. Menard, Gordon felt that education was an essential liberating force for the masses and the island. He denounced the excessive spending on prisons and the militia, and campaigned for the education budget to be increased beyond £3,000 per year. Gordon felt, like Menard, that it was the duty of the state to provide quality education for the people; that simultaneously 'with the abolition of slavery they [government] should have had an educational measure' (186). He advocated the establishment of schools and colleges across the island (169) (*Falmouth Post* July 29, 1859) and consistently urged the people at public meetings and campaigns to do everything they could to ensure that their children received an education because they had to be prepared and be 'qualified to fill the highest positions in society' (*Falmouth Post* July 29, 1859).

George William Gordon had a burning desire to see Jamaica develop.[13] Needless to say, he wanted very much to see civilisation making strides in Jamaica like in other countries where, according to him, revolutions, steam communications, railways, telegraphs, etc., were being developed and used to elevate their people and increase their material prosperity. He felt, however, that the motive force to develop the wealth of the island had to be 'the small settlers' (Parliamentary Debates Vol. IX, 306). Unlike Bigelow,

Sewell, and other free competition advocates who generally felt that Jamaica's socio-economic advancement was best served by the development of a white middle class, Gordon felt that Jamaica's development 'will be greatly brought out in time by the small settlers of the colony, who are gradually growing into importance'(306). The free competition advocates' choice of a white middle class was connected to their racist bias against blacks and their ability to produce a middle class of their own. Gordon believed in blacks' ability and proclaimed it to the Jamaican Parliament:

> At present the great benefit being done by this class of our population is only imperceptibility creeping on, but in time it will be materially felt, and there will spring up among us a good, steady, and industrious middle class.

Gordon, a firm advocate of free labour, was of course, talking about people like Paul Bogle, George B. Clarke, Samuel Clarke, Emanuel Goldson, Robert Miller, and William Kelly Smith, the own-account blacks who constituted his main political support. He was talking about the tradesmen who complained at the May 1865 Underhill meeting in Spanish Town about 'the cost of manufactured articles imported with which [they] have to compete' with their locally produced items.[14]

Gordon was also referring to the small farmers who were responsible for 'one half the coffee and nearly the whole of the pimento now exported' (Underhill 1862, 290). Gordon felt these people were being kept down by a system which had not facilitated 'the transfer of land' but clogged it with 'restrictions and placed it in the hands of the Crown' (Parliamentary Debates Vol. VIII, 227). These 'small settlers,' he felt were being fettered by an entrenched, preponderant sugar economy and sugar interests whose 'whole respect is for sugar and rum' (258).

Needless to say, it was Gordon's contention that Jamaica could not prosper under an economy so dominated by sugar and the class of sugar producers. For him, the answer to a more national-oriented and responsive economy, was in the removal or serious reduction of the special status of sugar and the privileges of its 'producers', while favouring a more diversified economic regime centred around the activities of 'small settlers'.

Gordon's economic nationalism was part of a tendency that emerged among Jamaicans in post-slavery society. Generally speaking, it was an expression of the desire of Jamaicans to reshape the economy to conform more to their aspirations. Although the expression of economic nationalism shared a common anti-plantocratic platform, individuals and sectors clearly had different interests and emphases. For example, there was Samuel Holt, that advocate of black proprietorship, self-reliance and self-employment of

Black River, who told the people at a meeting in Porus, 'not to work for the white man, and that they must form an agency in England, and send their produce there direct' (Eyre 1971, 111). Then there was William Wemyss Anderson, a friend, solicitor, and business associate of Gordon who was convinced that Jamaica's economy would be best served by copying the American model of the capitalist mode of production.

This Scottish abolitionist who made Jamaica his home, advocated close economic ties with the US because of 'their proximity and many valuable qualities, to aid us by their energy and agricultural skill, in developing the abounding and varied wealth of our soil' (Anderson 1851, 6).[15] An advocate of two-way investment between the US and Jamaica, Anderson believed that with the right method of production and an economic policy directed at national development, Jamaica should be raising its own food without having to import the same.

> On the subject of the expediency of raising our food on our own soil – the case against Jamaica is most remarkable, and I believe unique. With the finest soil and climate in the world, and a half idle population, we are eating daily the corn grown upon the soil of America. We ought to raise every article of corn, corn-meal, rice, beef, and pork, salted and smoked, lard and butter, candles, soap, and oil. We have been actually importing coconut and castor oil from the East Indies! How can there be the least prosperity among us so long as we stand disgraced before the world by such anomalies as these? (19–20).

Then there was Robert Osborn who felt, like so many Jamaicans in post-emancipation society, that:

> This history of the country shows the indelible fact that it has been the system of the planters, for three-quarters of a century past to take everything away from the country and to return nothing to it, except what is necessary to keep up their estates. (qtd in Heuman 1981, 67).

George William Gordon's radicalism was not just linked to the House of Assembly where it was felt he could say almost anything since he was protected by parliamentary privileges. This man's parliamentary views were expressed in the letters he often wrote to the press and in speeches at the public meetings he helped to organise across the island. In a letter called 'The State of the island,' intended for public display, and a device, mass produced, to assist in the mobilisation of residents of St Ann and St Thomas-in-the-East to public meetings in their respective parishes, Gordon pleaded impassionedly to the people to come forth and stand up for their rights. To the people of St Ann he said:

> People of St. Ann's! Poor people of St. Ann's! starving people of St. Ann's! Naked people of St. Ann's! You have no sugar estates to work on, nor can find other employment. We call on you to come forth; come, if you be naked; come forth and protest against the unjust representations made against you by Mr. Governor Eyre and his band of Custodes. You don't require custodes to tell your woes, but you want men free of Government influence. You want men with a sense of right and wrong, and who can appreciate you (Eyre 1971, 219).

Turning to the people of St Thomas-in-the-East, Gordon said:

> People of St. Thomas-in-the-East, you have been ground down too long already; shake off your sloth and speak like honourable and free men at your meeting. Let not a crafty jesuitical priesthood deceive you. Prepare for your duty. Remember the destitution in the midst of your families, and your forlorn condition. The Government have taxed you to defend your own rights against the enormities of an unscrupulous and oppressive foreigner, Mr. Custos Ketelholdt...This is not the time when such deeds should be perpetuated; but as they have been, it is your duty to speak out and to act too! We advise you to be up and doing, and to maintain your cause. You must be united in your efforts. The causes of your distress are many, and now is your time to review them. Your custos, we learn, read at the last vestry the Despatch from Mr. Cardwell, which he seemed to think should quiet you; but how can men with a sense of wrong in their bosoms be content to be quiet under such a reproachful despatch. Remember that "he only is free whom the truth makes free." You are no longer slaves, but free men. Then as free men act your part at the meeting...Try to help yourselves and heaven will help you (Eyre 219).

George William Gordon's radical ideological position was not an isolated phenomenon linked to 'a sadly erratic politician' with a 'Utopian philosophy' (*Falmouth Post* July 29, 1859), or a man 'essentric in his views and notions of the people's rights,'[16] or that 'confirmed talker against time' who 'preaches, sports, jests, and dallies for hours' because 'his great pleasure' was to 'hear himself talk' and 'swell the volume of Parliamentary Reports' (*Colonial Standard* February 20, 1865). Gordon's thought represented part of a radical shift by significant sections of the Jamaican population away from liberal and conservative ideas and solutions to the socio-economic and political problems confronting the island.

Radical ideas emerged and grew especially towards the end of the 1850s following on the Westmoreland and Trelawny riots of 1859; the great religious revival at the ending of the 1850s and the beginning of the 1860s; the Underhill meetings of 1865 and a serious shift to the right in the island's politics under the authoritarian rule of Governor Edward Eyre, 1862–65.

The Jamaican masses and the coloured elites had long favoured liberalism over conservatism and revolutionism in political thoughts and political actions. That favouritism might have emanated from the fact that Britain, Queen Victoria and the British Anti-slavery Society were perceived by many Jamaicans as supra class forces, standing incorruptibly above the internal conflicts in the island and fairly adjudicating between planter and labourer; black and white; indeed, a non-partisan force that blacks felt they could appeal to against their white adversaries.

After all, it was Britain that proclaimed the abolition of the slave trade in 1807 while the planters and merchant slave traders opposed it; Britain proclaimed emancipation, while the planters fought every inch of the way to prevent it. Similarly, the dissenting missionary groups and leaders such as William Knibb and Thomas Burchell sided with the enslaved Africans, sometimes to their peril, to oppose slavery, while the planters and the Established Church supported slavery.[17]

Missionary societies, especially the English Baptist, also played a central role in assisting blacks to establish free villages, acquire land and the franchise, and create a system of education, while the planter class and its allies fought to prevent or restrict their implementation.[18] Thus, in the struggles with their immediate antagonists, the plantocracy/slaveocracy/neo-slaveocracy, the blacks came to value the practical and ideological support of those white people in England and Jamaica who sided with them against the practices and ideas of the planter class.

The support of the black majority for liberal positions, which they benefited from, was cultivated over many decades, and probably acted as a break on the development of a nationalist movement in the island. By liberal positions I refer to the views of whites who, opposed the slavery and neo-slavery measures of the conservatives, supported a basic humanitarian regime for Africans, spoke on behalf of blacks whom they regarded as less civilised than Europeans, but were equally or more opposed to black radicals like Sam Sharpe and Paul Bogle taking things into their own hands.

Liberalism, therefore, stood between the conservatism of the plantocracy and the revolutionism of blacks. The hold of liberalism on the people was undeniably deep but breachable. One such breach was the 1831–32 anti-slavery insurrection led by Sam Sharpe, who disregarded the advice of William Knibb and the English Baptists not to rebel against slavery. The other major breach was to come in 1865.

So deep, however, was the belief in liberalism, that Sam Sharpe, the revolutionary who broke with it or set it aside for revolutionary activities, felt sure that the English soldiers in the island would not side with the slaveocracy against the rebelling blacks (Hart n.d., 268–69). Paul Bogle, George William Gordon and Samuel Clarke were to make that mistake again 33 years later. Gordon's response to the Queen's (British Government's) reply to the petitioners of St Ann, was indicative of the deep belief that even the most revolutionary-conscious Jamaicans had in British liberal institutions and British justice. Gordon said:

> We know that our beloved Queen is too noble-hearted to say anything unkind, even to Her most noble subjects, and we believe that Mr. Cardwell and Her Majesty's ministers are gentlemen too honourable and honest in their intentions wilfully to wound the feelings of Her Majesty's Colonial subjects; but we fear they have been deceived and misled, and the consequence is a serious grievance to our people (Eyre 1971, 219).

Gordon, Bogle and Clarke would die on the gallows proclaiming themselves loyal British subjects like one of their fellow countrymen, Richard Clarke, who shouted 'God bless the Queen' while being whipped by British soldiers in St Thomas-in-the-East. Even so, an ideological breach was made in post-emancipation society favouring radical views and solutions in opposition to liberal and conservative ideas.

Such were the views of one man who went by the pseudonym 'Dux'. In a reply to an editorial carried by the *Falmouth Post*, which, among other things, blamed the Westmoreland riots and the destruction of toll gates on the 'inflammatory harangues delivered at monster gatherings by...a small band of factionists,' Dux asked, 'what then is the destruction of a few toll houses' compared to the great battles for liberty in England and France?

> Nay it is a praiseworthy demonstration and if "the people" of Jamaica would always show such admirable resistance to oppression and ill constituted measures the "collective wisdom" of wealth and respectability would respect the rights of the people more, or if a few of those contemptuous writers of your politics and opinions were physically dealt with, you would not jabber such trash and hypocrisy as was spoken last session, we want Robespierres, Dantons and a few other men of that stamp or even of the Haytien...kind, then would Jamaica be a happy Island. Until there be a revolution of blood to free the land of political plagues whose creed is one of injustice and oppression, until such be, there will be no hope of regeneration for Jamaica (qtd in Schuler 1980, 103).

Dux, like Gordon, was obviously influenced by the ideas of European Bourgeois revolutionaries such as Locke, Paine, Robespierre and Danton, as well as the revolutionary battles for liberty against feudal monarchical absolutism in France and England, and exemplified by the French Revolution. Information on revolutionary leaders, revolutionary upheavals and revolutionary ideas from the perspective of Europeans were certainly not lacking, though restricted in Jamaica.

Some Jamaicans did have access to Locke's *Two Treatises of Government*, Charles Darwin's *On the Origin of the Species*, Adam Smith's *Wealth of Nations*, and of course, the Bible, among other publications. It was, however, from the newspapers that a much larger section of the Jamaican population got a wealth of information on revolutionary activities, and revolutionary ideas, reprinted from the foreign press by the Jamaican press. From articles reprinted from the *Anti-Slavery Reporter, Telegraph, Pallmall Gazette, Leeds Mercury, Daily Scotsman, London Times, Morning Advertiser, Daily News, New York Herald, Liberator, Harper's Magazine, New York Tribune*, Jamaicans learned about the 1848 revolution in France; the 'Civil War' in America, 1861–65; the 'Indian Mutiny,' 1857–59; the anti-colonial struggles of the Fenians against British rule in Ireland; the rise and fall of the Paris Commune, 1871, as well as ideas of white radicals and liberals such as Jean-Jacques Rosseau, François-Marie Voltaire, Wendell Phillips, Abraham Lincoln, Charles Darwin and John Bright.

Like Dux and Gordon, the knowledge of international politics influenced political ideas and actions in Jamaica. Hence, when dozens of rebels took Hire's great house at Amity Hall, they roared, 'Hip! Hip, hurrah! We have taken Sebastopol' (Royal Commission 1866, 847). Then there was the note found in St Mary, which stated, among other things, that:

> In the whole of St. Thomas-in-the-East, old man and maiden, young men and children, them all taken up and shot by the soldiers. In all the life of Napolien, none like this. Innocent lives is taken (873).

Dux's reference to the Haitian Revolution suggested that the only successful black revolution in the African Diaspora continued to have a positive impact on the growth of radical consciousness in Jamaica.[19] The Haitian Revolution continued to invoke fear in the minds of whites and was cited as a main reason for the nature of the suppression in Jamaica in 1865.

Another way in which radical views were expressed in post-emancipation society was through the Revival/Warner tradition. One example of this was the message from 'a placard which was stuck upon a wharf gate in the town of Lucea, Hanover.' It was first carried in the *Falmouth Post* and reprinted in the *County Union*, June 20, 1865. The author of the placard, 'A son of Africa', warned:

> Nearly a year since I saw the vision. I heard a voice speaking to me in the year 1864 saying, "Tell the sons and daughters of Africa that a great deliverance will take place for them from the hand of oppression", for said the Voice,

"They are oppressed by Government, by Magistrates, by Proprietors, by Merchants," and this voice also said, "Tell them to call a solemn assembly and to sanctify themselves for the day of deliverance which will surely take place; but if the people will not harken I will bring the sword into the land to chastise them for their disobedience and for the iniquities which they have committed. And the sword will come from America. If the people depend upon their arms and upon our Queen, and forget Him who is our God they will be greatly mistaken, and the mistake will lead them to great distresses." At that time, I kept silent, but yet the thought of what the voice told me was always bearing on my mind to speak about it. Shame or fear seems to have kept me back, but the Great Being who rules all things reminds me again to proclaim it aloud. The calamity which I see coming upon the land will be so grievous and so distressing that many will desire to die. But great will be the deliverance of the Sons and Daughters of Africa, if they humble themselves in sackcloth and ashes, like the children of Nineveh before the Lord our God; but if we pray truly from our hearts, and humble ourselves, we have no need to fear; if not the enemy will be cruel, for there will be Gog and Magog to battle. Believe me. A SON OF AFRICA (849).

The language and method of this placard, bore the hallmark of Native Baptism/Myalism/Obeahism and other aspects of the Warner tradition in Afro-Jamaican Christianity, a tradition which formed an important basis of the ideological position of Paul Bogle's movement, and had a significant influence on George William Gordon's political thought.

Liberalism Moved Closer to Conservatism

The growth of ideological radicalism in post-slavery society was part of a process which saw liberalism move closer to conservatism. In practice, English Baptist ministers as well as ministers from other denominations who once opposed flogging, gave support to the plantocracy who passed a Whipping Bill in the House of Assembly in 1865 (883). Baptist, Moravian and Anglican ministers were at one in expelling many black members of their congregations for engaging in religious practices considered African, and for behaviour deemed immoral.[20]

For their part, thousands of blacks who once flocked the English churches began to stay away (Underhill c. 1865, 49–50, 53–55, 61–62, 64–65, 68). They stayed away because they could no longer afford to buy 'church' clothes. They also stopped in response to the racism of English ministers who showed contempt for black personhood and cultural expressions. Moreover, they stopped because they derived more satisfaction of self and spirit from relying on themselves in the tradition of their ancestral praxis, especially when things got harder.

This reliance was referred to by a British Navy Commander in Jamaica, Bedford Pim, as 'the rude notions of socialism in the masses which the GEORGE WILLIAM GORDONS and the PAUL BOGLES lately sought to explore for their own purposes' (*Colonial Standard* April 4, 1866). Dissenting ministers co-operated with planters and government officials to report to them the attitude of their congregations to the ruling classes as well as to persuade the masses from acting politically on their own behalf.[21]

By 1865, when the pace of antagonism between the people and the ruling classes reached fever pitch, liberal reformers, some of them to the left of the political centre, began to pull back from George William Gordon because they feared or disagreed with the increasing tempo of his radicalism.[22] Perhaps one of the best stated ideological justifications for liberalism's common ground with conservatism against radicalism in post-emancipation society found expression in a sermon delivered by prominent Baptist missionary leader, David J. East to his congregation at Rio Bueno, Trelawny, during the suppression in 1865:

> And what is it but the force of the law and Government, in the case of multitudes, that restrains these evil passions from overleaping all bounds? But for Civil Government, whose wife, or daughter, would be safe from the filthy and abominable lusts of the fornicator and adulterer? But for Civil Government, whose reputation would be safe from the false witnessing of the perjurer? But for Civil Government, whose house, land or property of any kind, would be secure for a single hour from the cupidity of the prowling thief, of the violence of the open murderer?

All this made it easier for the authorities to execute George William Gordon and for it to be justified by the right-wing press, clergy and state actors. The *Falmouth Post* (October 21, 1865) insisted: 'There can be no sympathy for, no extension of mercy, to George William Gordon.' For its part, the *Gleaner* (November 8, 1865) stated that:

> George William Gordon, an enemy to himself, his country and his Queen has been like the vampire of South America, flying from parish to parish, fanning his unconscious victims into sleep, and sharpening the fangs that were to destroy them in their fancied security at home.
>
> If ever a villain lived, George William Gordon was one, and if from the days of Judas Iscariot down to the present days, a man was ever guilty of death in its most ignominious form – George Gordon has been the man.

Notes

1. A *Gleaner* correspondent writing out of Montego Bay said, 'I am informed that Bogle was in this parish three months ago with George W. Gordon, while he was travelling through this side of the Island, for the purpose of addressing Meetings' (*Gleaner* October 19, 1865).
2. Browns gained their freedom earlier partly because of their own efforts, but especially as a result of the desire of the white slave-owning plantocracy to forge an alliance with coloureds to counter the tide of black emancipation struggles.
3. Duncker noted that John Swaby, the Sambo who, in 1828 owned 217 slaves and 331 livestock, studied at Charterhouse, one of England's most prestigious public schools, and was 'remarkably well educated' (42).
4. Except probably for the Walton School in St Ann, Duncker said free coloureds were generally allowed in schools with white students. Coloureds were first admitted in the Wolmers Free School in 1815 when three brown students were placed on roll alongside 111 white students. By 1830, whites accounted for 88 students and coloureds 194.
5. He was said to have secured a loan of £1,000 from a 'white lady', that 'was probably the foundation of his business ventures' (Hart 14).
6. Qualifications for candidacy to the Assembly 1840: an annual income of £180, from land or real property worth £1,800, or both real and personal property worth £3,000 (Wilmot 277). Qualification 1858: annual income, after payment of all just debts, of one hundred and fifty pounds,... or an annual income of two hundred pounds from land, freehold office, or any business, or an annual income of three hundred pounds from any freehold office or business, or the payment annually of land tax, or other tax on houses, tax on horses, mules, asses, meat cattle, breeding stock and spring carriages, and still and cart licenses, export duty paid by the produce or any one or more of them, to the extent of ten pounds or upwards. See *Laws of Jamaica 1858–1859* (Jamaica 1877), 1,143–44.
7. Joseph Stone Williams, Advocate-General of Jamaica, member of the House of Assembly, felt that the 'vestry system' 'is a source of so much agitation that I don't think the Colony, under present circumstances, can allow it to go on, the more so as the intelligence and respectability of the country is becoming fast lowered' (Royal Commission 1866, 851). Obviously, this white legislator felt that respectability of the country was becoming fast lowered because the black people were being allowed to get into areas of the state that were the preserve of white and coloured folks.
8. For his commitment to the people, he was called a 'traitor' and 'Judas' by the coloured middle and upper classes and the white population.
9. Eyre was probably the most centralist and autocratic pro-plantocratic Governor to assume office in post-slavery Jamaica.

10. One of the most outrageous acts of corruption was the 'Tramway Fraud' which rocked the political system. See Ansell Hart, *The Life of George William Gordon*, (Jamaica: Institute of Jamaica, n.d.), 48–51.
11. This case referred to the legal battle between George William Gordon and Baron Ketelholdt. Gordon took legal action against Custos Ketelholdt for expelling him from the St Thomas-in-the-East Vestry.
12. The Bill had its second reading on April 22, 1863. See *Parliamentary Debates VIII* (1863): 210.
13. In reflecting on the state of Jamaica over the past 30 years, Gordon said in a speech in the House of Assembly:

    Oh! What revolutions have occurred during that time! What changes have not marked the affairs of mankind during those thirty years? Important steam communication has been established, railways have been laid down; telegraphic wires have been erected, and the peoples and governments of every country have rapidly progressed, except poor Jamaica. While civilisation is making its strides in other lands, nothing is done to elevate our people; to develop our resources; to increase our material prosperity; to extend education; but I believe that the time has now come when there is to be a change. See *Parliamentary Debates IX* (1863): 143.

14. Andrew Lewis, a Jewish member of the Assembly representing St Catherine reported that at that Underhill meeting which he chaired, there were complaints of 'want of labour generally, and the cost of manufactured articles imported with which tradesmen have to compete.' He said, 'if stuff is imported into the country manufactured, the duty upon it would be four per cent; but if they manufactured the article in the country, the raw material imported would bear a duty 12½ per cent. We would get a copper pan imported for an estate, and the duty upon it would be four per cent, but if an artisan were to buy the copper and manufacture the pan he would have to pay 12½ per cent for the copper instead. They complained of that as a great evil' (Royal Commission 1866, 839).
15. William Anderson travelled to the US to observe that country's methods of production. On his return to Jamaica he had a lecture 'before the Colonial Literary Society, on Monday the 17th day of January 1850' to give his impression of his visit.
16. According to Gordon's contemporary, Dr Fidds, a Kingston medical doctor, quoted in [Sidney] Olivier, *The Myth of Governor Eyre* (London: Leonard and Virginia Woolf at the Hogarth Press 1933), 94.
17. Some 11 Baptist chapels were burnt by persons connected to the plantocracy and the Colonial Church Union. The burning was quite intense after the defeat of the uprising led by Samuel Sharpe.
18. Read Charles V. Carnegie, ed., *Afro-Caribbean Villages in Historical Perspective* (Jamaica: African-Caribbean Institute of Jamaica, 1987), 1–19; Inez Knibb Sibley,

The Baptists of Jamaica 1793 to 1965 (Kingston: The Jamaica Baptist Union 1965), 14, 16–22; and Swithin Wilmot, 'Baptist Missionaries and Jamaican Politics, 1838–54', in *A Selection of Papers Presented at the Twelfth Conference of the Association of Caribbean Historians* 1980, ed. K.O. Laurence (UWI, St Augustine: Association of Caribbean Historians, 1986).

19. For more on the impact of the Haitian Revolution on Jamaica, see Patrick Bryan, 'Emigres, Conflict and Reconciliation: The French Émigrés in Nineteenth Century Jamaica' *Jamaica Journal* 7, no. 3 (September 1973): 13–19.

20. Both the liberal and conservative British churches exhibited racist contempt for the cultural expression of the black masses (Curtin 1955, 158–77). Bedford Pim, a militant ideologue of the plantocracy praised the English Baptists who 'disclaim any spiritual connexion with their black pupils in Jamaica.' He said black 'revivals and prayer meetings were 'more characteristic of a meeting of monkeys,' (*Colonial Standard* January 10, 1866). Meanwhile, Baptist missionary, Benjamin Millard said, 'members of the church were excluded for different matters such as those having connexion with their own churches' (Royal Commission 1866, 782).

21. Revd William Claydon, for example, held meetings with his congregation in May 1865 for the purpose of an 'inquiry into the causes of the then present distress, and with a view of removing impressions which had taken possession of the minds of the peasantry that the estate managers were determined to withhold work from them' (Royal Commission 1966, 833). Other ministers like Thomas Lee read the 'Queen's advice' to their congregation and 'urged' the people 'to follow it, and return to industry, and so on' (Royal Commission 1866, 605).

22. The proprietor and editor of the *Sentinel* refused to carry a report on the Kingston Underhill meeting because he felt 'the speeches were not fit for publication' (Royal Commission, 554). For his part, Robert Bruce, one of Gordon's closest political allies, felt it necessary to write to George William Gordon to tell him that he would not attend any more meetings because he 'did not like the way he [Gordon] spoke.' Bruce felt the meetings 'have a bad effect on the people' (Royal Commission 1866, 729).

8 'Buccra Can't Catch Duppy, No, No': Marching into War Oh with the Spirits at Morant Bay

> I heard a Voice speaking to me in the year 1864, saying, "Tell the Sons and Daughters of Africa, that a great deliverance will take place for them from the hand of Oppression; for, said the Voice, they are oppressed by Government, by Magistrates, by Proprietors, and by Merchants." And this Voice also said "tell them to call a solemn Assembly, and to sanctify themselves for the day of deliverance which will surely take place."
>
> — 'A Son of Africa'

> No one can hope to appreciate the thoughts and feelings of the black man who does not realise that to him the dead are not dead but living.
>
> — P. Amaury Talbot

In the early 1920s, one man who experienced the Great Revival in the 1860s told the American Folklorist, Martha Beckwith: 'I remember the St. Thomas rebellion and the revival in 1860. It was taken up by the whole world. Now today there is Bedward' (qtd in Murphy 1994, 124–25). In this man's estimation, the Great Revival could not be separated from Paul Bogle and the violent political confrontation in Morant Bay, in 1865. The spirit and mood of the Great Revival, it would seem, flowed into that political confrontation.

Having witnessed torrents of cathartic rituals of pain and hope unfurling flocks of wings of freedom, dream and determination and having made a casual connection between the Great Revival and the Morant Bay War, this man, in his thought and feeling, was experiencing déjà vu in the 1920s with Alexander Bedward and his movement.

This déjà vu then, was the reliving of an urgent engaging band of masses of people, this time led by Bedward, commanding, fashioning and working a spiritual and temporal world for redemption rooted in a Revival order with its African aesthetic and anti-colonial refrain. This Revival order which manifested itself in the early 1860s as the source of the faith, fortitude and agential culture of black radicalism in post-slavery society, was anchored in a rich subterranean universe of Pan-African Jamaican episteme, spirituality and creative and aesthetic culture.[1]

The island-wide mass meetings of the mid-1860s that bore the name of Edward Bean Underhill, English missionary and a secretary to the *Baptist Missionary Society*, were like a re-enactment of the all island religious meetings associated with the Great Revival at the beginning of the early 1860s. Each set of meetings was initiated by the dissenting British clergy in Jamaica, but each time these meetings were taken beyond the expectation of the clergy by the black masses. The Great Revival of Christianity was transformed into an African Jamaican order in the form of Zion or (18)60 and Poko or (18)61, while the Underhill meetings or conventions, became fora for the political mobilisation and expression of black freeholders and labourers.

The activities of the black masses, including the so-called *New Agitation Movement* of 1858, the riots of 1859, the Great Revival of 1859 to 1862 and the Underhill conventions of 1865, constituted the social political portfolio of an increasing agential flow of black determination for change. But the process by which change was envisaged, was increasingly pointing in the direction of popular armed uprising, which tradition and portfolio experience and methodology associated with the riots of 1859.

Compact with the Ancestral Spirits

Perhaps the single most important indication that the struggles of the grass roots political movement in St Thomas-in-the-East was edging towards an armed phase began in September 1865 with the systematic swearing in of people at meetings held in communities across the parish. The trigger for this shift appeared to be the refusal of Governor Edward Eyre to meet with a deputation led by Paul Bogle to present grievances on behalf of the people of St Thomas-in-the-East. The deputation was composed at a mass meeting at Morant Bay which passed a dozen resolutions regarding the deteriorating state of their social, political and economic condition and the need for redress.

This swearing in, or taking the oath, was designed to solicit from a selective number of persons, their ultimate commitment and loyalty to a cause which increasingly required an engagement involving life and death. This commitment had to be ritually sworn to the ancestors and ancestral spirits and, if broken by any person so sworn, that person would be visited by a curse from the spirit(s) or sanction(s) from his comrades, or from both.

Organised oath-taking was not just aimed at persons who were considered to be committed to the struggle but needed to be sworn into a fraternity or organised state of the living in communion with the ancestors to denote the higher degree of seriousness, loyalty and commitment required for political action involving life and death. Even black persons who were considered to be working for the other side, such as policeman William Fuller, were made to take the oath to cleave from the white and cleave to the black.

In this context, oath-taking was administered as a form of intimidation and control to secure the neutrality, if not loyalty, of blacks who were deemed to be in the camp of the enemy.[2] It was not the expectation that one, having being made to perform a ritual of oath-taking, would break the promise, knowing what the consequences could be in the belief system and culture of the black majority. It is within this context that the warning by George Craddock, an oath administrator, must be viewed. Craddock, a leader of the Bogle movement, told recruits he presided over in an oath-taking ceremony 'not tell to anybody' what they had pledged or their 'belly would swell' (Royal Commission 1866, 22). The spiritual sanction of which Craddock warned, represented one source of ensuring compliance, the other source was human agency like the decapitation that Fuller was threatened with.

History has shown that most, if not all, premeditated insurrections and aborted insurrections in Jamaica up to and including the Morant Bay War, involved as a principal requirement of their preparation, the administering of oaths to intended insurrectionists and to neutralise others.[3] In the preparation for war against Bakra in St Thomas-in-the-East, those taking the oath were required at a minimum to kiss the Bible. At other times, the oath-taking exercise seemed to be more complex and required a deeper level of involvement and commitment.

One of these complex oath-taking ceremonies was described by Policeman James Foster who went to Stony Gut with other policemen, including William Fuller, to arrest Paul Bogle and saw it performed. Foster said he:

> saw seven men go into Paul Bogle's room, they all had cutlasses. Paul Bogle spoke to the men in a language I did not understand. The men all took the oath. They kissed a large book, the Bible. Paul Bogle gave each of them a dram of rum and gun powder which they drank. I saw the rum and powder mixed myself in a large bottle (Eyre 1971, 53).

This African Jamaican oath-taking ceremony, presided over by Paul Bogle in Stony Gut, incorporated rituals embracing Christianity's holy book as used to elicit truth telling in the island court system. Truth telling in this context was to abide by what was sworn to be upheld: to cleave from the white and to cleave to the black. The ritual part-taking of 'a dram of rum and gun powder' seemed to suggest the summoning and invocating of an aggressive spirit, a warrior spirit – likely to be in the realm of the Kongo tradition. The social, political and economic situation required an aggressive medicine, like war oh!

The use of the mixture of gunpowder and rum in rituals pertaining to African Caribbean spirituality was not new. In the Lemba-Petro order of *Vodun* in Saint Domingue (Haiti), Moreau de Saint-Méry, the French creole writer, noted in 1797 that 'the blacks mixed well-crushed gunpowder in the cheap rum they drank while dancing' (qtd in Thompson 1984, 179). The purpose for drinking this mixture, was to aid these blacks to become and to dance in the same sharp, sudden aggressive staccato manner of *Dom Pédre*.

Today in Haiti, *Dompédre* who was likely to have been a historically important *Oungan* (priest), 'is a powerful god who is normally greeted by the detonation of gunpowder' (180). The type of warrior spirit dance or aggressive medicine that the consumption of gunpowder and rum symbolised can still be found in the *Kumina* pantheon today in Jamaica. It can also be observed in the working of the *Bongo Seal* (fire altar) in *Revival* where adherents may dance not only around the fire but with the fire.

But we did not have to go to eighteenth century St Domingue (Haiti) to find examples of the ritual consumption of gunpowder mixed with rum as part of a ceremony to invoke the spirit of aggression and indeed justice in a compact with the living for political struggle. We could have looked to eighteenth century Jamaica.

In 1765, five years after a man was acquitted in a trial for participating in the 1760 Tacky (Taki) led anti-slavery insurrection in the parish of St Mary in Jamaica, he was again arrested for planning a 'fresh' insurrection to take place immediately after the Christmas holidays, in that same parish. According to one report:

> Several of the leaders met in St. Mary's in 1765 when the solemn fetish oath was administered. Into a quantity of rum, with which some gun powder and dirt taken from a grave had been mingled, blood was put, drawn in succession from the arm of each confederate… this cup was drunk from [by] each person, and then came the council. It was agreed that during the ensuring Christmas holidays the rising should take place, and that in the meantime all were to obtain companions (Hart 1985, 151).

To 'obtain companions' meant to recruit persons to the cause being planned: the overthrow of slavery. The principal recruiting tool was the oath-taking ceremony, directed at signing up persons to the cause of revolution by engaging (or intimidating) them into a ritual compact with the living to work and to journey with aggressive spirits (deities and ancestors) for radical political agency. By engaging in such compact, the persons so engaged were expected to be endowed with the agential power of the spirits or to face life threatening sanctions for breaking the oath, i.e., disrespecting the spirits.

Figure 6.   Remains of the Steps of Paul Bogle's Chapel in Stony Gut. Photo by Clinton Hutton.

The language spoken by Paul Bogle during the oath-taking ceremony which James Foster did not understand, was likely to have been Ki-Kongo. Ki-Kongo was taken to St Thomas-in-the-East by Central African speaking indentured labourers beginning some 25 years prior to the Morant Bay War. Paul Bogle must have learned this language as well as other elements of the oath-taking ceremony he oversaw from speakers of Ki-Kongo. Indeed, his teachers were likely to have been some of the 'old Africans who were buried at Stony Gut' (Schuler 1980, 161) and were certain to have lived there during Bogle's time.

Moreover, William Lake, one of the policemen who was sent to Stony Gut to arrest Paul Bogle recognised a number of indentured African labourers who were living at John's Town, seven miles from Stony Gut, helping on that day in Stony Gut to prevent the arrests (161). Perhaps some of these Africans also participated in the oath-taking ceremony presided over by Paul Bogle.

One of the most powerful symbols of this oath-taking ceremony presided over by Paul Bogle, was the seven cutlasses, one each borne by the seven men being sworn. These cutlasses symbolised the Ogou/Ogoun/Ogun type spirits; being invoked in preparation for war and re-creation. The cutlass (machete) as well as the sword were symbols of this order and are much used in invocations across Jamaica today in *Revival* and *Kumina*. It is often seen in *Revival*, especially in the order of St Michael or Archangel Michael, as a Christian representation of the Ogoun-like African diaspora warrior spirits.

The cutlass, the symbol of the Ogoun-type spirits, is regarded above all as the agent of destruction and creation. The cutlass was sworn to in the oath-taking ceremony in Bogle's chapel in a similar manner to which people swear on this symbol of Ogoun in Yoruba social, religious and judicial life, and in a manner in which Christians are sworn on the Bible. In the oath-taking ceremony observed by policeman James Foster, in Stony Gut, both the cutlass and the Bible were used to swear on, an indication of the creative methodology of Deacon Paul Bogle's Native Baptist Church. It may also be that the administrators of oaths were hoping to strengthen their position by incorporating different spiritual realms on their side.

What can be concluded here is that Deacon Paul Bogle, the Native Baptist leader, was in the description of the oath-taking ceremony that he presided over at his chapel in Stony Gut, of the order of 61 *Revival*, of *Poko* (*Poko-Kumina/Pukkumina*), the result of the (re)fashioning or (re)working of *Kumina*, *Myaal*, and especially the George Leilean tradition of Christianity.

This outwardly Native Baptist deacon was inwardly a *Poko* leader, an expression of masking, an important ontological, philosophical and political device employed in the making of the African diaspora in the Americas.

This device, masking, is still evident in *Revival* today. In the last 15 years that I have been studying/photographing/engaging *Revival* across Jamaica, the old titles denoting leader such as Captain, Shepherd and Mada (Mother), are being replaced and/or used interchangeably with Bishop, Reverend, in much the same way Deacon/Deaconess was used in Bogle's time. The logic here appeared to have been rooted in the need and efforts by black people to secure a place of respectability and status in society by manipulating the symbolic order of whiteness. Not because Paul Bogle was designated Deacon meant that he fitted neatly into the ontological category that Devon Dick (2009) constructed for him and the historical political/event of which he was a key player.

Masking then, was an important component of the system of imagining, creating and constructing knowledge, identity and social conduct in the epistemic, ontological, aesthetic and agential terrain of the black masses. It is within this context that we should locate and examine the semiotic meaning and expression of the flag of the movement led by Paul Bogle.

This flag, 'white with a red cross and a piece of black cape sewed on' (*Gleaner* November 22, 1865), seemed like the flag of England minus the black cape, an adoption of the standard of St George of Lydda, the Roman soldier martyred for being a Christian, April 23, 303 AD and acknowledged as the Patron Saint of England by the end of the fourteenth century. Regarded as a symbol of the triumph of good over evil, this prominent military saint in the Christian pantheon, was re-worked or reinterpreted in the African pantheon of spirits as Ogoun or Ogoun-like. In the *Petro* order of Vodun, St George has been used as a mask for Ogoun.

In the meanwhile, the African warrior spirit that was invoked and fed with rum and gunpowder in Stony Gut in 1865, seemed to be journeying in this time in the *Revival* tradition as St Michael or Archangel Michael. The symbol of this Ogoun-like/Shango-like spirit is dominantly expressed in the ritual use of the cutlass, but also the sword, axe, saw, gun, fire, rum, blood sacrifice, extreme aggressive dance performance and the crack of the whip.

Interestingly, at a *Kumina* ceremony that I attended and photographed one night in Port Morant, St Thomas in the 1990s, one of the male adherents was dressed like a policeman. This was an unmistaken representation of the Ogun-like spirit. His dance (rapid, aggressive pelvic movements performed in a sexual manner on the females) was in accordance with that spiritual realm. This policeman/Ogun-like character is regularly seen in Jonkunu masquerade.

Moreover, the Christian cross denoting the crucifixion of Jesus Christ for the redemption of sinners in Christian cosmology, might not be such in the deeper semiotic reading of the cross on the flag of the Bogle-led movement. It might have been a symbol of the crossroads. It might be reflective of a symbol of one of the multiplicity of Kongo 'emblems of the cross-roads and the union of the worlds of the living and dead,' to use Robert Farris Thompson's formulation (Warner-Lewis 2003, 167).

The vertical line of the cross, denoted the centre pole (*poto mitan* in Haitian Vodun), a bridge or passage linking the community of the living from above, with the community of the dead from below in a reciprocal relationship between both worlds. The horizontal line of the cross represented the boundary or *Kalunga*, the primordial body of water separating the world of the living above from the world of the dead below.

The place of the cross-roads in *Kumina* and *Revival* cosmologies remains significant as symbols, signs and rituals in the geography, architecture and language of these orders. *Kumina* and *Revival* adherents still conduct rituals at the cross-roads. The rituals (those that I have witnessed) begin with the circling of the roads three times where they crossed. A basic graphic Kongo representation of the circling of the cross-roads is an encircled cross. The representation of the flag of the Bogle-led movement, as bearing a stylised Kongo cosmogram posing perhaps as the cross of St George, the warrior spirit, is not far-fetched.

Why, for example, was a 'piece of black cape sewed on' to a flag that appeared to be an imitation of the English flag, transforming it into a standard bearing the three primary colours of Kongo spirituality: red, white and black? In any event, the flag of the Bogle movement was a battle symbol in broad daylight.

As can be seen from my analysis and discussion above, policeman James Foster's description of the oath-taking ceremony presided over by Paul Bogle, has become an important basis for us to journey into the knowledge system of the Morant Bay War. In this journey thus far, the cosmological roots of the people's rising on October 11, 1865 are becoming apparent.

The meaning and administering of oath in pursuance of black anti-plantocratic insurrection in Jamaica emanated from the heart of the belief system which emerged and evolved from the creative, cultural, spiritual, emotional and cognitive activity of Africans. It was a common belief among Africans that an inseparable, reciprocal relation existed between the ancestral (spirit) world on the one hand, and the world of the living on the other hand. These two worlds constitute the population of the African community: a community whose viability rested on the reciprocal relationship of both halves. Blacks conceived that the spiritual world and the world of the living constituted one reality on a continuum where they pay 'homage to the power and spirit that once dwelt in those now dead and that lives on after them' (Alleyne 1988, 61). Awolalu and Dopamu (1979) noted that in the West African belief system 'since the ancestors are no longer visible in the physical sense, some element of enhanced power is attributed to them' (275). Awolalu and Dopamu asserted that in this belief system, death has given the ancestors 'more potentialities, and has greatly enhanced their dignity, power, and prestige.' Consequently, the ancestors

> possess considerable power both for good and for evil. Sickness and misfortune of every kind can be attributed to the influence of those offended among them. They can influence rainfall or bring good harvest; they can promote prosperity or cause adversity; they can also give protection and general well-being or cause disruption and calamity (Awolalu and Dopamu 275).

On the one hand, the oath-taking ceremony, like the one presided over by Bogle, was a compact for joint endeavour by the living to combine their efforts with the enhanced power of the ancestral spirits to protect them against the power of the white oppressors and their agents and to rain calamity on them in what both blacks and whites saw as an impending war. On the other hand, the guarantors of the compact to march into war with the ancestors against the plantocracy and company were the ancestral spirits invoked in the oath-taking ceremony.

A violation of this compact by anyone who took the oath meant a violation of the covenant with the ancestral spirits. This violation black people understood and feared could be attended to with serious sanctions either from the world of the living or the world of the spirits.

It was in this context, as noted above, that George Craddock, a leading figure in the Bogle movement and administrator of oaths, warned those who had sworn 'not tell to anybody', or their 'belly would swell' (Royal Commission 1866, 22). Another example, though in the tradition of *Vodun* in Haiti in the eighteenth century, applied to the Jamaican context of oath-taking and secrecy in 1865. According to Moreau de Saint-Méry, a contemporary of that period:

> A new oath, just as abominable as the first one, requires each one to remain silent on what has transpired, to concur on what has been concluded, and sometimes a vase, containing the still-warm blood of a goat, will seal on the lips of the participants the promise to suffer death rather than reveal anything, and even to administer death to whomever may forget that he had solemnly bound himself to the oath (qtd in Fick 1994, 59).

In another apparent oath-taking ceremony said to have taken place a 'month before the rebellion', Joseph Rose reported that Charles Farmer told him that 'he had seen blood sprinkled at Bell Castle Chapel, Manchioneal and that was a sign that there was going to be a row soon' (Eyre 1971, 52).

Feeding and Feasting with the Spirits

The oath-taking rituals in Bogle's chapel at Stony Gut and apparently at Bell Castle Chapel in Manchioneal both had a feeding component indicated by the use of the gunpowder and rum mixture and the blood mixture. The feeding of ancestral spirits was a key component of the spiritual/religious system developed by enslaved Africans in the Americas, in general, and the Caribbean, in particular. This feeding of the ancestors and their gods was practised in simple and complex rituals by enslaved Africans before Christianity was introduced to them in the Americas. These feeding rituals continued after slavery was abolished and are still practised in Jamaica today, even by persons who do not belong to any organised African spiritual order,[4] including Christians.

The 1854 description of a *Myaal* liturgical complex by Moravian pastor J.H. Buncher, indicated the importance of feeding the ancestral spirits to its articulation.

As soon as the darkness of evening set in, they assembled in crowds in open pastures, most frequently under large cotton trees, which they worshipped, and counted holy; after sacrificing some fowls, the leader began an extempore song, in a wild strain, which was answered in chorus; the dance followed, grew wilder and wilder, until they were in a state of excitement bordering on madness.

Some would perform incredible evolutions while in this state until, nearly exhausted, they fell senseless to the ground, when every word they uttered was received as a divine revelation (qtd in Murphy 1994, 118).

Although worshipping under the cotton tree is not widespread today, this tree still remains significant in African Jamaican spirituality. In 1865, one specific cotton tree bore some significance to the clash at Morant Bay. It was under this large cotton tree that the crowd which marched from Stony Gut under Bogle's leadership stopped and congregated for its final meeting before it entered Morant Bay on October 11. The general belief among Africans and their descendants was that the ancestors liked to congregate under the cotton tree. A plausible conclusion that can be drawn here is that the assemblage from Stony Gut congregated with the ancestors under that majestic cotton tree.[5] From there, they marched into war, just around the corner at Morant Bay.

The basic architecture of the liturgy described by Buncher, although mired in his language of prejudice, is easily recognisable in *Revival* and *Kumina* today. The feeding of the ancestral spirits employing blood sacrifice, libation, banquet and various other means, represented an important component of African Jamaican liturgical expression with significant meaning for knowing, being, doing and freedom.

The gathering of several hundred persons at a set-up in Stony Gut on the night of October 10, 1865 until the next day when they marched down to Morant Bay, was in part, a kind of feeding/feasting ceremony with the ancestors which, as it turned out, has had significant historical, social and political implications. The Haitian Revolution which commenced August 1791 began with two meetings/ceremonies/services, nay feasting rituals. The first of these meetings took place on August 14, 1791 at the Lenormand de Mézy sugar estate in Plaine-du-Nord and the second took place on August 21, 1791 at Bois Caïman. In the first meeting, a bull was sacrificed under the direction of an *Oungan* (*Vodun priest*) and a large feast held (Hutton 2005, 79 and 81). At the Bois Caïman meeting, a black pig was ritually killed under the direction of a *Manbo* (*Vodun priestess*) and the blood consumed in a compact to overthrow slavery (80–81).

These oath-taking rituals to engage aggressive medicine spirits to cure the social ills heaped upon blackness by whiteness were simultaneous rituals of protection from the agency of these social ills directed at the existential viability of Africans and their descendants as free, equal, sovereign people. Paul Bogle, who was born in slavery and was at the advanced side of his teen years by 1838, was not immune from these rituals, rituals that were also invoked for domestic purposes. These rituals were sometimes performed:

> under the sacred cotton tree...but sometimes in a yard over a spot where Obeah [was] believed to have been buried." A blood sacrifice of fowls was made; adepts wore headwraps "tied in fantastical manner" and waistbands tied "as tightly as possible" (Warner-Lewis 2003, 192).[6]

That obeahmen and women were involved in the Morant Bay War and its preparations, was not the making of news when taken against the backdrop of the history of black anti-slavery insurrections, where obeah practitioners always seemed to play an important role. What made news was how Arthur Wellington, a reputed obeahman and ally of Paul Bogle who 'raised him to captain',[7] was executed and his head displayed on Colonel Francis Hobbs's orders. Hobbs was out to teach black people as lesson that would make them question the viability of their cosmos.

Hobbs held that 'Obeism' and the deepest religious fanaticism had much to do with this rebellion, especially in Somerset, [where] 'Arthur Wellington bewitched [the people]'. Hobbs was furious that Wellington 'had immense power, and was much dreaded, and persuaded the people [that] they could not be wounded or killed by the buckra' (Royal Commission 1866, 1,129). He thus had him shot and decapitated and his head displayed on a pole in public because Wellington 'set himself up to be invulnerable to bullet shot, and I wanted to show them that no amount of incantation could prevent him from being shot' (764).

Several other alleged obeahmen were also executed. They included Charles Walker for 'rebellion' (1,137), George Williams for 'rebellion and plunder' (1,136), John Grant for 'sedition and murder' (1,139) and John Bartley 'for making images' (979). Images such as the ones allegedly made by Bartley were protective artefacts endowed by obeah practitioners with the power of ancestral spirits to protect the people from 'buckra'.

Hobbs who committed suicide by jumping overboard the ship taking him back to Britain, admitted that the people's beliefs in the protective power of the obeahman and obeahwoman worked. It worked because, as the black schoolmaster, Mathew Joseph said, 'many of the common people have great confidence in obeah; they believe them to be almighty, that they can do anything' (109). The view then, as it is now, is 'belief kill and belief cure'.

No assessment of Bogle's spirituality/religiosity and world view, broadly speaking, would be complete without understanding the place of obeah in it, because in this world view, 'nature is one threshold across which the spirit world crosses into the world of the living' and one can acquire the power of spirits and control both worlds' (Chevannes 1998, 24). It was the obeahman/woman who was 'invested' with the 'knowledge' to 'control the spirit world' (24), hence the importance of his/her agency in black anti-slavery insurrections and in the Morant Bay War, the first insurrection in Jamaica in the post-slavery era.

Food offerings, feeding/feasting rituals were and still are the central expressions of reciprocity in the relationship between the world of the living and the world of the spirits. In this respect, Karen McCarthy Brown noted:

> In the Vodou view of things the living, the dead, and the spirits are all dependent on one another. No group is, or could be, self-sufficient. "The living" (*vivan-yo*) need the advice, warning and protection provided by ancestors and spirits. The ancestors and spirits, in turn, have to be fed and honoured if they are to muster the strength and will to protect the living. From one perspective, a family is a single vast organism encompassing a group of *vivan*, as well as their ancestors and inherited spirits...No effort on the part of the living is too great, if it 'feeds' (and pleases) the spirits and ancestors...(McCarthy Brown 1995, 206).

In this relationship Sterling Stuckey (1987) noted, 'faith in the continuing influence of the dead on the living was as great as faith that the living influenced the dead' (42).[8] That faith was and still is classically demonstrated in the feeding ritual. Some of these feeding rituals have become services of aesthetic grandeur, amazing works of art such as the banquet style Revival table that I have been photographing for over 15 years.[9]

The rituals of feeding and feasting with the ancestral spirits in a continuous display and performance of a community of reciprocity in the culture of the African diaspora, were traceable to death and the various forms of wake and burial rites developed to deal with this issue. In wake and funeral rituals practised by enslaved Africans in the Caribbean, food was prepared for both the living and the dead.

In one example in Jamaica, John Taylor writing in 1689 noted:

> When those slaves die [African people] make a great adoe at their Burials for having cary'd them to the grave, in a verey mournfull Manner, all both Men and women which accompany the Corps, sing and Howle in a sorrowful manner in their own Language, till being com to the grave, into which they gently put the Corpes, and with it Casavar bread, Roasted Fowles, sugar, Rum, Tobacco & Pipes with fier to light his pipe withal, and to sustain him in

his Journey beyond those pleasant hills, in their own Countrey, whither they say he is now goeing to live at rest.

Then Taylor noted that:

They filled up the grave, and Eat and drink thereon, singing in their own Language verey dolefully, desiring the dead Corps to Acquint their Father, Mother, Husband, & other relations of their present condition, & Slavery, as he passes thro- their Countrey, towards the Pleasant Mountains, which Message they bellow out to the dead Corps in a doleful tune (Pigou 1985, 101–102).

Writing in 1808 about funeral rituals among Africans in Jamaica, James Stewart stated that:

At their funerals they use various ceremonies, among which is the practice of pouring libations, and sacrificing a fowl on the grave for the deceased; a tribute of respect they afterwards occasionally repeat. During the whole of the ceremony, many fantastic notions and wild gesticulations are practiced, accompanied with a suitable beat of their drums, and other rude instruments, while melancholy dirge is sung by a female, the chorus of which is performed by the whole of the other females with admirable precision, and full toned, and not unmelodious voices (Pigou 103–104).

Death and the Cosmological Roots of Freedom

Death never meant the end of existence of the deceased or his/her role in the community; hence, the belief that the dead must be continued to be fed. Death meant the birth of a new existential state of being – an ontological transformation of being and agency whereby the corporeal self or body dies, releasing the spirit self which it housed, thereby increasing the population of the ancestors, one of the two component parts of the black community – the population of the living being the other part. And with each death, an increase in the population of the living was assumed in wake rituals, including erotic music and dance mimicking sexual intercourse performed by participants to symbolically produce the next generation of the living as the next generation of the living dead received its rites of passage to the community of the dead.

In the cosmological culture of enslaved Africans, dying was simultaneously birthing: the releasing or freeing of the spirit self from the European enslaved corporeal self. This spirit self, or the ontology of free being in African diaspora metaphysics, cannot be subjected or enslaved, because as the funeral song of enslaved Africans in nineteenth century-Jamaica stated, 'Buccra can't catch Duppy, no, no' (D'Costa and Lalla 1989, 49). Bakra (Buccra) could not catch duppy (dopi) because, as noted in another funeral dirge song by enslaved Africans in Jamaica:

> Oh! The Great big ship of deat' will carry
> Him safe to him far off home
> Oh! Aldo we grieb an' mourn
> Oh, We know him 'pirit
> Gone back to him own home
> In Africa
> No no' slabe driber wip fe him
> Only home, an' lub ones, ober deh
> (Clerk 1934, 4).

The view that death meant freedom from slavery because, once the corporeal abode of the spirit died, that spirit was released and aided by the appropriate funeral rituals, returned to its pre-slavery state of freedom in ancestral Africa, was a commonly held belief among enslaved Africans and their descendants. In this respect, John Taylor noted that Africans were 'naturally rooted in this Oppinion' and 'that all the Argument in the World [could] not move them to disbelieve it.' Taylor stated that Africans:

> Are soe fully possest with this strange Oppinion that being dead they shall certainly return to their own Countrey...that verey often many of them having binn affronted, have either starved themselves to death or else have cut their Throats, that soe being free from their servitude, they might return to their own Countrey and there enjoy rest (Pigou 101–102).

Meanwhile in 1740, C. Leslie wrote that enslaved Africans 'look to Death as a Blessing'. Furthermore, Leslie wrote:

> 'Tis indeed surprising to see with what Courage and Intrepidity some of them will meet their Fate, and be merry in their last Moments...They are quite transported to think that Slavery is near an End and that they shall revisit their happy native Shores, and see their old Friends and Acquaintances...When a Negro is about to expire... his Fellow-slaves kiss him, wish him a good journey and send their hearty Recommendations to the Relations in Guiney [Africa] (Pigou 103–104).

And again in 1808, James Stewart came upon the cosmological roots of freedom in the funerary culture of enslaved Africans in Jamaica. He wrote that:

> the poor creatures cherish the hope that after death they shall first return to their native Country, and enjoy again the loved society of kindred and friends, from whom they have been torn away in a luckless hour (Pigou 105).

The cosmological roots of freedom, faith and the reciprocal relationship between the living and the dead in the funerary culture of enslaved Africans in Jamaica did not disappear with the end of slavery. It did not disappear even as Dick (2009) noted that 'the memory of African religious expressions was fading due to fewer persons coming directly from Africa' and 'the deliberate policy of the missionaries to obliterate African religion and culture' (93). Neither did it disappear during the reign of terror performed on the Jamaican masses during October to December of 1865 any more than ancient European spirituality and culture ended with Christianity, or from shaping the ontology of Christianity. It exists today, in Jamaica, in the belief system of the masses, including many Christians and in wake rituals and other social practices.

'The Holy Ghost Has to Come by the Spirits'

In his book, *The Cross and the Machete: Native Baptists of Jamaica – Identity, Ministry and Legacy*, Devon Dick referred to the outbreak in Morant Bay on October 11, 1865 as the 'Native Baptist War', denoting its authorship and belief system to the Native Baptist adherents in St Thomas-in-the-East, under the leadership of Deacon Paul Bogle. In Dick's conceptual and theoretical approach, he absolutised the Christian references in the Bogle movement and minimised, marginalised or ignored its African/African diaspora references.

In the meanwhile, Colonel Francis Hobbs, who had the obeahman, Captain Arthur Wellington shot and decapitated and his head displayed on a pole in public to prove to the black masses 'that no amount of incantation could prevent him from being shot', took the opposite view to Dick. He absolutised the African references in the Native Baptist Church and ignored the Christian references. According to Hobbs:

> If ever there was anything calculated to endear a man to the Established Church (or, indeed, to any recognised and regular kind of religion), it is a week's campaign in St. Thomas-in-the-East, Jamaica. The place swarms with Native Baptist "chapels;" their ministers are the leading rebels (unable in many cases to read or write), who rant, excite, and poison the minds of their flocks against the powers that be. At the door of these wolves in sheep's clothing lies the responsibility of all this rebellion,...Let those who doubt this statement visit "Somerset," "Mount Lebanus," "Mount Pisgah" – the hotbed of the rebellion, and account for this, in a province of wealth, in any other way than fanaticism; and it is the fact of this being the case that has from the first made me take a graver view of the rebellion than those who considered

it a question of mere discontent about local wages (Royal Commission 1866, 1,122).

Although William Gardner the missionary historian abhorred the religious practices of the Native Baptists in Jamaica, he recognised the Christian and African references in the make up of that religion. Indeed, the source of his abhorrence was the African/African diaspora (Myaal) references in the Native Baptist Church. In 1873, he wrote:

> With few exceptions, native Baptist churches became associations of men and women who, in too many cases, mingled the belief and even the practice of Mialism with religious observances, and who perverted and corrupted what they retained of these: among them sensuality was almost entirely unrestrained (Murphy 1994, 123).

To William Gardner, the African component of the Native Baptist Church, Myaal was not religious; it was a 'perverted' and 'corrupted' agent which was mixed with 'religious observances,' that is, Christianity. The implication here is that the Native Baptists were not Christians. Devon Dick appeared to disagree with Gardner, since he saw in the Native Baptist Church the ontology of orthodox Christianity (Dick 2010, 127–41). That is to say, the Native Baptist Church was devoid of African references by engaging in the 'right practices and correct beliefs concerning Christianity' (131). In this conversion, the 'Native Baptists were the successors to the Africans who had their own interpretation of scriptures' (126).

Spenser St John, who became the British chargé-d'affaires in Haiti, in 1863, held views about Vodun that were similar to William Gardner. According to St John:

> Although he [the Vodun adherent] follows the white man's religion to a certain extent, he does not in consequence forsake his serpent-worship, which appeals to his traditions, to the Africa of his nursery-tales, and, above all, to his pleasures and passions. The Vaudoux priest encourages lascivious dancing, copious drinking, and the indiscriminate intercourse of the sexes, but he at the same time inculcates the burning of candles in Roman Catholic churches. He keeps a serpent in a box in his temple, whilst the walls are covered with the pictures of the Virgin Mary and the saints. No other brain but that of a negro could accept such a juxtaposition of opposing beliefs (St John 1971, 142).

St John's assertion that 'No other brain but that of a Negro could accept such a juxtaposition of opposing beliefs,' reflected his judgement on the epistemic nature and conceptual compass of the African as confused, incoherent and childlike: a state of nature without any sense of a rational order. Such 'juxtaposition of opposing beliefs' was reflected in Paul Bogle's Native Baptist practices as observed in the oath-taking ceremony in Stony Gut, that he presided over in 1865 and seen in Revival today.

But what St John posited as an epistemological disorder and Gardner saw as an agent of perversion and corruption, was a way of thinking, knowing and creating central to the philosophy and existential viability of the African diaspora. A core tenet of this philosophy of knowledge, being and praxis in the world view of Revival, was uttered by Bishop Raleigh Christie at a thanksgiving ceremony at his church in Yallahs, St Thomas, Jamaica in 2013. He said: 'The Holy Ghost has to come by the spirits.'[10] In this conceptual and operational principle, the spirits of Africa are required to pave the way for Christ to enter: another 'juxtaposition of opposing beliefs'.

In this profound statement, the way to Christianity, to Christ, has to be paved or cleared by the spirits, so too the way to freedom, healing and a better life in post-slavery society. That was what the oath-taking ceremony presided over by Paul Bogle was about: the mobilisation of the community of the living and the dead (the spirits) to go into war at Morant Bay against the ruling elites and their allies.

According to Dick: 'Africans who believed in African religions had no creed to recite, and had no sacred scriptures to study but only had to live the life' (Dick 2010, 92). Furthermore, he noted that although the expectation would be that 'through oral tradition, the religious beliefs and practices of African religion would have been disseminated among persons who would become members of the Native Baptist groups,' the 'extent of this influence seems minimal because when the JNBMS (Jamaica Native Baptist Missionary Society) was formed in 1839/40, the memory of African religious expressions was fading due to fewer persons coming directly from Africa' (93).

In this logic, the British abolition of the slave trade was in one sense bad, because it prevented new generations of Africans from being taken into slavery where they could come to know Christ. In another sense, it was a good thing, because it prevented Africans and their descendants in Jamaica from receiving a constant flow of African religious culture, making it easier for Christianity to germinate and grow.

I find both points to be problematic in this logic. On both counts, the Africans were mostly to be blamed for the extinction of their ancestral spirituality and religiosity. In the first place, their culture of conducting their religious life fettered the trans-generational transportation of such. Secondly, the 'minimal' influence of the African spiritual and religious presence had nothing to do with the religious/cultural genocide carried out by European missionaries against African religious practices, the assumed ontology of

Satanism and barbarism from which Africans, thanks to the Middle Passage, were extricated, to give them a chance to become free, redeemed humans in Christ.

Regrettably, these two positions undermined Dick's view about 'the deliberate policy of the missionaries to obliterate African religion and culture' (93). At the same time, he mounted a robust and important critique of the role of the English clergy for its support of slavery, the empire of racial superiority and global domination (111–19). While this was an important step, to a certain extent, to obviate one source of the problematic, that is, missionary culpability in cultural genocide, Dick silenced the culture of ingenuity weaved by Africans to prevent it.

Figure 7. The cutlass is still pervasively used in Revival and Kumina rituals in Jamaica today. Photo by Clinton Hutton.

In this framework of silence, the African spiritual and religious references and their importance to the epistemic, ontological and cultural architecture of Jamaica is silenced in *The Cross and the Machete*. An open-minded knowledge of the conceptual and methodological approach Africans fashioned to realise the creative, epistemic, aesthetic and agential corpus of this culture of ingenuity and especially its subterranean expressions, could have perhaps assisted Dick in his epistemic and analytical judgement.

Then he would have had to answer why the machete, which became an icon of Christianity in Edna Manley's sculptural depiction of Paul Bogle/Native Baptist, which Dick endorsed (XIII–XIV) and reproduced on the cover of his book is not being used as an invocating/liturgical icon in the Baptist Church. Yet, the cutlass remains a sacred instrument, pervasively used in Revival and Kumina invocations across Jamaica today. It remains an icon of spiritual warfare, truth, authority and symbol of the warrior spirit(s) in the liturgical culture, especially of the St Michael order of Revival.

Perhaps then, Dick would be able to say why some Revival churches are named 'Baptist' – the classical historical example of this being the Jamaica Native Baptist Free Church of prophet and healer, Alexander Bedward. This Revival church was established in August Town, near Kingston in the last decade of the nineteenth century. It had strong support from St Thomas people. It is not a stretch to suggest that Bedward saw himself and his church as the inheritors of Bogle and his church. The clue to this is to be found in a sermon he was reported to have made in which he referenced Paul Bogle and the 'Morant War' as a warning to the 'white wall' which was 'closing round the black wall' to take heed because the black wall 'shall crush the white wall' (Chevannes 1995, 39).

The epistemic, cultural and creative bases of the ingenuity complex fashioned by Africans to combat cultural genocide included an open-ended approach to thinking, knowing, doing and creating, what Barry Chevannes (2006) referred to as 'an open-ended adventure of imagination' (77). In this open-ended epistemic paradigm all can be included in the weaving of a redemptive universe once all came to it by way of the spirits, to use the conceptual and operational principle posited by Revival leader Raleigh Christie.

It was on the basis of this open-ended episteme that aspects of Christianity were woven into Myaal/Native Baptist/Revival. So too, aspects of Hindu cosmology, including the ontology of the goddess Kali, articulated in the concept, 'coolie dopi', an aggressive spirit that would have easily fitted the identity of the Ogunn-like/St Michael-like warrior spirits invoked in the oath-taking rituals in the movement led by Paul Bogle in 1865, 20 years after East Indian indentured labourers were brought to Jamaica and many of them sent to St Thomas-in-the-East.

Also included in the ingenuity complex of the Africans and their descendants is the concept rooted in the aphorism: 'Play fool to catch wise' (Plie fuul fi kech wiz). One cannot really pretend to be stupid to trap those who claimed themselves to be wise, 'without perfecting the art of performance, of flattery, mimicry/impersonation and deception, of feigning characters and roles, of code switching' (Hutton 2007, 129). In this social milieu, black people developed a double personality complex with double consciousness – two minds, one modelled on the white ontological construction of blackness and hence on white people's expectation of black people as servants of white people. The other was the sovereign ontological construction of blackness with its own inner transcript in the service of itself (Hutton 2005, 43–51; 2007, 128–30). An understanding of the cultural, ontological and epistemic imperatives of this ingenuity complex should allow us to have a better appreciation of how meanings were framed and articulated by Africans and their descendants in the Americas in general and in Jamaica, in particular.

All designations, 'Native Baptist', were not the same, although Dick appeared to have moved to that position. For him, the two known associations of Native Baptist Christianity in Jamaica, the Jamaica Native Baptist Missionary Society and the Native Baptist Communion, were orthodox Christian associations largely in the Lielean tradition. The Native Baptist Communion was led by Richard Warren and George William Gordon. Paul Bogle, who was baptised in this church, became a deacon.

To be sure, there were some Native Baptists who fitted Dick's category of orthodox Christianity. They included members of the Jamaica Native Baptist Missionary Society founded in 1839/1840. Dick noted that this society 'was largely a breakaway from English Baptists' (Dick 2010, 125). These 'Native Baptists had amiable and beneficial relationships with the governor, mayor and other government officials' (130). Some Baptists in the Warren/Gordon Native Baptist Communion would have belonged to the above category of Baptist who had the 'right practices and correct beliefs concerning Christianity' (131).

Despite this, they were treated like second class humans by the Orthodox/British Baptists. These Native Baptists tended to be more progressive than the British Baptists and had to battle for their space. They were more centrally organised, more in line with the European churches, while the masses of Native Baptists of the Myaal/Revival type were organisationally diffused in the way Revivalists and Rastafari are organised today. The majority of

Buccra Can't Catch Duppy, No, No

Native Baptists in Jamaica in 1865 would not fit Dick's category of orthodox Christianity.

Despite Dick's designation, one elderly man who witnessed the Great Revival of the early 1860s linked it to Paul Bogle and the Morant War in his utterances to Martha Beckwith in the early 1920s. Moreover, he linked it to Alexander Bedward as a continuation of the Great Revival or an extension of its principles. At the time of the outbreak in 1865, and the commission of inquiry into its causes and suppression in 1866, the term Native Baptist was better known than Revival, which just came into use. But that did not prevent one of the commissioners from making the link between Native Baptist and Revival.

James Taylor, a resident of Stony Gut who was arrested during the suppression and given 100 lashes for being a drummer, was questioned about his participation in 'revivals' in Paul Bogle's chapel.

22, 511.	What did you do at the revivals?	– I never did anything but sing hymns.
22, 512.	Did you eat?	– No, never eat.
22, 513.	Did you drink there?	– No.
22, 514.	Did you smoke there?	– No.
22, 515.	Did you dance there?	– No.
22, 518.	Did you ever pray?	– Me sir?
22, 519.	Yes you.	– Yes, sometimes me pray.
22, 520.	Our loud I mean?	– Yes.
22, 521.	Did you ever see vision?	– No, I never worked at that myself

(Royal Commission 1866, 447).

The questions that the commissioner asked James Taylor were not arbitrary. They were likely to have been informed by what the commissioner was told about the characteristics of Revival/Native Baptist in general and in Bogle's chapel in particular. These questions were aimed at ascertaining information about the African or Myaalist identity of the Revival/Native Baptist church and perhaps its propensity for inciting, promoting and organising disobedience and insurrection against law, order and civility.

All of these questions revealed in 1866, what I know today and have been photographing during the last 15 years as key, accurate expressions of Revival iconography, better known as Native Baptist and Myaal in Paul Bogle's time. The name Native Baptist as a public designation for Myaal, seemed politically appropriate as a mask for a most sacred expression of the sovereignty of self. That expression of the sovereignty of self was deemed to be a state of perversion, corruption and 'unrestrained sensuality by polite society in which Africans needed to negotiate their humanity, but which was determined to free Africans from themselves – from their ontological state of nature.

That was why Africans had to develop a double personality complex with double consciousness, so that they could play fool to catch the wise, or having one mind for the boss to see and another mind for what they knew themselves to be – what Spenser St John called 'juxtaposition of opposing beliefs' that 'no other brain but that of the negro could accept'. St John's over-generalisation adorned with prejudice aside, the conceptual and methodological approach outlined above, was/is central to the creative ethos of the African diaspora and black existential philosophy.

It is this realisation, to a certain extent, why Chevannes (1995/1998) highlighted the concept and method of dual membership' (8), and Besson (1995/1998) spoke of 'parallel commitment' (58) in the making, sustenance and development of African Jamaican spirituality and religiosity over 200 years. In the conceptual and methodological complex of dual membership and parallel commitment, people of African descent in Jamaica must pretend to be Christians in public while maintaining Africa spirituality and religion subterraneously; or use Christian signs and symbols to explain, justify, mask-reveal African spiritual/religious beliefs; or to merge-juxtapose Christianity (and other entities such as Hinduism and Islam) with African spirituality and religion; or a combination of the above. Revival, Vodun, Orisha, Spiritual Baptist, Kumfa, Lukumi, and Myombe are living examples of this African diaspora construction. Such was Paul Bogle's Native Baptist church.

Notes

1. The Great Revival was in the beginning a Christian revival spreading island-wide across various denominations: Baptist, Moravian, Presbyterian, Wesleyan/ Methodist and others. It saw an urgent and rapid increase in church attendance and membership, and provided an atmosphere for revival of African spirituality from below, superseding in breadth and depth the Myaal revival of the early 1840s. This African revival, facilitated by a Christian upsurge, would have a major social, political and ontological impact on developments in post-slavery Jamaican society.
2. In one example, Policeman Fuller was told that if he did not take the oath as he was directed to swear, 'they would take off his head' (Royal Commission 1866, 81).

3. See Richard Hart, *Slaves Who Abolished Slavery Volume 2: Blacks in Rebellion* (Kingston: Institute of Social and Economic Research, University of the West Indies, 1985), 51, 225, 237, 251; Great Britain, *Report of the Jamaica Royal Commission, 1866, Part II: Minutes of Evidence and Appendix.* 1866 (Shannon: Irish University Press, 1966), 22, 80, 1,126; Governor [Edward] Eyre, *Papers Laid Before the Royal Commission of Inquiry.* 1866 (Shannon: Irish University Press, 1971), 53; Dianne M. Stewart, *The Three Eyes for the Journey: African Dimensions of the Jamaican Religious Experience* (Oxford and New York: Oxford University Press, 2005), 38, 40, 43, 55–56, 76, 104, 129, 158–59, 223–24, 262–63, 270, 279. Oath-taking as a method of recruitment for war was not confined to Jamaica but practised in the African diaspora across the Americas. The Haitian Revolution was a classical example of this.

   This practice also denoted the Mau Mau uprising in Kenya against British colonialism in the tenth century. See David W. Throup, *Economic & Social Origins of Mau Mau 1945–53* (London, Nairobi and Athens: James Currey, Heinemann Kenya and Ohio University Press, 1987), 120 and Tabitha Kanogo, *Squatters & the Roots of Mau Mau* (London, Nairobi and Athens: James Currey, Heinemann, Kenya and Ohio University Press, 1987), 5, 116–20, 126, 127, 129, 130, 136, 137, 144–45, 148 and 172.

4. In bars across Jamaica and at other spots where alcoholic beverages are being consumed, it is fairly common to see a person pouring a small quantity of the drink on the floor/ground for the ancestors before he begins to drink for himself. This practice continues unabated even when the person pouring the libation cannot explain the reason for his ritual. So engrained is this memory of praxis. The rituals of putting out food for the ancestors also continue across Jamaica, perhaps less so in individual households as was the case when I was a boy. However, this tradition is strong in Revival and Kumina rituals.

   Outside of Jamaica feeding rituals are practised. See Kean Gibson *Comfa Religion and Creole Language in a Caribbean Community* (New York: State University of New York Press, 2001), 53, 104, 107, 108, 117, 137–38, 144, 151 and 155; Sandra T. Barnes, ed., *Africa's Ogun: Old World and New* (Bloomington and Indianapolis: Indiana University Press, 1997), 69, 240–41, 360; Karen McCarthy Brown, 'Serving the Spirits: The Ritual Economy of Haitian Vodou', in *Sacred Arts of Haitian Vodou*, ed. Donald J. Cosentino (Los Angeles: Regents of the University of California, 1995), 205–12; J. Omosade Awolalu, *Yoruba Beliefs & Sacrificial Rites* (New York: Athelia Henrietta Press, Inc., 1966); Maureen Warner-Lewis, *Guinea's Other Suns: The African Dynamic in Trinidad Culture* (Dover, Massachusetts: The Majority Press, 1991), Chapter 6.

5. Considered sacred by Africans and their descendants, the silk cotton tree and its domain became a site of worship and for gathering with the spirits. It was/is viewed as a bridge connecting the world of the living with the world of the ancestors. Its roots were/are treated as altars and were/are often decorated with fabric and other paraphernalia and food for the spirits.

According to Warner-Lewis:
> In Jamaica a tale was told of slaves who had buried their money at the root of silk cotton trees. At those sites gold chains and gold tables come out of the ground and spin around at midday. But these treasures cannot be culled because they are attached by chains to the ground. The booty can only be accessed with the help of the dead. They would appear in dreams advising a person to place rice, rum and goat meat as offerings to them at the base of a silk cotton tree. See Maureen Warner-Lewis, *Central Africa in the Caribbean: Transcending Time, Transforming Cultures* (Barbados. Jamaica and Trinidad and Tobago: University of the West Indies Press, 2003), 272.

In Revival other trees are consecrated and used in invocations. For more on trees in worship see Robert Farris Thompson, *Face of the Gods: Art and Altars of Africa and the African Americans* (New York: The Museum for African Art, 1993), 123–28.

6. Here, Warner-Lewis is using references from the eighteenth to the nineteenth century, especially having to do with Myaal upsurges (revivals) in the 1760s, 1831–32, 1842 and 1860–61. In three-quarters of these cases, the upsurges coincided with or preceded uprisings of the enslaved and their descendants: the Taki-led insurrection of 1760 and an aborted uprising of Taki followers in 1765, the Sam Sharpe-led anti-slavery uprising of 1831–32 and the Morant Bay War of 1865.

7. The title of a male Revival leader in the Poko tradition is 'Captain'.

8. David Lan has written a beautiful and insightful book about the national liberation war that led to the liberation of Zimbabwe. Sterling Stuckey's statement: 'Faith in the continuing influence of the dead on the living was as great as faith that the living influenced the dead,' represents a similar theme and episteme upon which Lan revealed to us the cultural and cosmological roots of a guerrilla movement which rose up against the white minority racist regime in Rhodesia between 1966 and 1980 and won independence.

In this liberation war, where the majority of the combatants were Shona people, Maurice Bloch notes in the preface to Lan's book that, the 'Shona have always seen the relation between their past and their present mediated by their ancestors. The young fighters therefore had to enter into a dialogue with these ancestors, to justify and explain their actions and to seek ancestral help' (xiii).

The world view and cultural and ritual practices of Paul Bogle and the people who marched to Morant Bay on October 11, 1865, bore some resemblance to that of the Shona in Zimbabwe as far as the relationships of the living to the dead were concerned. That is why Lan's book, *Guns & Rain; Guerrillas & Spirit Mediums in Zimbabwe* (London, Berkeley and Los Angeles: James Currey and University of California Press, 1985), is conceptually and methodologically important to me in some understanding and theorising of the Morant Bay War.

9. See Clinton Hutton 'The Revival Table: Feasting with the Ancestors and Spirits', In *Jamaica Journal* 32, nos. 1–2 (2009): 18–31.
10. This statement was made on Monday morning (October 12, 2013) near 2:00 a.m. Bishop Christie was endeavouring to bring Sunday, the first night of the annual thanksgiving feasting table to an end. He said: 'Kids have to go to school. [Adults have to] go to work. We are not going to stretch [it] out till a morning. Unless of course the Holy Ghost dictates it and the Holy Ghost has to come by the spirits.'

    Meanwhile, on March 1, 2012, Bishop Guthrie stated the reason for his attire at the First Quarter Revival Convention at Watt Town, St Ann: 'I robe according to my angel.' This statement fits in the same conceptual framework and logic of Christie's statement. Perhaps it should be noted here that in the 1840s, years before the Great Revival of the early 1860s, adherents of Myaal were referred to as 'angel men' or 'Mial people'. Both designations meant spirit. Angel has become a main name for spirit in Revival.

9 'Take a Thousand Black Men's Hearts for One White Man's Ear': The Suppression of the Black Jamaican Masses in 1865 – A General Survey

[We] slaughtered all before us;
We left neither man or woman or child.

– *British soldier*

You caught me on the loose
Fighting to be free
Now you show me a noose
On the cotton tree
Entertainment for you
Martyrdom for me

– *Third World*

Figure 8. Morant Bay Massacre. Drawing by Clinton Hutton.

The suppression of the black peasantry occasioned by the October 11 events exposed the brutishness of Englishmen who regarded themselves as most civilised. First among the measures employed by them, against the people was the physical elimination of so-called 'rebels'. According to official statistics 439 persons from over 30 villages and towns in and around St Thomas-in-the-East were killed by forces under the command of Governor Eyre and his military officers (Royal Commission 1866, 1,135–42). However, sufficient evidence has come to light to suggest that more than 439 people were executed or died as a result of the activities of the suppressionist forces. Within 16 days of the revolt came a press report that 'the total number of rebels destroyed, was one thousand and thirteen' (*Gleaner* October 27, 1865). Both the *Gleaner* and *Colonial Standard* newspapers had correspondents travelling with the armed detachments throughout the declared martial law zone.[1] The figure of 1,013 deaths would have therefore had a definite basis in reality. While this was the case, however, it was also quite possible for the newspapers and military officers among others to exaggerate the figures to suit their political agenda. The number of people killed could have been deliberately exaggerated to reassure the white and upper sections of the coloured community that the authorities had things under control so as to arrest the initial panic and paralysis experienced by some of these people. It was also done to signal to the majority of the black population that risings among them would be utterly defeated.

If politics played a key factor in influencing the deliberate inflation of the number of executed, it also played a similar role in influencing the deflation of the figure. When the perceived black threat was uppermost, before the British public knew what was happening, the ruling classes reigned indiscriminate violence against the black population and boasted of the hundreds and, indeed, thousands of black rebels that they destroyed. At that time the possibilities were greatest for exaggerating the number of people killed. On the other hand, when the perceived black threat was eliminated, when reactionary violence was on the wane and important sections of British public opinion, having heard of atrocities committed in Jamaica became outraged, the number of people killed was deflated. Even so, the deflated figure of 439 seemed too low and the outer limit of the inflated figure of 3,000 killed seemed too high. Commodore McClintock's estimate that '1500 lives would perhaps be a modest compilation' of the number of blacks killed looked more realistic (Robotham 1981, 10).

The official number of persons who died as a result of the initiatives of the suppressionist forces certainly did not take into account persons who died as a result of severe flogging. The official statistics did not include children who died as a result of the suppression even when the evidence was available. One indication that children were also killed was revealed by a British soldier who participated in the suppression. In a letter to his parents, this soldier wrote:

> I must tell you that when the rebels broke out there was but 300 of our regiment in this place, and the rebels was to look at them about seven to one of us. But by theire surprise we slotered all before us; we left neither man or woman or child, but we shot down to the ground. I must tell you that I never see site like it before as we taking them prisoners by a hundred per day we save them for the next morning for to have some sport with them. We tied them up to a Tree and give them 100 laishes, and afterwards put a shot into their heads,..I seen from fifty tow sixty men shot and hung every morning (Olivier 1933, 278).

Some contemporaries of Governor Eyre did not believe the official figures. Henry Bleby, author of the book *The Reign of Terror*, which was published in 1866, was categorical in his rejection of the official number of black people killed. Without reservation he wrote:

> This is a strong figure of speech, but it contains words of appalling truth. There is reason to believe that the facts as to the amount of life sacrificed in Jamaica, under the sanction of ex-Governor Eyre, and by the agencies he set to work for that purpose, far surpassed what was proved on oath before the Royal Commission (120).

Bleby, a British Minister of religion who lived in Jamaica at the time of the suppression, insisted that the figure of 439 killed 'is reason to fear, very far short of the reality' (121).

A further look at the official statistics revealed that, of the 439 people executed, 430 or over 97 per cent were males. The wide margin between the number of men killed compared to women was no accident. There was a conscious decision by the authorities to eliminate the men because they were deemed the primary threat to the rule of white males. This was no accident since European patriarchal thought regarded state power as the highest expression of masculinity, a position that could only be held by men and challenged by men whatever their class or race.

On October 18, 1865, for example, Lieutenant Colonel Elkington sent a despatch to Colonel Hobbs ordering him not to take any prisoners. According to the despatch:

> Hole is doing splendid service with his men all about "Manchioneal," and shooting every Black man who cannot account for himself. (60 on line of march.) Nelson at Port Antonio hanging like fun, by Court martial. I hope you

will not send in any prisoners, civil law can do nothing (Royal Commission 1866, 1,120).

The command not to take prisoners was repeated on October 19:

> You will make "Monklands" your head-quarters, and patrol from thence (without fatiguing your men), hunting out all the rebels you find, and the Major General hopes you will deal in a more summary manner with them, and on no account forward prisoners to this place (1,122).

Colonel Hobbs, who obviously was having fun despatching black skins, dutifully obliged his superiors. On October 20, 1865, without any fear of retribution or recrimination, he reported the following:

> I accordingly shot nine of the Fonthill rebels in a chapel, where their leader commenced with prayers and ended with blasphemy and sedition; and I there adopted a plan which has struck immense terror into those wretched men, far more than death, which is, I caused them to hang each other. They entreat to be shot to avoid this, which appears to me to be by far more dreadful an ordeal to them than death (1,122).

Hobbs ended his report by expressing his appreciation to his superior for supporting and encouraging the campaign of terror he and his men were waging against the Black population. He said, 'Your letter of approval of our proceeding has gratified us much, and encouraged us for fresh energies' (1,122).

Witnesses to the campaign of executions told chilling stories of their observations. In an incident in Monklands where 13 men were executed, Anthony Bicknell, a coloured resident of Mount Lebanus described his observations:

Figure 9. Col. Francis Hobbs. Courtesy of the National Library of Jamaica. Restoration by Ainsley Kerr and Clinton Hutton.

> I did see the bodies. I buried the body, and one was shot and did not kill; and he was put into the hold, and they ordered to cover him; and then they covered him, and when he was in the hole he cried out, "I am punished," and one of the men took a pick and stuck him two times before he died (1,122).

In another incident Augustus Lake, a reporter of the *Colonial Standard* described the execution of George Marshall, who was hanged on October 18, 1865.

> He was a very thin man and rather sick. After being tied to the gun by order of the provost Marshall, he was ordered to receive 50 lashes. On receiving the 47th or the 48th he turned round and ground his teeth. The Provost Marshall saw him, and ordered him to be hanged immediately....his back was like a bit of raw beef, bleeding very profusely. He was taken down, thrown on his back, his hands and feet tied, a rope put round his neck and thrown over a rail, and then he was hoisted up as you would a barrel of flour...after he had been suspended about three minutes a huge white stone was taken and put between his arms which were tied behind him (275).

Of course, the effects of executions are not measured merely by tallying the number of persons killed or by describing the methods of killing employed. The social, economic and emotional losses suffered by the relatives, friends, neighbours of the executed, and indeed the community, were profound. Then there was the trauma and the psychological wounds inflicted on those who had witnessed these killings and had to live with the memories.

Hundreds of people were witnesses to the executions that took place between October 14 and November 13, 1865. Indeed, no attempt was made to despatch any of the victims in a clandestine manner. This was deliberately done to drive terror into the hearts of the masses, to demoralise and turn them against each other and to imprint in them a feeling of total helplessness and subordination to the ruling classes.

The administration of executions in full view of the public was not only frequently done, it was a matter of policy. Officers in charge of operations were instructed to have prisoners witness the executions. In a 'Field Force-General Orders' issued by Brigadier-General A.A. Nelson on October 22, 1865, the Commanding Field Officer told Lieutenant Jones, Commander of the Royal Artillery Detachment that he 'will be pleased to see that the prisoners now in gaol are present when the execution takes place' (1,116). In this regard, John Lutus, a black tailor who was detained in Kingston and taken to Morant Bay confirmed that while he was in detention; 'we were taken out every morning to witness the executions' (854).

Morant Bay, the main site of executions, was blanketed with an awful stench emanating from dead bodies, stirring up fears of an epidemic. A reporter of the *New York Daily Tribune* (November 17, 1865) noted, for example, that:

> There is one continual scene of hanging day by day, and it becomes a matter for consideration whether the burial of so many people (packed, as I heard a Blue Jacket say, "like sardines") in the town is not likely to produce some serious epidemic here. Already the effluvia arising from the graves in which these dead bodies are interred pervaded the entire town, and it was not without difficulty that one could avoid getting nauseated. This ought to be looked after. It is a matter of vital importance.

Many of those killed left behind many children to the material and emotional care of their relatives – especially of their mothers. Among the many examples to come to light included Cecelia Stewart's husband who was executed leaving her their three children to maintain (271). Dougald Lindsay, husband of Emily Lindsay of Stony Gut, was shot leaving her with five children (335); Simon Wilson, killed at Chigoe Foot Market left Frances Wilson with the four children of their marriage (352); and Anthony Bicknell's son, shot and killed leaving his two children to his father to support (112).

Flogging as a method of coercion was used with devastating and indiscriminate frequency in the military zone. Once a principal symbol of slavery, the whip was brought back as a tool of mass terror and humiliation. Like during slavery, the whip was the most widely used instrument to inflict physical damage to the person of large numbers of men, women and children. Hundreds of black people had their backs reduced to 'raw beef'. As a result, several victims died from flogging, while others suffered permanent internal and external disfigurement to the point of irreversible disability.

Although the feature of the whip, or cat, was left up to the initiatives of its creator, John March, who 'could not bear the sight of flogging,' said the typical whip was made of nine lengths of cord attached to a stick handle. In most cases, each length of cord was wrapped closely from the end to a certain distance up with plain brass wire. The wire was so closely wrapped around the cord that it could not be easily seen (252).

The administration of each stroke of this whip usually left nine bloody trails as the wire wrapped tails sunk into the victim's back. A man who received 100 lashes would end up with 900 stripes on his body. Whipping was not just catting of itself or by itself. It was a package of rituals designed to terrorise, demoralise and humiliate the victims and to teach them a lesson: never to raise their hands at white people.

It was not uncommon for a whipped victim to have his or her back washed or dressed with salt or pickle.[2] In one such incident, Elizabeth Collins of Long Bay related that the back of her 22-year-old daughter, Charlotte Scott, was 'well blooded up' and 'washed...with salt pickle' (Royal Commission 316). In another case, William Onslow, labourer of Stanton, described how he was whipped and had salt administered to his wounds: 'A sailor, and some of them held me by the head and some held my feet, and they gave me 25 lashes again, and took fine salt and scoured my back with it' (134).

Another element of this package involved the stripping of the victims of parts or all of their clothing before they were flogged. No discrimination was made according to the sex and age of the victims.

Then there was the practice of gagging the victims to prevent them from screaming when they were being whipped. In one incident, Alexander Gray, a black peddler, said he witnessed several whipped victims at Manchioneal gagged with stones while they were being flogged by soldiers. Gray said the stones used were 'hard stones they paved the street with; stones that they break with hammers' (342). In another incident, the Reverend Alexander Foote, a coloured Wesleyan minister residing in Manchioneal, spoke about two men he saw flogged and gagged.

> I don't know whether a soldier or a sailor that put stone to the mouth of a man who was bawling out. The man was making a great noise and bawling, and they called to him to be quiet, and one of the soldiers or sailors took a stone and put it to his mouth, and told him to hush, and put it over his mouth, and the man struggled and held back his head, and I think the stone cut the mouth of one of them and it bled (475).

The wholesale flogging of people frequently led to an impious ceremony to send the victims packing. John March, a resident of Bath described one of these ceremonies that frequently took place in Morant Bay:

> There was a road immediately opposite to the flogging post, and the soldiers were on either side, forming an avenue and they had to run through that avenue, and the soldiers were prepared, some with large sticks, and some with heavy clubs, as large as [a] chair leg...the flogging post was nearly at the right hand of the Court-house, and they ran from there, and as they ran through the avenue of soldiers, the soldiers struck them on the ground; I saw many felled to the ground by the blows (253).

Flogging was widely administered either by itself or to complement or supplement other methods of punishment. An example of persons receiving flogging as a punishment by itself involved 72 people who were detained but not formally sent to terms in prison. These detainees collectively received 5,560 lashes at an average of 77 each. Cases where flogging was used to complement or supplement other types of punishment fell in two main categories. The first category comprised those persons who were whipped before they were executed. Alick Taylor and Toby Butler who received 100 lashes each before they were hanged, belonged to this category (464). The other category comprised those who were sent to prison in addition to being 'catted'. Of the 68 males confined in the General Penitentiary under sentence of court martial for rebellion offences, for example, 59, or 85 per cent were to be flogged. These 59 prisoners were to receive 3,149 lashes (at an average of 53.4 each) and 264 years imprisonment or an average of 4.47 years each.[3]

It was evident that a principal motive for applying the 'cat' was to inflict the maximum possible level of humiliation and psychological pain to the victims as well as to those witnessing the ordeal. It is within this context that the flogging of John Ricketts of Darlingford and hundreds of other victims should be seen. Having received 100 lashes, he was forced to politely accept his fate: 'when they had give me the 100, the doctor [Major] made me bow down before him and say "I am much obliged to you, sir"' (579).

Hundreds of people were detained and imprisoned during the violent conflicts of 1865. They were held for periods ranging from a few hours to 20 years. According to the official statistics, 994 persons, including 179 who were subsequently executed, were taken to Morant Bay between October 13 and November 13, 1865 (1,145). At Manchioneal, Captain Hole tried 150 prisoners during his 17-day stay in that community (1,133). At Port Antonio, 38 prisoners were sentenced to a total of 118 years in the Port Antonio District Prison (1,147). Those prisoners did not include many others who were detained for short periods of time. Over at the General Penitentiary in Kingston, 68 persons were sent to serve 313 years in connection with the rebellion. Sixty-three or over 90 per cent of those prisoners were sentenced for 'traitorous and threatening language' (1,145–46).

Figure 10. One of the three canons at the fort behind the Morant Bay courthouse where persons were tied, stripped of their clothing and whipped. Photo by Clinton Hutton.

Fire was also used as a vital tool employed by the upper classes to subjugate the labouring classes in the military zone. Houses from over 50 rural towns and villages were put to the torch. Entire villages were burnt off the face of the earth. Among them were Stony Gut, Somerset, Fort and Barracks. On October 19, 1865, directives were given by Colonel Hobbs to a party of 'sea men, marines and artillery' and others, to have Stony Gut 'utterly destroyed' (1,024). The result of Hobbs's order was described by Harvey and Brewin who visited that village in 1866:

> [T]he head of it [the village] was conspicuously market by four white, roofless walls, the remains of Paul Bogle's chapel. The village had been entirely desolated, the sites of the houses being simply denoted by a fire-blackened patch of ground: the cocoa-nut and other valuable fruit-trees had also been partially destroyed (Harvey and Brewin 1867, 11).

Meanwhile at Somerset, 101 houses were torched (Royal Commission 1866, 1,144). In this village, which 'impressed its destroyers as the highest example they had ever seen of negro prosperity and luxury, every house was destroyed, except two standing together near the lower entrance to the village (Harvey and Brewin 1867, 12). According to the official tally, just over 1,000 dwellings or about 21 per cent of the 'negro houses' were destroyed (Royal Commission 1,144).

The average 'negro house' in St Thomas-in-the-East was thatched and wattled and had earth floor. The sizes of these houses ranged from 10 feet long by eight feet wide to 24 feet by 24 feet (Royal Commission 1866, 1,144). The black household had an average of five persons. In contrast, planters and overseers who never dug a cane hole or cut a root of cane in their lives, lived in spacious mansions and great houses built primarily by the labour of black people. Dwellings like the 'very comfortable furnished house' of Samuel Shortridge, owner of two sugar estates, attorney of 'six of the largest estates' in the parish of St Thomas-in-the-East and Magistrate of that parish, had 16 to 18 windows' (22). These houses contained silver plates, pianos, queen or king size beds and armchairs, among other things.

The consequences of the mass destruction of the 'negro houses' were indeed far reaching. In the first place, it meant the loss of shelter to more than 20 per cent of the population of St Thomas-in-the-East.[4] The loss reduced family cohesion, stability and solidarity. Throughout the length and breadth of St Thomas-in-the-East and, to a lesser extent, from Portland came testimonies of the homeless. From Long Bay, Elizabeth Berry pleaded for her house to be saved: 'I went to the Constable and begged him as the young man [sweetheart] had been shot and was dead, and I had nowhere to live with my seven children, not to burn the house' (284).

From Fonthill Sophia Davis also pleaded but to no avail.

> I had nine children in the house. My husband saw the soldiers come, and he ran into the bush, for fear they should shoot him. I sat down with my little child at my breast, then I rose with the child in my arms, and said, "Massa, I beg you not to burn my house with my nine children" (249).

Many people with no roof over their heads had to take to the bushes and face the consequences of the elements. This was particularly hard on young children, pregnant women and old people. Several persons died from exposure. Thomas M'Lelland 'lost two of his children from severe cold taken during martial-law' after the house and all he had in it was burnt by soldiers in Somerset (Harvey and Brewin 1867, 87). In another incident, Abraham and Sarah MacKindo lost one of their children who died in the bush from 'cold' after their house was torched by soldiers (Royal Commission 1866, 501).

The indiscriminate burning of 'negro houses' was usually accompanied by one or a combination of more than one of the following: the pillage and looting of the contents of the house; the pillage and looting of some of the contents and the destruction of the remaining articles; the destruction of all the contents of the house; the firing of buildings such as mills, shops, schools and chapels; the theft or destruction of domesticated animals and crops; the seizure of the provision ground, i.e., the plot of land planted with food crops; and the looting of wedding rings and money.

The sum total of these practices revealed a determined scorch-the-earth policy by the suppressionist forces. This regime was directed at liquidating the small but nonetheless material base that black men and women had built up after emancipation to enable them to be more independent of the plantocracy. It was designed to push the African back materially to pre-emancipation conditions. The many testimonies of some of those who suffered revealed the essence of that policy. Henry Minott, a black carpenter did 'not save as much as a pin head'. All his carpenter's tools and clothing were consumed in the fire that consumed his house (270). Rochester Cousin from Muirton did not fare better. When he took his clothes and 'crockery ware' from his doomed house, his assailants threw them back inside the raging fire (570). Over at Williams Field, George Hamilton lost his house and shop where he sold 'salt provision.' A tidy sum of £82 that he had made from sales in his shop was also lost (570). The hands of the suppression would go to any lengths to rob their victims as Richard Clarke revealed. While under rap at Morant Bay he said he witnessed the following:

> A woman was being marched from the Court-house to the gallows. She had a small portion of money in her possession – the amount I cannot tell, and her daughter, a little girl, was near. She called her daughter and, wanted to give her the money. Ramsay [Provost Marshall] turned round, and said, "What is that?" the soldier said, "The women is calling her daughter to take some money." He said to the girl, "Go away." After the woman was hung on the gallows, I saw Mr. Ramsay and the rest of the officers surround the woman on the gallows, and the sailor were taking away the money from her off the gallows (72).

The plunderers themselves spoke of their successes in pillaging the black population. On this score, Lord Olivier, making use of information written by Private Atkins, wrote the following:

> The soldiers,...had stolen about £700, apparently in cash, found and taken. Colonel Hobbs also carried off all the horses, mules and donkeys that he could get hold of (besides consuming pigs, turkeys and fowls), and after using as many as he could for his officers, and for transport, sent the rest to Up Park Camp to be sold...Colonel Hobbs also impounded the whole of the coffee crop at Somerset and the adjoining villages (Olivier 1833, 280).

In another example, 'Capt. Henry Ford in Command of the St Thomas-in-the-East Irregular Troop' reported, among other things, that:

> We quarter on the enemy as much as possible, small stock, turkeys, &c, we take ad libitum; other supplies we give receipts for. We press all the horses and saddles we can find, but the black troops are more successful than ours in catching horses; nearly all of them are mounted (*Gleaner* October 27, 1865).

In real social terms, the scorch-the-earth regime led to mass hunger, nakedness and homelessness.

British military officers also used the occasion to test the capability of their military hardware. One such test was carried out on Arthur Wellington. In response to a despatch from John Elkington, Deputy Adjutant General, Captain Spencer Field wrote a reply on behalf of Colonel Hobbs:

> I have the honour to state, that Colonel Hobbs, the night before the prisoner was executed, stated that he intended to test the power of the Enfield rifle at long ranges. The following day, at about 2 o'clock p.m. the prisoner was taken up a hill, a distance of 400 yards or thereabouts, and tied to a tree. The provost sergeant in charge of the prisoner acted as a marker, and signalled the seventh as having passed through the rebel's throat, the ninth or tenth shot entered his heart, or thereabouts (J. Peel; War office February 11, 1867).

Take a Thousand Black Men's Hearts for One White Man's Ear

Figure 11. The spot where Arthur Wellington was executed and decapitated – National Gallery of Jamaica – Edna Manley's Bogle: A Contest of Icons (2010). National Gallery of Jamaica, September 26 – November 13.

Notes

1. These newspapers were praised by the military for their reports on the suppression following October 11, 1865. *The Colonial Standard* October 17, 1865, for example, 'acknowledged with thanks the flattering approbation which his Excellency, the Commander of the Forces, has been pleased to convey to us on the correctness of our Bulletin'.
2. Salt pickle in this case referred to the very salty liquid or brine content of containers used for storing/reserving fish, pork and beef.
3. Calculated from statistics in the *Royal Commission Report 1866*, 1,145–46.
4. One estimate put the homeless at 'no less than 5,000 persons' (*Colonial Standard* August 8, 1866).

10 'He set my house on fire, and I was in Childsbirth':
The Suppression of the Black Woman

> She preferred her freedom, and accepted its greater responsibilities with equanimity. It was this unconscious sensuality which proved the greatest obstacle to the development of their character.
>
> – *William Pringle Livingstone*

> I had got his breakfast ready to take to him, and before I take it to him he was shot and they put a rope round his neck and hung him up on a tree. I began to bawl. I said: 'Wilson, is that the way you are going to dead wrongfully, and leave two little children to me to maintain?'
>
> – *Frances Wilson*

The suppression of black women constituted a main plank of the overall strategy to pacify the Jamaican masses. Before looking at the methods, forms, scope and reasons for the suppression of black women in 1865, let us first take a look at the position of the African Jamaican women in post-slavery society. By so doing, a better insight into the enormity of the impact of the suppression of black women on the African family can be appreciated.

According to the 1861 census, females made up 179,097 or just over 51 per cent of the black population of Jamaica, which numbered 346,374. Blacks accounted for over 78 per cent of the population, coloureds 18 per cent and whites a mere three per cent (Higman 1980, 16).

In St Thomas-in-the-East, there were 23,230 blacks of almost even sex distribution. Females comprised 11,819 or just under 51 per cent, while males accounted for just under 50 per cent. The white population of that parish comprised 282 persons or one per cent, while coloured people accounted for 2,717 or ten per cent of the population (16).

Both sexes of black people emerged relatively equal in post-slavery society, because both were in the main starting from the zero of things, coming out of a system that allowed the majority of Africans little or no access to personal, social and private property. Yet, despite their relative equality in poverty and property relations, the black male emerged in post-slavery society with an economic edge over the African woman. Unlike his female counterpart, the black man journeyed into emancipation with a wider range of skilled jobs,[1] and the potential for more training and higher income. This was mainly due to the patriarchal nature of the society which favoured even oppressed black males while promoting the domestication of post-slavery black women.

The African woman had to endure the brunt of the domestic work in the post-emancipation black household. Domestic work – cooking, washing, sewing, ironing, carrying water, caring for children, and some forms of agriculture – was in some ways a major source of hindrance to the progress of the woman. It fettered her access to public life; politics, education, sports, professional training and employment, the economy, and made her more dependent on men. Without having to consistently do the housework, the man was considerably freer to pursue public goals. Consequently, the domestication of the woman freed the man to be the master of society. And the more the black male (like other men) prospered economically, the more engaged he became in the public sphere, the more he developed into a middle-class person and beyond, the more he required his wife to withdraw to the private/home sphere.

The obvious progress that emancipation brought to the black population also generated its own set of problems. Emancipation brought a far higher degree of sovereignty to the black family than could be anticipated under slavery. Men and women could establish intimate relations with whomever they pleased and marry and cohabit with whomever they liked without the consent of a white master. Mothers and fathers could bring up their children the way they wanted without the veto power of the slaveholder.

This sovereignty over progeny must have been a main factor for what could be regarded as the exodus of women from the estates after emancipation. However, the mass departure of black women from field labour was attributed to their desire or preference for housework and child rearing. Accordingly, it was reported in the *Falmouth Post* (September 23, 1859) that one Revd Barrett and Sir Lionel Smith, the island's first post-slavery governor, were of the view 'that immediately after emancipation, the greater part of the women,...withdrew from field labour and betook themselves to the duties of home' while the children were 'drafted off to school, instead of to the canefields'. These black women were not endeavouring to substitute estate subjection for domestic subordination. The issue was more complex than that. The making of a more sovereign family and, consequently, a more sovereign people, for which the women played the leading role, was one of the main battle sites upon which the struggle for freedom, sovereignty and identity took place in post-slavery society.

Certainly these women (and men) would have wanted to make up for the many generations that the black family lost its sovereignty to slavery. In this context, emancipation had a causal effect on the increase in domestic work among black women and men, but especially the women.

Domesticity, however, did not become the lot of the post-slavery black woman. She regained her capacity for domestic and other kinds of work which the slaveholder forcible took and used for his/her own benefit. She thus arrived in post-slavery society with the capacity for both domestic and other kinds of work in a manner that was wider than the man's repertoire. She was provider (breadwinner) and homemaker.

As provider and homemaker, the African Jamaican woman played an equal, if not superior role to her male counterpart in the production of food for immediate household consumption and for sale in the island's markets. Black women were road builders and repairers. They also loaded coal on to ships and carried basket loads of produce to weekly markets for sale.

A US citizen who visited the island in the early 1870s, captured in his travel article for *Harper's New Monthly Magazine* (March 1872), a picture of working black women:

> Idleness is the one great curse of Jamaica, which has at once destroyed the prosperity of the island and degraded the people. The little work which is accomplished is done mostly by the women. Barefooted and bare-armed, with their frocks wrapped in a roll round their bodies, and their heads tied in the handkerchief universally worn by both sexes, they toil from morning till night at the severest labor, and never seem to repine at their lot. They may often be seen carrying head loads of fruit or vegetables to market, while the men ride after them on otherwise unburdened mules. I saw a dozen black and brown women mending the carriage road in a part of the Bog Walk; and, besides their ability as road-makers, they are excellent hands at coaling a ship.... these coal-carriers are among the most industrious people in Kingston, and they work with a steadiness and alacrity that are surprising to one who has heard nothing but stories of negro idleness from the White people. They carry twelve head-loads of coal on board a steamer for one penny,....much of the labor of coaling the trans-atlantic ships is done at night (554).[2]

This report (despite its language of prejudice) left no doubt that black women performed equally to, or indeed better than, black men (white men too) respecting a wide range of jobs which were regarded as 'male jobs'. This the women did along with their role as homemaker, effectively making them the category of workers doing the longest hours and probably performing the hardest work in the colony.

While most black women came to post-emancipation society in the role of provider and homemaker, their men were mostly required to be provider. Black women became breadwinner and homemaker in post-slavery Jamaican society because, historically and traditionally, most of them performed those roles. They also carried out both functions because slavery so reduced the economic capabilities of both black men and women alike, that reliance on one sex (male) alone for breadwinning (even when the prevailing ideology placed emphasis on a strict division of labour between male and female) would make little economic sense.

The black man's material condition was so poor that he was incapable of breadwinning on his own. At the same time, his female counterpart's condition was so similar that she could not allow homemaking to prevent her from becoming a provider as well.

Another reason for the newly emancipated woman becoming a provider seemed to emanate from her desire never again to be a slave to anyone. After being a slave for a white plantation patriarchy, the black woman was in no mood to become a domestic slave for a black patriarchy, just as the black man was in no mood to become a neo-slave to anyone in post-emancipation society.

Her ability to provide for herself and her children constituted a principal barrier against domestic enslavement. She was intent on providing for herself and her children even if it meant doing a wide range of 'male jobs' for ridiculously low and deliberately depressed wages. Such wages, many black men would not consider working for, because, among other possible reasons, they regarded them as women and children's rates to which they were not about to subject their manly status.

The white colonial plantation patriarchy which could identify with the black patriarchy's psychology and notion of its place, vis-á-vis, black women in post-slavery society, kept wages exceedingly low (below the perceived levels which black men would consider and accept as men's rate) by using immigrant labour and a deliberate preference for women's and children's labour to increase profit and put pressure on the African Jamaican male.

Although the fact pointed to a massive departure of men from the estates as well, more women than men did so even though both sexes despised the system that kept them in slavery. This hatred for the past and hence the desire of not wanting to associate with it, does not sufficiently explain why more women than men abandoned the estates after slavery. Other explanations, like those given above, had to do with the role of women in the newly emancipated black family. This role was not just a domestic role. It was highly political and ontological to the building of the family/community and hence to the culture and agency of black sovereignty.

The woman's position in the post-slavery household was strengthened also as a result of the continuation among the enslaved population of aspects of African beliefs that accorded motherhood a higher place in society. Unlike fatherhood, motherhood was a source of authority and power (Diop 1962, 37–38), with its own mythical and cosmological foundations.

A black family/black household did exist under slavery. However, African beliefs/myths/customs/conventions/rituals/attitudes respecting family/kinship relations, etc., in so far as they represented the development over millennia of the emotional experience, the collective consciousness and psychological feelings of a people played a significant role in shaping the family that was to emerge after slavery.

These non-material factors which existed within the black person were not easily destroyed, not even by generations of slavery. Such factors were certainly underestimated by Fernando Henriques who credited slavery as the single most important factum shaping the black family that was to emerge after slavery (Henriques 1968, 23). The idea that the condition of slavery (imposed on a transported people) was the predominant actor giving rise to notions respecting post-slavery family types, was certainly one-sided since it ignored or underestimated the fact that the outlook of the enslaved Africans was also shaped by myths, beliefs and mores of the ancestral homeland from whence they were transported. Accordingly, Barry Higman's caution respecting the methodological approach to discussion on the slavery and post-emancipation family is timely. He said:

> Most sociologists and historians have adopted a functionalist position, seeing within the period of slavery economic and demographic conditions capable of explaining the family patterns which emerged. These conditions relate particularly to the economic marginalisation of the male and the consequently central role of women in the family (Higman 1980, 41).

Higman's caution is quite relevant in so far as the functionalist approach did not explain or seem to be able to explain satisfactorily the superstitious and mythical reverence that black society had for motherhood. This reverence existed in pre-colonial Africa. It existed despite slavery and thus cannot be explained by it. The functionalist approach did not explain why, despite slavery, there 'is on the whole a strong sense of family, and a folk interest in terms of relationships'. It never explained why 'every man is "brother" to every other, and every old women is "nana" (grannie) or "auntie"' (Beckwith 1969, 46). The answer lies in pre-colonial black African realities (and the continuation of such by the dispersed) where the 'African calls his father's brother, father, or his mother's sister, mother,' because 'he knows that they will serve as his real parents in case of death, illness or extinction' (Diop 1952, 46). This reality which led Maurice Delafosse to conclude that in Africa 'there are no orphans among the negroes' (46), was the same reality passed down to African Jamaican women who 'reared children, whether or not they had given birth to them' (Brodber 1986, 26).

Therefore, any attempt to explain the black family by primarily focusing on the impact of slavery on blacks, and without reference to and an examination of the beliefs and experiences associated with the African family in its various manifestations, must lead to faulty conclusions.

The functionalist approach which saw in slavery the marginalisation of the black male and the elevation of the black women to the centre of the family largely represented a Euro-patriarchal notion of the family. According to this view, in a real, civilised or superior type of family the women and children are subjected to the rule of the man. Man must exercise power over the family if there were to be 'any common family interest', 'community of property', 'mutual trust' and stability, (Livingstone 1899, 53–54).

According to the logic of nineteenth-century Euro-patriarchal thought, the problems that plagued the black family, the reasons for its instability, underdevelopment and backwardness had to do with the centrality of the African woman in that family, and until she was stripped of her powers, there could be no progress for the black race. The black woman's equality with the black man's, her economic independence and her sexual freedom had to be overthrown by man if a true civilised black family were to emerge in post-slavery society.

Livingstone, who shared this view, was certainly not letting the black male off the hook with his share of blame but the woman was regarded as the main ontological obstacle even if this opinion were not explicitly stated.

> The women were no more disposed to marry than the men. This was largely due to the relative position of the sexes. Both were on an equality. The women earn their own livelihood, and lived their own robust, independent life. There was no wooing, and winning, and permanent companionship thereafter, they gave themselves to each other as they pleased. To be married was, to a woman, to become a slave, with slavery, with its dark associations, was as yet but a stone's throw in the past. She preferred her freedom, and accepted its greater responsibilities with equanimity. It was this unconscious sensuality

which proved the greatest obstacle to the development of their character (46–47).

The implicit implications of Livingstone's statement were no different from the explicit statements of Pim and other patriarchal European thinkers. The black woman (like the white woman) should not be a provider and a domestic; rather, her work should be confined to the realm of domesticity since it was the natural duty of the male to be the provider. Indeed, the extent to which civilisation went beyond savagery and barbarism depended on the extent to which the man was able to become the provider and subject the woman to domestic work. Such was the logic of European-patriarchal thought. Isabel Maclean appeared to be championing this view when she wrote in 1910:

> The women and girls have a great deal of hard work to do, but you must remember that it is not so very long since the Jamaican negroes were a heathen people, a savage race, over in Africa. Now, in all savage races there is an idea that women are intended to be the slaves of men, and Christianity and education in Jamaica are gradually rising women to their proper and honoured position in the world, yet all the old heathen ideas and customs cannot be rooted out just at once (Maclean 1910, 48–49).

That black women had 'a great deal of hard work to do' was not disputable. This hard work, however, did not emanate from the idea that black women came from a heathen and savage race in which males forced them to do 'men's work'. Rather, it came from the fact that both the white and black patriarchies were opposed to men doing domestic work. For Maclean, like so many other men and women who subscribed to the racist patriarchal notions of male–female relations, the answer to ending 'hard work' and allowing black women to rise to 'their proper and honoured position', must be found in the liberation of women from 'men's work', and their domestic enslavement, rather than advocating for joint responsibility.

The role of the black woman in post-slavery Jamaica was also defined by the plantocracy and post-slavery officialdom, which placed enormous restrictions on black men and women in their bid to acquire property and socio-political power. Hand in hand with the colonial state, the plantocracy subordinated women to the rule of men even while ensuring that black men remained in a degraded emasculated patriarchy. The black woman was paid less than her male counterpart for doing the same work.

No matter how much property she acquired, no matter how much tax she paid, the black woman, like all other races and classes of women, could not vote or run for public office. However, a property-less husband could vote and run for public offices on the basis of his wife's property,³ because state power was viewed by the European plantation patriarchy as the natural occupation of man, since man was ontologically a political animal and the maker of history.

Although they viewed African men as the main threat to white power, the ruling classes were, if necessity required, willing to allow black males a stake, however restricted and symbolic, in the post-emancipation state than to surrender the same right to white women. They allowed Jewish, coloured and black males the right to vote and run for political offices whilst white women, coloured women, Jewish women, along with black women, were denied this right.

This seemingly contradictory Euro-patriarchal attitude to political power appeared to have been dictated by tactical and strategic considerations aimed at preserving white domination. To this end, the ruling patriarchy resolutely attended to the promotion of the (colour and gender) division of black Jamaicans and the preservation of the appendant status of white women, the perceived weak link in the defence of European hegemony.

In response to the peculiarities of their enslavement, political activism became a feature of the life of black Jamaican women in ways it could not be for white women, who were made to feel that that role was unlady-like in public.

Women and the Morant Bay War

Although women played a leading role in the upheaval in St Thomas-in-the-East, and might be credited for casting the first missile in 'the war' at the Bay,[4] the politics of the black masses in post-slavery society in general and in Paul Bogle's movement in particular, was dominated by men. In a sense, this politics was to an important extent, the politics of the black male. Women, it would appear, were not allowed to drill, take any oath of allegiance to the movement and its activities, sign letters or petitions respecting public matters,[5] or to march along with their men in the same formation, to Morant Bay on October 11, 1865. They had to walk on the side (Royal Commission 1866, 202). The organisational regime of the movement, 50 men to one captain and possibly one secretary for each district, was, to a large extent, based on the need of black men to strengthen their cohesion and unity to better confront the patriarchal ruling classes that stood in their way. There is no known female captain or secretary of the movement, although on several occasions during the conflict, women demonstrated that they had the final say as to whether a perceived enemy lived or died.[6] Women showed deep resolve to fight at Morant Bay on October 11, and while there, some seemed to have exhibited more resoluteness than their menfolk in seeing the battle through to its conclusion. Cecelia Gordon, citing one example of black women's resoluteness, spoke of the following incident:

> They came on the wharf road and the men came on the Four Mile road, and the women said, "Now, you men, this is not what you said in the mountain. You said you would come to the Bay and do so and so, and now you leave all this work to the women; go to the Parade and see what Volunteers do to the men there" (180).

The female rebels had their way, because 'When the women spoke to the men they divided again, and returned to the Parade' (180).

Contemporary literature/reports had little to say about the leadership role of women in the Bogle movement. This reflected the anti-feminist bias of the overwhelming majority of post-emancipation writers who were men as well as the subordinate political role that black women held in the political movement representing them. Despite that state of affairs, however, there were several indications to suggest that women did, on occasions, play a leading role in Bogle's movement. A.E.K. Mudie's assertion that to his 'knowledge...one of the concubines of Paul Bogle went up in the month of September to a negro village, known as Wilmington, and endeavoured to obtain a house to hold meetings, but the residents were persons in communion with the Established Church, therefore she met rather a cold reception' (Eyre 1971, 92), was one indication that women were doing up front organisational and agitational work for the movement.

The Suppression of the Black Woman

The impact of the suppression of the African woman could not be separated from the primary role she had to play in the organisation, management and stability of the newly emancipated black household. Women witnessed and experienced the horrors of the war against the black population and had to live through it with all its attendant emotional and psychological consequences.

The liquidation of hundreds of black males and the looting and burning of over 1,000 'negro houses' meant extreme pressure on black females to reconstruct the black household following the suppression. Many black women suffered the additional pain, stress and trauma associated with sexual violence or the threat of it from the white male-directed military and para-military forces. As females performing the biological and social functions of conceiving and giving birth to children, pregnant women and mothers with young children suffered the additional trauma visited upon them by unbridled repression.

The relatively fewer executions meted out to black women seemed more to be the result of a deliberate policy by the authorities to keep as low as possible fatalities among black females. Against the background of the patriarchal notion of the natural superiority of men over women and hence the view that men ought not to tarnish their masculinity by beating up on members of the weaker sex, there appeared to have been three main considerations for limiting the use of the death penalty for women.

The first reason seemed to have been a fear that killing a higher proportion of women and children might provoke a negative response from the black population (especially the men) across the island and push them into support for the rebels. This fear was later born out in part when blacks in various parts of the island were outraged by news that women and children were being hit or killed (Royal Commission 1866, 883).

Figure 12. Morant Bay after October 1865 with the burnt out courthouse in the background. Photo courtesy of the National Library of Jamaica. Restored by Clinton Hutton.

The second reason seemed to stem from a conscious or unconscious desire by the colonial authorities not to provoke negative British as well as world opinion against the notion that Great Britain, the leader of world civilisation, was practising the opposite in its colonies, torturing and murdering women and children in Jamaica. Indeed, criticisms denouncing British hypocrisy over the sanguinary proceedings in Jamaica were not long in coming. On November 20, 1865, for example, Karl Marx wrote to Frederick Engels on the 'Jamaican Affair':

> The Jamaica affair is typical of the meanness of "true Englishmen." Those chaps have no business rebuking the Russians. But, says the brave *Times*, these damned rogues enjoyed "all the liberties of an Anglo-Saxon Constitution." For a fuller exposure of English hypocrisy after the American war we only lacked the Irish affair and the Jamaica butcheries (Marx and Engels 1978, 322).

In his reply to Marx on December 1, 1865, Engels stated, among other things, that: 'Each successive mail brings ever more startling news of the Jamaica infamies...The spirit of the British army has at last emerged unblushingly' (323).

The third and most obvious reason was a deliberate move by the authorities to use women to achieve military and political objectives over black men. Firstly, they used the women to appeal to their menfolk to come out of hiding and surrender to the suppressionist forces. After the initial counter offensive against the black population, most of the men went into hiding. Orders were given then to the soldiers not to use excessive and unnecessary force, including execution against women. Instead, women were used to lure the men out of hiding. In one of the several cases to come to light, Colonel Alexander Fyfe ordered women to appeal to their husbands and sons to come out of hiding. According to Fyfe:

> I said to them "Now, go into the woods, and tell your husbands and sons all to come out. I do not wish the Maroons to go in. If they do, and [they] do not surrender, they will be shot" (Royal Commission 1866, 901).

In another case, Eliza Berry told how she was used to lure her husband, Joseph, out of hiding, unaware that he would have been shot. According to Berry, one David Mayne, a shopkeeper and citizen of high standing in St Thomas-in-the-East, ordered her to appeal to her husband to turn himself in to him [Mayne].

> Mrs. Berry, I have heard that your husband is gone away, and we have no charge against him, so you have better send and call him and let him know, and when he comes, tell him I am at the Bay side, and he must come to see

me, and I will clear him with Mr. Codrington, for they have no charge against him (283).

When Eliza Berry took her husband out of hiding and accompanied him to Mayne, the shopkeeper ordered a black soldier and constables to shoot Joseph Berry.

Secondly, the women were used as a bargaining chip in exchange for their men who went into hiding. There are several examples of women being 'detained' or kidnapped in exchange for their men who were in hiding. George Bryan spoke of one such case where a man, having hid in the bushes from the soldiers, was forced to give himself up when his wife was held. Bryan noted that the man:

> hid himself in the bush as he heard the soldiers shot all the people, and he heard that Mr. James Codrington sent to take up his wife, and his wife was big with child, and he did not wish her to be hurt, so before they kill his wife, he came out to be killed himself (214).

In another case, Cecelia Stewart said orders were given by one 'Mr. Bowen' to detain her husband and in case he could not be found Constable Collins was to 'keep' her instead (271).

Thirdly, they pressured the women to reveal the hiding locations of their men to the military and para-military forces. This objective was usually accomplished by the use of torture. In one example, Polly Levingston, an old woman of Stony Gut was flogged, tied around the neck, choked and kept in the rain 'the whole day' in order to extract from her where Paul Bogle and other men were hiding (350).

Among the women killed were 16-year-old Amelia Stewart, daughter of Hannah Aspitt, who was shot by Maroons in Thornton and died one week later; Ellen Dawkins, executed for 'rebellion and assisting in murder'; and Justina Taylor, Mary Ann Francis, and Letitia Geoghegan, for 'rebellion'.

Mrs Letitia Geoghegan, as she was addressed, was clearly a leader and commander of events at Morant Bay on October 11, 1865. She was not only executed for this, her son James Geoghegan, a highly respected Captain in the movement was also executed.

While fewer females were killed, many women and children suffered the consequences of the execution of men. Firstly, there was the horror and trauma suffered by many women who witnessed the killing of their mates, fathers, brothers, sons. From Barracks, Charlotte Ross described how her son was killed in her house by soldiers.

> The soldier came to the door mouth; I rise and say, "Sir, it is a sick person; it is a son that is sick," and... as I say so, the other one fire off, and the young man

drop down, and they said they were truly sorry, it was an innocent person; but they can't help it, it was done already; them doing their duty (932–33).

In another incident, Mary Lindsay of Mount Lebanus spoke of one of her brothers who was shot 'and the crow eat him up' (916). Meanwhile, in another occurrence, Ann Mitchell witnessed her schoolmaster/bowl maker husband, Charles Mitchell, of Harbour Head, killed by a group of soldiers and 'book-keepers who dressed themselves in regimentals': 'One shot him in the side and took out his guts...and Depass [book-keeper] shot him...and his brains were scattered' (102).

Apart from the horror, trauma, stress and psychological consequences occasioned by the liquidation of husbands, sweethearts, breadwinners, and fathers, hundreds of black women had to physically and mentally cope with the task of reconstructing their lives. According to the *Colonial Standard*, quoting Alfred S. Churchill, President of the British and Foreign Freedmen's Aid Society, 'it is estimated that no less than 5,000 persons, principally women and children, are at the present time homeless' in St Thomas-in-the-East. Churchill revealed that nine months after the suppression of the peasantry his society received letter from a man in Jamaica requesting help for the people of St Thomas-in-the-East. The letter stated the following:

> That aid be given – 1. For the immediate relief of hunger, nakedness, and destitution. 2... material help to those who are desirous of rebuilding their homes. 3. Aid in building or repairing mills, school rooms and places of worship, etc. (*Colonial Standard* August 8, 1866).

The elimination of black males removed an important source of moral, psychological and material support from the African family. In this regard, Frances Wilson, mother of four children and the wife of Simon Wilson of York, expressed the essence of what probably most mothers in her position would have felt when their children's fathers were executed. Early one morning Frances took breakfast to her husband who was placed in detention in Chigoe Foot. On her arrival, she heard shots.

> I had got his breakfast ready to take to him, and before I could take it to him he was shot and they put a rope round his neck and hung him up on a tree;...I began to bawl,...I said, "Wilson, is that the way you are going to dead wrongfully, and leave two little children to me to maintain?" (Royal Commission 1866, 352).

There were also the hardships occasioned by the short or long-term imprisonment of hundreds of men locked away from assisting their families. Among them were James Fraser, sentenced to five years' hard labour; Joseph Scott, ten years in prison and Richard Newill, three years in penal servitude and 50 lashes. For their part, Fraser and Scott also received 100 lashes each along with their prison terms. If they and others served out their sentences, the chances of some of them coming out useless could not be discounted. Evidence has shown that some of the persons whipped died or became dependent on their family. In one incident, the father of Mary Mitchell from Pera died some time after he was flogged. She said her father's 'back mortified and break out' before he died, without seeing a doctor.

> [I made] fum poultices, from bush; boil it up. Picked bush and pounded it, and put it on. As it was getting bad we took it off, and put on other things. We could not get a doctor at that time. No doctor see him (953).

Others like Richard Clarke, were lucky to have seen a doctor or to have survived the 'cat'. However, some became virtually useless to themselves, their women and families. Clarke lamented his new status after receiving 100 lashes:

> I went to Dr. Phillippo, and he says the kidney is injured. If I was in a private place I could show the situation I am in. I am a poor man. The doctor says I am not able to support even myself. I have been obliged to live upon my family. I am breaking out all over enough to face the dead (73).

Still, others like Richard Rodon fared better than Clarke. Rodon was unable to work for two weeks after he was given 150 lashes. That resident of Barney was flogged by a team of black and white soldiers on orders from Stewart, the Estate overseer. Rodon's mother had to treat his back by bathing it with 'boiled bush and castor oil' (406).

Women also received their share of imprisonment and lashes.[7] While on a tour of the prison in Port Antonio in 1866, Harvey and Brewin found a number of female prisoners:

> We found in the prison between twenty and thirty prisoners under sentence of court martial, chiefly women, some of them mothers of families who knew not what had become of their children (1867, 15).

Hundreds of them had bloody trails etched across their backs, not because they necessarily participated or sympathised with those who rebelled, but simply because they were black and had to be reminded of who was in charge. Indeed, David Mayne had Charlotte Scott of Long Bay whipped, 'because it was martial law and you [Scott] shall be flogged' (Royal Commission 1866, 461). While whipping was a hated symbol of slavery for the black male, it was both a symbol of slavery and male domination for the black female.

The stories women told of whipping conveyed a chilling picture of the barbarity of this instrument of subjection. Ann Galway, a resident of Manchioneal, who was whipped on Codrington's orders said: 'He gave me

25 on my back, and tied me on a cart wheel, and took salt, and washed my back' (580).

The flogging of the black female was the source of two types of humiliation. In the first place, she was flogged by a male (black, coloured or white) and in the second place, she was stripped partially or totally of her clothes before the whip was administered. Charlotte Scott's experience with the 'cat' was typical of the lot of hundreds of women in St Thomas-in-the-East.

> I was going to Port Antonio with a bowl of coconut milk upon my head, and as I passed I saw Mr. Codrington at his shop. I said "good morning! And by the time I passed he sent a Constable after me to take me, and they smashed my bowl;...They stripped me...they took off all my clothes and left my back bare (461).

The representative forces of British colonialism and the planter/merchant alliance did not seem to care much whether the black women they were suppressing were pregnant or had young children. Some of the most gruesome stories to come to light had to do with the treatment meted out to black mothers and mothers to be. John Elisha Grant, stiller man of Albion Estate who was detained and made to dig graves for executed blacks, related the following incident which allegedly took place near Stony Gut in November 1865.

> When we got to a house a person was grunting in the house, and directly a soldier went up to guard the house, and when the woman was grunting he said, "You bitch, I will let you grunt for something," and directly I heard, "Oh, oh." I went to the door and saw a female naked in the house, and a baby came out from her in the house, about this [one foot long], and at that time the soldier shot an old lady and a little boy in the house....Six fired in the house and six fired the top of the house (55).

The old lady was apparently helping the 'naked female' with the delivery of her baby when the 12 soldiers of the 6th Royal Regiment struck.

In another incident, Esther Williams, labourer of Weybridge Estate, told how 'Mr. Codrington' came to her enquiring about Milligen, her common-law husband: 'He set my house on fire, and I was in childbirth' (564). Although she was visibly pregnant and pleaded for her house to be spared by saying 'I don't know where I go to live with my picanniny,' the hands of suppression burnt her house. Williams then started out for her sister's house, and 'By the time I got to my sister's house the child dropped [born]' (565).

In other incidents, Mary Ann Kidd of Arntully told how a woman who 'was in the family way' was hanged in Morant Bay (934), while Jane Wilson, realising the soldiers had set her house on fire with her two children, 'ran into the fire before it dropped down, and took out the live child and the dead child out of the house' (146). Meanwhile, Fanny Junior 'who was heavy with child' was detained and given 19 lashes (464). So too, was Charlotte Carr who was detained and 'flogged into the street of Bath'. She was eight months pregnant (976). In yet another incident, Elizabeth Millett had to flee Prospect, her district of residence when her sweetheart was killed: 'I tied my child behind my back and another in my hand, and went to Mr. Espeut at Leith Hall' (978).

The wholesale burning of houses made fatherless children homeless children, mateless and/or whipped women homeless women, as it was almost certain that a man executed would have had his house torched by men who faithfully carried out the policy of the authorities. But it was not only the houses of persons executed which were destroyed. Those houses which people fled to escape Governor Eyre's men became 'suspected rebel' houses. Besides, a homeowner did not have to flee; the house was destroyed just the same. The black women were left to tell the tale. Sarah MacKindo related how her house at the Barracks in Trinity Village was burnt by white soldiers.

> They were all round the house, and two of them came into the house, and said, "My good woman, come out! Where is your husband?" I had at that time a young baby. One old man came and put his hand upon my shoulder, and said, "My good woman, your house is going to be burnt; come out with the baby." Another one said, if I did not come out he would blow out my brains (500).

Sarah's husband, like most of the men, took to the bushes. Without a house and with nowhere to go, she hid in the bushes with her children. One of them died about a week later from exposure.

> I was in the bush eight days [with] the baby. The child took cold, and the inside of the child went bump, bump, like a watch beating. [It was raining] and the poor child died, all through rain. I was afraid to make a fire to dry myself (501).

The African-owned house was a symbol to both the black own-account/ labourer-peasants and the white planters. To the African, it was a material requirement for freedom. It was the anchor from which to develop a stable and independent household. To the planter, it was a symbol of the erosion of his power, a symbol of too much independence from the desires and influence of the plantocracy. The 'negro house' contained most, if not all, the personal belongings of the black family such as clothes, furniture, tools, utensils, jewellery, money and important papers. Outside the house were the family's domesticated animals, crops, mills, fire place, leisure spots, etc. In other words, in and around the house of the African stood elements constituting a main basis for the black family to develop socially as an independent entity to resist the encroachment of the former slave master.

During military rule, a spontaneous policy of coercive labour without remuneration was thrust upon the black population by the plantocracy. While the emergence of coercive labour without pay seemed to have come spontaneously, the urge for this regime had deep roots in the defunct chattel slave epoch. The desire to force a repressive regime of labour upon the black masses was not confined to the plantocracy in the east alone. The new political situation strengthened the ruling classes across Jamaica. Over in St James, more than 100 miles due west of the 'war zone', Colonel Whitfield requested 250 soldiers from Kingston because 'the negroes [were said to be] rude, sulky and disinclined to labour' (*Gleaner* November 24, 1865).

Both men and women were coerced into working. However, it would appear that women were the main victims of forced labour in the east – since more men were either in hiding, detention or killed. Most of the evidence of men forced to work came from those in detention. In some areas, like around Bath, women were ordered to work in lieu of being flogged. According to John Hamilton, a carpenter of Bath, Mr. Kirkland, the Magistrate 'never chastised them, but set them to work on the roads, and let them go without flogging' (Royal Commission 1866, 483).

There were women who were refused pay by their employers for work they did prior to the outbreak. Mary Williams, a labourer at the Holland Estate was one such person. Wages owed to her for two weeks' work were withheld by the estate management (248). Others were forced by use of arms and threats to work without pay. Peggy White, for example, was 'bound' to work on the Portland road for two months for the Maroons (528). In another incident, Mary Ann Taylor, an old woman, was coerced into working on the road for five weeks. According to her, she received 'not a quatty' for her labour. Instead, 'every morning and evening they gave me a piece of saltfish but no victuals at all' (537).

Older women were subjected to the same regime of suppression meted out to younger women. In one incident, Maria Robinson's three adult sons were executed. This senior resident of Mount Lebanus had a 'grandchild' who 'was a big man'. Robinson was robbed and made homeless with the rest of her family (938–39). In a way, the consequences of military rule rendered the older women (and men too) less able to cope in the new situation. It would

He set my house on fire, and I was in Childsbirth

have been certainly more difficult for them to face the elements or to rebuild their houses. It would have been very difficult for them to get food and to replace their clothes and household articles. Their difficulties would have been compounded if they were troubled by ailments and other vices of old age. Indeed, these would have been further compounded if those women were widows or without children, relatives and friends. Nancy Forrest of Somerset Village was very much in this position:

> an old widow, who lost her husband in Kingston some ten years ago. She was invited during last year by her cousin, Louis Graham, to come over and stay with him: she did come, and he provided for her. He was shot, and his as well as her house and furniture, etc., were burnt by the soldiers; and she is now left without any friends or means of support (Harvey and Brewin 1867, 87).

Eliza Betty of Stony Gut was in almost a similar situation.

> [She was the] widow of Edward Betty, who died a year ago. She is aged and sickly; was lying in her house sick when the Maroons ordered her out, and burnt it with all she had in it (85).

Elsie McFarlane, a resident of Coley, was more fortunate. She had the assistance of her sons in coping with her losses.

> [She was the] widow of Robert, who died about four years ago. Her house, and all she had in it, was burnt by the White soldiers. Her sons have been subjected to similar losses, but they are helping her to put up another house (85).

Sexual Violence

The use of sexual violence as a form of coercion, intimidation and control was an integral part of the suppression of black women. Women like Chloe Munro were victims of sexual violence. She was raped by a soldier in her Font Hill home. On October 20, 1865, a group of soldiers went to Munro's house while her husband 'gone to bush'. After they 'took out everything out of the house' one soldier remained inside. According to Munro, the soldier said:

> "You must go on the bed," and I said I would not go. He fix me against the wall and drop his breeches and pulled my clothes. I called to my mother; him fix me on the wall, and I took my knee and shove him off; he tore up all my front. I can't pea pea [urinate] for two days (Royal Commission 1866, 932).

In another report, Revd Henry Harris, a member of the English Baptist Society residing at Belle Castle, told how in two separate incidents 'soldiers forced' two girls. With respect to one of the victims, Revd Harris reported how a man 'met the girl crying' shortly after she was sexually assaulted. The

Baptist Minister, who knew both girls, said he spoke to the mother of one and the guardian of the other following the incidents (961). In another case, the intended victim, Sarah MacKindo, was luckier. Having robbed her, set fire to her house and left her family of six without a roof over its head, two of the soldiers decided to rape her:

> One held one hand, and the other the other...They say I must go into the bush. One said they only wanted one round [with] me, and the other one said they only wanted two. They were dragging me into the bush, and as I was making such a noise the Officer came up,...and asked what they were doing with me, and they said nothing, only making a bit of fun with me (500–501).

Several women suffered the humiliation of having their heads shaven by the suppressionist forces. One of the several cases that came to light involved Elizabeth McIntosh, a resident of the neighbouring parish of St David, who was detained on Mr Smelly's orders and taken to Monklands in St Thomas-in-the-East. She was accused by 'Mr. Lescelles,' Captain Field, and Colonel Hobbs of laughing at a 'Miss Fowles'. For this 'crime', the captains and colonels of estate and army decided to punish her:

> [T]hey took me down to the tree and shave off my head...They cut off the four plait with the scissors, and shave my had quite off, they put a piece of string round my head, and they stuck feathers in it, all round; and when them done, they mix up a pudding with some lime, and fat, and put it on my head; then Mr. Smelly said, some of [the] constables should take me up to beg Mrs. Smelly's pardon, and then go up to Arntully and beg Miss Fowles' pardon (939).

There were cases of men who were shaved – though fewer than women. However, forced shaving of the black male's head might have had less humiliating impact on him than the women since the man was more accustomed to wearing his hair short.

The suppression of black women by men under the authority of Governor Eyre had within it a determined gender conflict. The whipping of 'a young woman,' ordered by Joseph Briscoe, a Maroon captain, because she 'was charged' by Peter Espeut, the son of a St Thomas-in-the-East estate owner, 'for taking six shillings to go to this Williams [Obeahman] and buy obeah to mix with some spruce to tempt young Mr Espeut' (1,030), had nothing to do with the suppression of the rebellion, but everything to do with the suppression of a woman who dared to want a serious relationship with this 'brown' son of a white planter, instead of being one of his mistresses.

John Mendes's justification for flogging Catherine Williams was an argument for male domination over the female gender. Mendes had

Williams punished because she 'had left her husband a long time, and has been living with several others. She is nearly a prostitute' (1,049). It would be highly unlikely that John Mendes or any other male under Eyre's command would justify flogging any man, rebel or loyalist, black or white for leaving his wife and living with several other women. It was highly unlikely that the man would be flogged even though the woman could not become a near or real prostitute without the participation and sanction of male society. Thus, while the black male was being suppressed for reasons of race and class, the black women was crushed for reasons of race, gender and class.

Notes

1. See Lucille Mathurin Mair, *Women Field Workers in Jamaica during Slavery* (Jamaica: Department of History, University of the West Indies, 1987).
2. The name of the article is 'Negro Life in Jamaica'.
3. In one example, the 1858 Act to 'define the qualification of members of the Assembly, and of elections,' stated that no person 'shall sit or vote in the assembly, unless he was...a freeholder in his own or his wife's right, and possessed, among other things, 'a clear income, after payment of all just debts, of one hundred and fifty pounds, arising from lands held by him in his own right, or in right of his wife.' See Chapter 18, Laws *of Jamaica 1858–1859* (Jamaica, 1859), 1,143.
4. James Britt, a brown Volunteer said a woman who 'was a sort of leader...first fired a stone, and several other women followed her, and then the men rushed right in' (Royal Commission 1866, 178).
5. It appeared that the government would accept petitions signed by women.
6. One report, for example, suggested that the plan to burn down the courthouse and force its besieged occupants out, emanated from a woman, Rosanna Finlayson, who said: 'They [the men] must go and get a fire stick and trash, and set the school-room on fire' because, 'if they set fire to the school-room the whole people would be burnt up alive.'
7. Among those sentenced were Esta McKayne, five years hard labour, Mary Bailey, five years, Ann Walsh, five years and Nelly Steel, 12 months hard labour (Royal Commission 1866, 1,147).

11 Factors Which Accounted for the Defeat of the People's Rising

> [T]he blacks in the West Indies and elsewhere are not yet sufficiently taught to enjoy the great blessings which white men have conferred upon [them]
>
> – *Falmouth Post*

> War oh, Guinea war, oh
> War oh, Guinea war, oh
> War oh, Guinea war, oh
> See the Maroon man a-come,
> Guinea war, oh
>
> – *Kumina song*

> You think a little
> Think a little...
> Innocent Blood
> Shed down there
>
> – *Culture*

The struggles of the majority of Jamaicans to reform post-emancipation society, was soundly defeated with the brutal suppression of the Morant Bay uprising. The defeat of the people's efforts to get rid of absolutism and create the material basis for their empowerment resulted from unfavourable local and international factors.

Internationally, the former enslaved population had no African centre of world power to match that of European power. Consequently, there was no black power centre to extend political, diplomatic, cultural and material support to Africans struggling against white supremacy and hegemony in the so-called New World. Connected to this was the fact that there were hardly any social forces within the white power blocks that were adequately prepared to struggle for, support or accept black sovereignty. While some Europeans were willing to struggle to end slavery, the majority of them were unwilling to have blacks taking

Factors Which Accounted for the Defeat of the People's Rising 205

matters into their hands and determining their own future as sovereign in post-slavery construction. One of the main reasons for the apparent change in the attitude of mainstream white abolitionists from supporting the abolition of slavery to opposing black self-determination in post-slavery society found expression in Sidney Levien's statement that black people had no justification to rebel because 'There is no freedom to fight for, no chains to throw off.'[1]

Imperial Unity and British Military Experience

The unity of the British against African self-determination in Jamaica was supported by other European powers, especially Spain. Although England and Spain had serious rows over Spain's continued trafficking in Africans for slave labour, which led the British Government to order its navy to seize Spanish slavers and free enslaved Africans intended for Cuba,[2] the Spanish authorities in Cuba placed two war ships and troops at Governor Eyre's disposal for use in the suppression following the Morant Bay outbreak in October 1865. Two Spanish men of war, the *St Lucia* and the *Andaluzia* (*Colonial Standard* October 30, 1865) arrived in Jamaica 'within a week or ten days after the breaking out of the rebellion' according to Henry Wesmorland, member of the Executive Committee and Custos of the parish of Metcalfe (Royal Commission 1866, 879). Indeed, one report said 'Two Spanish war steamers arrived at Kingston on October 21, from Havana, and were placed at the disposal of the authorities' (*New York Daily Tribune* November 17, 1865). According to another report appearing in a Jamaican newspaper, the Spanish military vessels were sent to the British colony when:

> The Governor of Cuba, on hearing from the Spanish Consul in this city [Spanish Town] of the disturbances

Figure 13. Governor Edward John Eyre. Courtesy of the National Library of Jamaica.

in St. Thomas-in-the-East, immediately ordered a large Friggate-of-war and another steamer, to proceed without delay to Kingston with dispatches to Governor Eyre, placing both vessels at the disposal of his Excellency (*Gleaner* October 23, 1865).

For his part, Henry Westmorland said the Spanish vessels came 'in consequence of our telegraphing to the Consul at St. Jago, requesting that he should communicate with the Consul at Havana' (Royal Commission 1866, 879). Whether the Spanish Consul in Jamaica requested military assistance from his government in Cuba to help Governor Eyre or the Jamaican government requested same, or it was a combination of both, the two colonial antagonists were united in opposition to black sovereignty. Obviously, the Spanish authorities who were still presiding over a slave regime in 1865 were as eager as their Jamaican counterparts to see the black uprising crushed as quickly as possible fearing its example might lead to instability in Cuba. In this regard, the November 7, 1865 issue of the *Colonial Standard* noted that 'The news of the Rebellion in this Island had been received in Cuba with great consternation, and a strong feeling of sympathy was aroused for the unfortunate victims of the bloody murders in Saint Thomas in the East.'

When the Spanish vessels of war arrived with their officers and troops, the officers were 'entertained' by 'His Excellency the Governor and Mrs Eyre at King's House', on the afternoon of Thursday, October 26, 1865 (*Gleaner* October 27, 1865). Two days later, those officers and the Spanish Consul in Kingston were given an 'Official entertainment' at King's House by the British military command in the island and the colonial government. According to one report:

> Major General O'Connor, CB, commanding the Forces entertained the following Spanish Officials at dinner, on Saturday evening last [October 26, 1865] – Don Bruno Bedan, Spanish Consul; Don Bastillio; Don Manuel Villalon; Don Luis Parja; and Don Nontes de Oca (*Gleaner* October 30, 1865).

The Spanish military forces were never brought into action against the people in St Thomas-in-the-East because, although the people's rising forced the authorities to seek or welcome military assistance from Cuba, 'the emergency' had not 'actually arisen' for Governor Eyre to 'make use of Spanish vessels or troops' (Royal Commission 1866, 879).

The US government, fresh from the civil war that ended slavery in all of the US was concerned about the peasant rising in Jamaica. In words which seemed to have reflected sentiments within the US government as well as influential sectors outside that government, the *Herald* newspaper said the

Factors Which Accounted for the Defeat of the People's Rising

violent confrontation in Jamaica 'becomes a matter of some importance in the reconstruction of our Southern States', when 'the working of emancipation culminated in an insurrection.'[3] The US Government was also concerned about the Spanish presence in Jamaica. In a report, the November 11, 1865 issue of the *Herald* noted that:

> The State Department at Washington has received official information on the facts... regarding two Spanish war vessels having been tendered by the Captain General of Cuba and accepted by the English officials to assist in quelling the rebellion (*Gleaner* November 25, 1865).

Furthermore, that newspaper noted that the US 'Consul in Kingston, Jamaica expressed the opinion that several months will be required to suppress' the rebellion and 'hopes an American war steamer will be sent thither immediately' (*Gleaner* November 25, 1865). The *Gleaner*, which reprinted the *Herald's* article, was pleased to tell 'Our American cousins 'that instead of "several months" less than a week was all the time employed in crushing out the rebellion' (*Gleaner* November 25, 1865). However, before the US government could be apprised of the new situation in the island, 'An American steamer of war arrived at Port Royal' on October 30, 1865 (*Gleaner* October 31, 1865). Another American vessel, the *Re-Union*, was used to evacuate families of the ruling classes from Portland (*Gleaner* October 19, 1865).[4]

It has not yet been ascertained what was the specific response of the French government to the Morant Bay outbreak. However, a French steamer, *Caravelle* participated in the suppression of the Jamaican people.[5] Official contact was made with 'the agents and Captain of the French Steamer' shortly after a meeting involving Governor Eyre, military and naval officers, members of the Assembly and the Executive Committee, was held at Head-Quarters House on the night of October 12, 1865.[6]

While the unity within and among the white power centres served as an epochal shield against black Jamaica embarking on the road of empowerment and self-determination, the defeat of the African masses was made possible primarily because of the overwhelming military superiority of the British colonial authorities.

The military officers were seasoned and experienced campaigners in effecting and maintaining colonial subjection against Non-Europeans around the world as well as waging war against colonial rivals. Needless to say, Bogle and his people had little or no experience in battling the colonial army and would therefore need the force of an island-wide uprising of the Haitian type, or protracted guerrilla warfare of the Maroon type to counterbalance and nullify the military and naval advantages of the colonial armed forces. This was not to be.

Over 40 military and naval officers, ensigns, corporals, sergeants, lieutenants, captains, colonels, major generals, with several hundred years of military experience, were used in the 'war' against the people of St Thomas-in-the-East. Inspector Gordon Ramsay of St Catherine was 'instructed with the command of the Police in the district of St Thomas in the East'. He was 'an old trooper' who had 'seen good service in the Crimea, and taken part in the celebrated charge at Balaklava' (*Gleaner* October 14, 1865).[7] Captain Bullock of the gun-boat *HMS Steady* was also 'a Crimean hero, and lost a leg there' (*Colonial Standard* 2 November 1865). So too was Colonel Hobbs who 'served valiantly at the siege of Sebastopol during the Crimean war' (Semmel 1976, 85). For his part, Major General O'Connor, Commander of the British Troops in Jamaica had about 40 years of experience, suppressing colonial peoples in the West Indies, Central America, Africa and Ireland.[8] And Brigadier General Nelson who was selected by Major General O'Connor to head the military forces against Bogle, got the job because he was 'an experienced officer of upwards of 30 years, and because...he had served under most distinguished officers, Sir William Knott, Sir Charles Napier, and others, and had been engaged in the Afghanistan wars' (Royal Commission 1866, 679). Nelson was promoted to the rank of Brigadier General because of 'distinguished services in Africa' (681). He also served as an officer in India and was decorated for the role he played in suppressing the Afghan and Indian fighters for national liberation (*Colonial Standard* December 6, 1865).

Meanwhile, Lieutenant Colonel John Elkington, Commander of the forces on the northern side of the island, had 19 years military experience. He joined the army in 1846 and was promoted to Lieutenant Colonel in 1859. He served in the 6th Royals in the Kaffir wars, 1847 and 1851–52. Elkington was Assistant Quartermaster General to the Ottoman Contingent from its formation in May 1855 to the end of the war. He was also an officer in the suppression of the 'Indian Mutiny' in 1858 and served with the China Expeditionary Force in 1860 (*Colonial Standard* December 6, 1865).

General Forbes Jackson, like Lieutenant Colonial John Elkington, was also a veteran of the suppression of the Indian Mutiny,[9] while Colonel Alexander Gordon Fyfe was a veteran of the suppression of the 1831–32 anti-slavery uprising led by Sam Sharpe in Western Jamaica.[10] For his part, Captain Algenon de Horsey, the Commander of the *HMS Wolverine*, which transported the first batch of troops to Morant Bay on October 12, was a senior naval officer with many years of experience.

Factors Which Accounted for the Defeat of the People's Rising

Of the estimated 1,000 troops stationed in Jamaica at the time of the outbreak, 500 were sent into war against the people of St Thomas-in-the-East. They were assisted by some 500 Maroons and about 1,000 volunteers and special constables. The remaining military detachments were held in reserve and/or deployed in Kingston and other parts of the island. They were joined by 1,200 troops brought into the island from other British colonies in the hemisphere during October and November 1865. This was in addition to the unspecified number of military personnel from Cuba and the US.

Of the troops brought in from other British colonial possessions, 500 white soldiers and 27 officers were sent in from Barbados and arrived at Port Royal on October 28, 1865 (*Gleaner* October 30, 1865). Another 200 troops from the 1st West India Regiment, Nassau, Bahamas, were sent to Jamaica and arrived in the island on October 28, 1865 (*Gleaner* October 30, 1865). Then another 500 soldiers from the 17th Regiment were dispatched from Halifax (Canada) and arrived in Jamaica on November 10, 1865 (*Gleaner* November 11, 1865). All told, about 4,000 British military personnel, merchant/planter militia and Maroons were mobilised against the black population across the island. This tally did not include the American and Spanish military and rural militia and armed private civilians operating outside of St Thomas-in-the-East, St David and Portland.

The troops who participated directly in the suppression at St Thomas-in-the-East were drawn primarily from the 6th Royal Regiment and the 1st West India Regiment. They included men from the Royal Artillery, the Royal Marine and the Blue Jacket. The Maroons played a major role in the suppression.

In terms of weaponry, the British forces in the colony possessed, among other things, the Enfield rifle which could hit a target with deadly effect upwards of 400 yards. They also commanded artillery or field pieces which were mounted for offensive and defensive purposes on military vessels and on land in St Thomas-in-the-East. Artillery pieces were used against people in St Thomas-in-the-East on at least one occasion. In contrast, the black masses were armed primarily with cutlasses, homemade spears, sticks, bottles, and a few old muskets taken from the Morant Bay police station, and rifles seized from the volunteers in front of the courthouse. The superior fire power of the colonial troops overwhelmed the people. Indeed, some rebels expressed the view that 'without firearms they could not contend with the [soldiers]' (Royal Commission 1866, 409).[11]

The considerable military experience of the officers, along with their superior armaments, was combined with military tactics of sheer terror and intimidation. These they inflicted on the people with wanton sadistic methods by men who believed that Africans were lesser humans which entitled white people to 'take a thousand...black men's hearts for one white man's ear' (427).[12] The calculated 'terror which martial law inspired' (871)[13] overwhelmed the people.

Many fled in panic leaving property and sometimes their immediate family behind. Friends and relatives denounced loved ones to save themselves. Some allegedly took their own lives and cheated the advancing terror.[14] Innocent folks voluntarily sought out military and paramilitary officers and entreated the suppressionists to whip them on the spot in lieu of sending them before the martial law courts.[15] It was, therefore, not hard to see why many people, including some who supported Paul Bogle, felt that 'all the Bogle should hang.' According to Henry Bogle, 'even the black people self say, no seed of Bogle must be left alive' (23).

Apart from the terror meted out to the people of St Thomas-in-the-East and parts of Portland and St David, a campaign of detentions of liberal-minded and reformist individuals of influence was simultaneously launched across the island by the authorities and private individuals in favour of the suppression. It was under this campaign that George William Gordon was detained, transferred to Morant Bay, tried and executed.

Among others to be detained were Noel Croswell, a Jewish businessman from Kingston; Caroline Pink, the only woman to be arrested as a 'political prisoner'; Maximillian Carto Benuzzi, a former soldier in the Austrian and Italian armies (he gave drawing lessons in Kingston); William Kelly Smith, editor and Isaac Vaz, proprietor of the *Watchman* newspaper; Revds Roach, Crole, Palmer and Harris; Emanuel Joseph Goldson, former Sergeant of Police, Kingston; Haitian exiles, General Solomon Jean, Emile Pierre, and Simon Lamoth among others; Sidney Levien, Editor, *County Union*, Montego Bay; William Silvera, Deputy Marshall of St Mary and St Ann; Dr Robert Bruce, Coroner, Vere; Alexander Phillips, a progressive Maroon associate of George William Gordon and a friend of Dr Bruce, secretary of the Underhill meetings, Vere; and Alexander Miller.

Thus, although the Morant Bay outbreak was confined almost entirely to one parish, its suppression became an occasion for an island-wide crusade against reform minded individuals, societies and institutions to foreclose on what was felt to be the gathering storm of island-wide black insurrection.

One of the institutions confronted by this all island reactionary suppression was the progressive press. As can be seen above, William Kelly Smith, Isaac Vaz and Sidney Levien, were men associated with two newspapers, the *Watchman* and the *County Union*. Another paper in this category was the *Sentinel*. These men were detained for the making and distribution of ideas that were deemed to be antithetical to civility and order in their newspapers.

Factors Which Accounted for the Defeat of the People's Rising

The *Watchman* or 'People's Paper' was situated on Peter's Lane, Kingston. It was highly influenced by George William Gordon and was edited by William Kelly Smith, a black man. That paper ceased operation on October 18, 1865, when it was closed by Police Inspector Nairne, who, accompanied by a Royal Artillery force, 'put the Government's seal on the door and left it strongly guarded'. The following day (October 19), the proprietor of the *Watchman*, Isaac Vaz, a coloured man, was arrested 'for complicity in the rebellion' (*Colonial Standard* October 20, 1865).

Also arrested were members of the *Watchman* staff, William Kelly Smith, John Sharp (George Sharp, Printer), and a correspondent named Miles. Miles was executed by the authorities in Morant Bay during the suppression. The *Gleaner* (October 20, 1865) reported Miles's arrest and stated 'that sufficient evidence will be brought to convict him.' This 'perfect firebrand in the parish for some time' before the October 11, 1865 outbreak, exposed through the *Watchman*, a case against magistrates of St Thomas-in-the-East who refused to prosecute a fellow magistrate, named Walton who severely supple-jacked[16] his female servant.

The *Sentinel* was in some respects similar to the *Watchman* in its political orientation. It was operated by a former editor of the *Watchman*, Robert Johnson. The *Falmouth Post* (November 24, 1865) noted that the 'types, presses, and cases of the late *Sentinel* newspaper' were 'seized' and the proprietor detained.

The *County Union*, which was owned and edited by Sidney Levien, a man of Jewish ancestry, exposed the dreaded condition of the labouring classes in St James and other western parishes in Jamaica. Levien was arrested for 'using language and publishing the most disloyal articles in his newspapers'. The *County Union* was closed by the authorities in Montego Bay and its printing press smashed. Levien was transported over one hundred miles from Montego Bay to Morant Bay to be tried under Martial Law and was lucky not to have been executed. The proprietor and editor of the *County Union* was handed over to Civil Authorities to be tried along with other 'Political Prisoners' as Martial Law 'expired' November 15, 1865.

While the suppressionist forces destroyed the capacity of the progressive forces to tell their side of the unfolding story through the press, the pro-suppressionist press was supported and encouraged to manufacture public consent by telling the elites' story. The *Colonial Standard* (October 17, 1865), for example, 'acknowledged with thanks the flattering approbation which his Excellency, the Commander of the Forces, has been pleased to convey to us of the correctness of our Bulletin.' In another example, a *Gleaner* correspondent on assignment with British military personnel occupying a section of St Thomas-in-the-East said, 'I feel myself bound to acknowledge the courtesy and facilities extended to me by the above named gentlemen', (Provost Marshall Ramsay and Captain Jones and other) 'officers of the Royal Navy. Everything has been done by them to further my views, consistent with their duty, and the emergency of the moment' (*Gleaner* October 21, 1865).

This 'national' crusade became politically viable because of the limited geographic scope and nature of the rising, which allowed the authorities to concentrate half of their military forces on St Thomas-in-the-East, St David and Portland, while simultaneously dispatching some of the rest around the island to support the initiatives of the ruling classes in the other parishes to intimidate the black masses and arrest influential progressives.

The single most important medium through which the suppression of the reformist movement across the island was achieved was the fleet of naval and commercial vessels at the disposal of Governor Eyre and Major General O'Connor. These vessels, numbering upwards of 20, were used to transport soldiers around the island,[17] deliver arms and ammunition to parish militia and private volunteers (Royal Commission 1866, 861–65), carry detainees to detention centres,[18] and transport troops from abroad to Jamaica.

Among these vessels were the gun-boat *Onyx* from which the Royal Marines used artillery pieces to send 'several shells' in the 'midst' of rebels at Bowden 'which speedily put them to flight (*Colonial Standard* October 17, 1865); the 21 gun warship *HMS Wolverine*; the 81 gun battleship *Duncan*; the 80 gun *Abaukir*; the *Galatea*, 26 guns; *Niger*, 11 guns; *Fawn*, 17 guns; *Cordelia*, 11 guns; *Nimble*, five guns, and the *Steady*, three guns. There was also the 1,700-ton commercial steamer, *Plantagenet*, which was also used to transport troops from Barbados to Jamaica (*Colonial Standard* October 17, 1865).

Bogle and his people had no comparable instrument of transportation, communication and warfare, and their rising was not broad enough to counterbalance the obvious advantages of the suppressionist forces in this sphere.

The defeat of the black masses was also assured largely as a result of disunity among the people and a dramatic depreciation of their will to continue the course of October 11 when the military struck and seized the initiative from them on October 13, 1865. For two days the rebels had most of the main centres of St Thomas-in-the-East under their control putting to flight and confusion, humbling, demoralising and eliminating members of the ruling classes and their allies in that parish.

That victory was short-lived, however, because what Bogle and his followers did for St Thomas-in-the-East on October 11 and 12, they, along with thousands of Jamaicans across counties, especially Middlesex and Surrey,[19] should have done for the other parishes. This never materialised because of the limited scope of Bogle's organisation and the uneven development of a revolutionary situation across Jamaica, as well as the low level of unity and cohesion among Jamaicans of African descent respecting the path to reform. Consequently, the colonial authorities and the ruling classes outside St Thomas-in-the-East, frightened and incensed by the October 11 events, went on a counter-offensive to 'crush out' the rebellion and adopt measures to prevent any rising outside the affected parishes.

The Unity and Agency of Elite Classes

Meetings reminiscent of the Underhill conventions earlier that year were called in earnest across the island. This time, however, they were convened by planters and merchants, and attended by 'gentlemen' of influence and power; their allies and others fearing the wrath of the ruling classes.[20] Unlike the Underhill conventions, however, the October meetings were entirely pro-government despite the unpopularity of Governor Eyre among important sections of the ruling classes prior to the outbreak.[21]

Those attending endorsed resolutions supporting Governor Eyre and his handling of the crisis. They endorsed measures to revive the volunteers units, establish private militia detachments and secure arms and ammunition from government to equip them.[22] These requests, which pointed to the strengthening of the state and the ruling classes at the parish level, were readily acceded to by a government which, a few months earlier, refused to act positively on the calls of the black masses for reform.

The October meetings demonstrated that the ruling classes were clearly united in their determination to bring about what one of their numbers, Henry Vendryes, called the 'pacification of the peasantry'. Even among perennial white progressives such as William Wemyss Anderson, the fear of black sovereignty seemed to have superseded their progressive beliefs and measures they had struggled for in favour of people of African descent. Anderson, who was George William Gordon's friend, business partner and legal representative, tried to have Gordon escape the hangman's noose by attempting to file a writ of habeas corpus, but was rejected. He, however, actively sided with the suppressionist forces. Anderson, who owned properties in St David and St Thomas-in-the-East, requested of Governor Eyre, 'a company of soldiers' to 'occupy the Port Barracks' and asked 'that some supply of arms be sent for the well disposed' (Royal Commission 1866, 1,862).

Estate proprietors, overseers, attorneys and lessees used their estates as centres for the detention, whipping, torturing and execution of people they regarded as rebels or troublemakers and also to settle scores with individuals over past conflicts and disagreements (316). Hundreds of planters, merchants, magistrates and their allies organised themselves in Special Volunteer detachments or reported for duty in the legally constituted Volunteer units of the various parishes to which some of them belonged.

Special Volunteer units like 'DeCordova's Irregular Cavalry' conducted military assignments in St Thomas-in-the-East, did guard duties in Kingston, and carried out other assignments in the city and Spanish Town. This cavalry was headed by merchant, Altamont DeCordova, and was equipped with rifles and swords supplied by the army.

Then, there was the Special Volunteer detachment founded by Henry Ford, a merchant who had businesses in Kingston and St Thomas-in-the-East. This company was made up of young men, 'Bookkeepers of estates, mostly white, or fair-coloured who would pass as white' (393). They hailed from the Plantain Garden River district of St Thomas-in-the-East, the heartland of that parish's sugar industry. Ford's Special Volunteers were celebrated by the planters of St Thomas-in-the-East and the merchants of Kingston for the atrocities they committed against black people in St Thomas-in-the-East.

There was also the 'Shortridge's Volunteers', 'A company of Volunteers composed of gentlemen...of St Thomas-in-the-East, and commanded by Samuel Shortridge, and Lieutenants H. Chisholm and George Donaldson.' This company 'was supplied with arms and ammunition, from the Ordnance, left for Golden Grove, via Morant Bay in HM Gunboat Steady' (*Gleaner* October 19, 1865). From the standpoint of the ruling classes, the Special and Regular Volunteers played a very important role in the defeat of the people. In St Thomas-in-the-East, the Volunteers, army/navy and Maroons constituted the principal strike force against the people, while in Kingston over 650 Volunteers were responsible for the safety of the city.

Apart from organising themselves in Special and Regular Volunteer detachments, the leading men in society conducted meetings with members of the labouring classes in a bid to enlist their moral, political and ideological support for the suppression, and to warn, intimidate, and discourage them from giving any support or sympathy to their own people. In one of several such meetings, Assembly man, newspaper proprietor, and former superintendent of the Mico Establishment, George Henderson, 'advised the people [of Port Royal] to be quiet, to get their arms and cutlasses, and to resist any attempt of the rebels to enter the parish' (Royal Commission 1866, 949). He told them that if they conducted themselves properly, 'the

Factors Which Accounted for the Defeat of the People's Rising

troops and the Government would protect them, but...if they joined the rebels in the end they would severely suffer for it' (949).

The pro-suppressionist activities of the planters and merchants were also extended to other areas including the illegal importation of arms and ammunition by a firm in Falmouth 'for the use of the estates' in Trelawny. According to a report in the *Colonial Standard* August 31, 1866:

> In November last, a Firm in Falmouth imported in a vessel, from New York, a case marked and entered in the manifest as iron monger, in which 20 revolvers and 20,000 cartridges were found to be contained. The custom-house officer who attends to the landing of goods, seized these arms and reported the fact to his supervisor, who communicated about it with the Customs Authorities in Kingston. Meanwhile the firm in question wrote to Governor Eyre and the Executive Committee, representing that the arms had been imported for the use of the estates which were defenceless, and to be sold to the Planters and others on these estates. The Executive Committee directed the return of the arms to the firm in question, only a letter of guarantee being taken that they should be returned when called for.

The pistols are by this time distributed to various persons.

Thus, all the evidence showed that the suppression of the people was done by the state authorities in partnership with the planters, merchants, middle-class professionals and significant sections of the clergy, among others. The pro-suppressionist partnership was also extended to the area of the transporting of troops, arms and ammunition. Several mercantile firms put their ships at the disposal of the authorities to transport troops from abroad to Jamaica or to different locations around the island.

The commercial steamer, *Plantagenet*, owned by the firm of Barclays and McDowell, was made available to the Governor and was used to transport 200 troops of the First West India Regiment from Nassau to Jamaica. Then there were 'the sloops', *Ranger* and *Stafford*, belonging to persons in Montego Bay, which were made available to the authorities and used to transport 'a detachment consisting of 27 rank and file, of the 2nd West India Regiment' to the town of Lucea in the parish of Hanover (*Gleaner* November 13,1865). At least two other mercantile firms, Arnold Malabre and Company and Davidson, Colthirst and Company, 'placed the Steam Vessels of their agencies at the disposal of his Excellency for the conveyance of troops to the scene of the disturbance' (*Falmouth Post* October 27, 1865).

The partnership among the ruling classes which helped to guarantee them victory over the black masses was largely absent from among Jamaicans of African ancestry. In the first place, there was no partnership between the politically and economically influential middle- and upper-middle-class coloured and the black population because, in the words of Henry Westmorland, 'the feeling of alarm' over the rebellion 'was shared by the white and coloured people of respectability' (Royal Commission 1866, 879). Westmorland further noted that the coloureds 'were with the white people to a man' and 'approved' of the arrests of a number of prominent men as political prisoners (880). These coloureds detested the action of the black masses as coarse, uncivilised and lacking the finesse and decorum befitting British subjects. Indeed, the coloureds appeared to be more afraid of black radicalism than extreme white conservatism.

Maroons Served the Suppression

While the outbreak and its suppression generated a high degree of solidarity and cohesion within the ruling classes and their allies, the black masses and their allies experienced a dramatic erosion of theirs. Paul Bogle had hoped that the Maroons, who up until the last anti-slavery uprising in 1831, sided with the slaveholders and the colonial authorities in suppressing the enslaved Africans, would have sided with their colour in the post-slavery epoch. But this was not to be.

The Maroons with whom Paul Bogle sought to form an alliance, joined forces with the colonial authorities and decisively shifted the balance of power in favour of the suppressionists. Bogle's resolve to get the Maroons to side with his people was matched only by the determination of the Crown to have them on the side of the white population. James Gall's statement on the Maroons probably reflected the apprehension of most whites at the prospect of the former guerrillas joining Bogle and relief when they continued the post-treaty tradition of supporting the British in suppressing dissent among the rest of the black population. According to a relieved Gall (1879):

> By the investion (sic) of Providence the Maroons, whose loyalty was doubtful, in consequence of their former rebellion which took upwards of twelve months to suppress, and with whom it was well known many of the rebel leaders had been tampering, happily decided to throw in their fortunes with the white people. Under the Hon. A.G. Fyfe, they did incalculable service. They protected Bath, captured the leader of the Morant Bay rebels, Paul Bogle, hunted out other notorious ring leaders, and by their general behaviour showed how valuable their services were, and how dangerous they would have been had their sympathies been directed the other way (195).[23]

The Maroons, who, over generations, evolved into a mercenary caste in the service of the Crown,[24] sided once more with the British, because the treaty

Factors Which Accounted for the Defeat of the People's Rising

obligations they had with that colonising power and the benefits they derived from it, remained stronger than any feeling of racial solidarity they might have developed for the rest of the black population. An explanation of the basis for the Maroons' services to the colonial government which continued after emancipation was given by the *Colonial Standard* on November 7, 1865:

> This noble race enjoy particular advantages, and numerous privileges, which were conferred upon them at the conclusion of the "Maroon War." They pay no taxes, and their officers hold Military rank with the British Army – while, on the other hand, they have, in consideration of these rights, promised, at all times to respond to the call of her Majesty in suppressing a rebellion or whenever she may require their assistance.

While the *Colonial Standard* highlighted the material basis of the Maroons' partnership with the Crown, there was an equally important and inseparable ideological dimension for that partnership. The Maroons at that time felt they were superior to the rest of the black population. That feeling of superiority emanated from the fact that for generations they were never enslaved in consequence of the battles they waged against the colonists which forced the British to sign a treaty with them in order to promote the stability and viability of the system of slavery.

More so, they felt superior because the Europeans, whom they considered, in some respects, to be superior to blacks, accorded them the special position of association and employment as an informant police caste which gave them power over the majority of the black population. The Maroons probably felt as well, that it was better for them to stick with the power they knew and were certain of, than to throw in their lot with Paul Bogle and blacks in a project that was not sure to succeed and thereby lose their position in the process.

At least 250, but probably up to 500 Maroons, were actively involved in the suppression of the people in St Thomas-in-the-East and Portland. One report noted that 'No less than 500 Maroons had arrived at Port Antonio and placed themselves under the command of their captain, the Hon. A.G. Fyfe, declaring that they would die in the service of the Government' (*Jamaica Tribune* October 18, 1865). The Maroons, who were armed 'after their own fashion,'[25] were rearmed by the military high command. In one example, '500 stand of arms' were shipped from Kingston to Maroons in Port Antonio.[26]

The Jamaican press and state officials had no doubt about the critical importance of the Maroons in suppressing the people. The *Colonial Standard* noted, for example, that 'it has been in a great measure in consequence' of the 'services' of the Maroons 'that the rebellion of 1865 has been crushed out in the bud' (*Colonial Standard* November 7, 1865). Meanwhile, Governor Eyre told a joint session of the House of Assembly and the Legislative Council that it was '[t]o the fidelity and loyalty of the Maroons it is due that the negroes did not commit greater devastation, and the Rebellion has not been a more protracted one' (*Gleaner* c. November 7, 1865).

Reports of the exploits of the Maroons, probably exaggerated at times, were celebrated in the Jamaican press. On October 19, 1865, for example, the *Gleaner* carried a report that the Maroons were 'already scouring the country for rebels dragging them from their concealment, and exterminating them whenever they have been found.' That paper further noted that 'over one hundred rebels are reported to have been shot by the Maroons in this mission already.' With undisguised glee, the *Gleaner* concluded:

> At an execution of the rebels, and while the dead bodies were hanging as a public example, the Maroons (we are informed by Col. Hunt) assembled around the gallows, where they had a war dance; the savage wildness of which was truly grand.

It was the Maroons who captured and delivered to the authorities the principal leader of the people of St Thomas-in-the-East and *The New-York Daily Times* celebrated the moment of his delivery and fate thus:

> This notorious rebel was brought into Morant Bay about 11 o'clock on the Tuesday following Gordon's execution. He came in escorted by a large body of Maroons, and his arrival was announced by the blowing of shells. The greatest excitement prevailed in Morant Bay when it was ascertained that the monster had really fallen into our hands, and was soon to meet the punishment he so justly merited. In appearance he was a man about 45 or 50 years old, black, with thick, heavy reddish lips, bleared eyes and very much pitted with marks of small-pox. His sullen countenance and dogged manner bespoke him a man capable of commiting all the atrocities with which he was charged (*The New-York Daily Times* November 17, 1865).

Perhaps the highest expression of gratitude that the white ruling classes and their allies showed to the Maroons in recognition of the leading role they played in the suppression, was the official reception organised for them by the State in collaboration with the merchants of Kingston and Spanish Town. On Monday, November 13, 1865, at 'about nine o'clock in the morning,' 249 Maroons,[27] fully armed and dressed in their camouflage battle outfit, entered Rock Fort, the approach to the city of Kingston.[28] They arrived after many hours trek from Portland and St Thomas-in-the-East. They were met at Rock Fort by a guard of honour and 'commenced their public entry into

[the] city' (*Gleaner* November 15, 1865). As they proceeded, 15 companies of uniformed Volunteers with arms, a company of pensioners of the West India Regiments, and members of the 'Fire Brigade' 'with two of the city Fire Engines' (*Gleaner* November 15, 1865), lined both sides of Windward Road leading into Kingston and fell behind the advancing Maroons, forming a procession of over 1,000 strong. The procession which moved to the music of the Kingston Volunteer Artillery Drum Corps, the bands of the Engineer Company and the 17th Regiment, had in its ranks many of Kingston's leading merchants.[29]

Monday, November 13, 'was everywhere observed as a holiday, marked with attention to the race for whose welcome it was given' (*Gleaner* November 15, 1865). The *Gleaner* noted that the procession of Maroons and Volunteers was enthusiastically welcomed by the people of Kingston.

> From every window, door, piazza, even the roofs of houses, smiles and waves of handkerchiefs from the fair sex greeted the advance of the true and loyal hearts who had sprang to arms in defence of their Sovereign – their country and their families. In many instances Bouquets were thrown on the Volunteers as they passed along (*Gleaner* November 15, 1865).

The Maroons were met and welcomed at the Kingston courthouse where a guard of honour of 100 soldiers of the 1st West India Regiment was drawn up. The welcoming party was headed by Governor Eyre and included Major General O'Connor; Vice-Admiral Sir James Hope, Commodore Sir Leopold McClintock, Custos Lewis Bowerbank; Edward Jordan, Secretary to the Governor, and 'many other gentlemen, Military and Civilians' (*Gleaner* November 15, 1865).

The Maroons were addressed by the Governor who congratulated them for 'crushing out a most atrocious and blood thirsty rebellion' and promised that the Queen of England would write to thank them for their 'loyalty and devotion' (*Gleaner* November 15, 1865). After, the Maroons 'sat down to a sumptuous repast,' and, according to the *Gleaner*, they expressed 'their entire satisfaction at the courtesy shown them' (*Gleaner* November 15, 1865). Many of them, 'were heard' to have expressed 'loyalty to their Sovereign and faithfulness to the white and colored classes of our beautiful land' (*Gleaner* November 15, 1865).

The next morning the Maroons went by train to Spanish Town and 'were received...with an ovation worthy [of] the Spanishtonians' (*Gleaner* November 15, 1865). The following day they left Spanish Town and travelled some 100 miles through the country 'to pay a friendly visit' to the Maroons of Accompong in St James.[30]

'Black Skin White Heart': Identity and Ideological Division

Another important factor leading to the defeat of the people was reflected in the antagonistic ideological, philosophical positions they held about their sense of self and place in the world – positions which transformed Africans into strangers to themselves and to fellow persons of African descent within and outside of their community. Many blacks, believing their position to be ordained, came to accept as truth the white racist conception of society and became conscious or unconscious agents of the ideology of white supremacy. In a display of white racist prejudice, one black resident of St Ann, for example, opposed Bogle's movement and the actions of the people of St Thomas-in-the-East on October 11 because 'Massa, black people too fool: ax dem what dem fighting fa, and dem no able to give you any reason' (*New York Daily Tribune* November 17, 1865), while another remarked:

> Take me word – tis the bery reason I say I neber will leave me parish – St. Ann for eber! Wen we see dem know too much s'mady come a dem village to talk wid we about de rights a de people; turn him way out a de village, and if him won go way, lick him till him sneeze (*New York Daily Tribune* November 17, 1865).[31]

Then there was 'A Negro' who wrote to the *Colonial Standard* protesting against the press and those who argued that the 'Morant Bay Rebellion' proved that all blacks were 'savages, cutthroats and devil incarnate'. He said:

> No one regrets the late rebellion of St. Thomas in the East more than I, neither do I believe that Her Majesty has amongst all her subjects any that is more loyal than I; I would stake my loyalty against that of the proudest son of English blood, or of English aristocracy. But really I cannot see how from PARTICULAR PREMISES men can draw a universal conclusion. The late rebellion of the East was the work of a few of the basest sort of negroes, men of no education and of any position in the country as was manifested in the brutal murder of Mr Price (*Colonial Standard* December 21, 1865).

This 'Negro' of the pen who obviously prided himself as a sort of honorary white man, noted that the majority of blacks in the island were men 'willing to sell their lives in protection of Her Majesty's dominion, and to show that they respect and honour 'the Power that be' (*Colonial Standard* December 21, 1865). He was obviously displeased and worried that the white society which he admired so much, benefited from and endeavoured to mimic could so categorise all blacks as to put persons like him in the same class as Bogle. However, his high level of education could not compensate for his low level of race consciousness and sense of justice, freedom and sovereignty. He,

Factors Which Accounted for the Defeat of the People's Rising

like white society, did not feel that blacks were capable of organising and planning the 'rebellion'. It had to be Gordon the coloured, who 'with a white wife in his arms, was the sewer of the seed of disaffection – the fanner of the flame of sedition' because black people were 'less aspiring' (*Colonial Standard* December 21, 1865).

Many African Jamaicans opposed Bogle and his methods because they felt that their progress depended on the 'blessings' white people 'bestowed' on black people. For them, post-slavery society needed the direction of a white ruling class. Hence, when Dugald Lindsay asked one Minott, a plough man, 'if war come, who you for, buckra or nigger?', Minott answered, 'You fool! Man, who this plough for? Who land this? Who cow this? Who pay me and you? No Buckra. You nigger got anything go give me?' (Royal Commission 1866, 49). There were some blacks, therefore, who opposed the confrontation (or any move for serious reforms) for more pragmatic reasons than for strictly race and class considerations. Thomas Cousins, for example, related the following conversation between himself and Richard Cousins, an alleged rebel who told him that they (the rebels) were going down the river to 'take in the crops' of sugar canes.

> I asked him how they could manage to take in the crops without buckra? He said it was not buckra making the sugar all the time, it was black people making the sugar. I asked them what would they do with the sugar after they had made it. He said they would send it to England. I said, "Send it to England? To whom, who do you know there?" (424).

Even if Thomas Cousins conceded that 'it was not buckra making the sugar all the time' but the black people who worked on the estate, he could not bring himself to support the rebels because, according to the logic of his argument: white people were needed to command the vital areas of the economy since they were the ones who had the connections in England and knew other things, who to send the sugar to.

The views voiced by many blacks against the Morant Bay outbreak, black radicalism and reformism meant that there was no consensus among the African majority for radical solutions to the problems that confronted them. The lack of such a consensus doomed the people to defeat in 1865. Doomed indeed, since many of them tended to respond to their position in post-slavery society in ways similar to how whites interpreted it and planned it to be. In a sense, some of these African Jamaicans could be described as black persons with the acquired consciousness of white plantocrats.

They thus developed a culture and psychology of self-denial and self-hate. Some of them felt, like the Europeans, that black people were 'too fool;' that they would never take themselves 'out a white people law so go trus...black nego' (*New York Daily Tribune* November 17, 1865); that they would join 'no party but that of white people, because [they] have grown up under them' (Royal Commission 1866, 87). The people's struggle for radical reforms was doomed to defeat because a significant amount of blacks at that time did not subscribe to the view that 'Buckra country' should belong to them (The Jamaica Committee 1866, 87), or that it was their time to 'turn buckra' themselves (61), or that it was time for them to have 'a black queen, not a white one (152), or that it was 'Blackman time now'.

Finally, the people's revolt was defeated because by day three of the confrontation they lost the initiative and began to retreat and disperse in confusion after last ditch efforts to maintain an organised force against advancing soldiers began to fall apart. Among the measures they took to counter the colonial armed forces were, firstly, to seize all firearms and ammunition in the possession of members of the ruling classes and other persons not with the uprising. On October 13, 1865, for example, several armed men went to Revd William Harty's mission house for one Mr Miller's 'gun and pistol'. Miller, an 'overlooker' of Serge Island estate, fled in fear of his life after urging his wife to seek refuge with their children at Harty's mission. Harty had the following verbal exchange with the rebels:

> I said Mr. Miller has no pistol, but Mrs. Miller brought a gun; they then said, "Minister, we don't come here to do you harm or do we wish to hurt your family, if you give us the guns;" they said they would not disturb us if we would give them the gun; Mrs. Miller was in a very excited state of mind, and I advised her to give the gun, and it was given to them.
>
> I asked them what they wanted with the gun; I had heard of them before; I said, "You are going about seeking these guns, what are you going to do with them?... they assured me that their reason for asking for the gun was that they might be able to contend with the soldiers (Royal Commission 1866, 409).

Secondly, they tried to encourage a mass uprising of the populace by appealing to the people to rise in arms and continue the momentum which was clearly in their favour on October 11 and 12. Reports indicated that the leadership of the movement was probably relying on armed uprising and industrial action to counter the military offensive. Five days before, an appeal was issued calling on the people to rise in arms, Paul Bogle was said to have told a meeting of his supporters, 'Don't go to any work.'[32]

That meeting was also addressed by George Craddock who, endeavouring to see that the people keep up the fight, told them that they had the country to gain from it. According to a report, Craddock told the people that 'they had been long trodden under sandals, and now they were about getting the

Factors Which Accounted for the Defeat of the People's Rising

country; it had long been theirs, and they must keep it wholly in possession' (144).

The people at that meeting were obviously in a high mood because, when Craddock asked them 'Where are your chaises and buggies; they make you pay taxes to drive them.' The people all said, 'Hear! Hear!' (144).

With all their efforts, however, organised resistance to the suppressionist forces fell apart. Paul Bogle was captured by Maroons and brought to Morant Bay on Tuesday, October 24, 1865 (*Colonial Standard* October 28, 1865). When he was taken, he was alone, a graphic example of the extent to which the movement was in disarray. He was 'taken before a Court Martial composed of Col Lewis, Lieutenant Col Hutchings, and Captain Espeut,' found guilty and hung along with his brother, Moses, and James Bowie in the archway of the burnt out Morant Bay courthouse that same day (*Colonial Standard* October 28, 1865). Paul Bogle maintained his dignity and defiance to the end and 'was very sullen at his trial and said not a word in his defence' (*Colonial Standard* October 28, 1865).

Notes

1. Quoted from the *County Union* 24 October 1865 in Great Britain, *Report of the Jamaica Royal Commission, 1866, Part II: Minutes of Evidence and Appendix* (Shannon: Irish University Press 1966), 201.
2. Several reports of British naval vessels intercepting and detaining Spanish vessels suspected of engaging in the slave trade appeared in both the Jamaican and foreign press. On November 27, 1860, for example, the *New York World* noted from the Jamaican press that 'The British war steamer Baraconta had brought two Spanish brigs, names unknown, captured on the way from Cuba to the African Coast.' The paper noted that 'Three other vessels, supposed to be slavers, were in sight at the time the above were taken but the steamer not having coal enough, could not pursue them. In a June 8, 1858 report, the *Falmouth Post* reprinted an article from the *Morning Journal*, which that paper lifted from the US *Gazette* of the capture of the 'Emelia,' 'a clipper of 800 tons' after it was chased for fifty miles by 'Sphynx,' accompanied by the 'Jasper,' Lieutenant Commander Pym.' That Spanish vessel 'which had long enslaved Blacks. The report said 'The 'Emelia' had a valuable cargo, and 2,400 doubloons in gold, and a crew of 40 men, and was commanded by a notorious slave captain who had been captured three times before. The *Sphynx* had to keep up a continual fire from her 8 inch gun before bringing the chase [to an end].'
3. Quoted in the *Colonial Standard* 17 November 1865. The *Herald* or the *New York Herald* was a daily published in the US from 1835 to 1924. That paper favoured a compromise between the North and South in the American Civil War.

4. Portland bordered St Thomas-in-the-East on the north. The *Re-Union* was commanded by one Captain Tracey (Royal Commission 1866, 59).
5. This vessel, for example, 'took a company of the 1st West India Regiment' to Port Morant, St Thomas-in-the-East during the beginning of the suppression according to the *Gleaner* 14 October 1865.
6. A Report published in the October 13, 1865 issue of the *Colonial Standard* noted that 'His Excellency the Governor arrived at Headquarters House in this city at about 9 'o'clock last evening when a Council of War was held and arrangements entered into with the agents, and Captain of the French Steamer....' It should be noted, however, that the meeting referred to at Headquarters House by the *Colonial Standard* was an informal gathering comprising the Governor, military and naval officers, along with a few members of the Assembly. The Council of War meeting was held the next day.
7. The Crimean or Eastern War, 1853–56, was between Russia on the one hand and Britain, France, Turkey and Sardinia on the other.
8. O'Connor joined the West India Regiment as an officer in 1827 and helped to maintain the system of slavery for 13 years before it was abolished in the British West Indies. By the time slavery ended, he was promoted to Deputy Assistant Adjutant General to the forces in the West Indies. He served in the Yucatan from 1848 to 1851 during the 'revolutionary upheaval' there. In 1855, General O'Connor led military campaigns in Africa where he, along with British and French troops, defeated 'a numerous force of Mahometans commanded by Omer-Hadajee, the Black Prophet. O'Connor was military Governor of Gambia from 1852 to 1859 (*Colonial Standard* December 6, 1865).
9. For General Jackson's role in the suppression of the Morant Bay outbreak see Royal Commission 1866, 118–122).
10. See Richard Hart, *Slaves Who Abolished slavery Vol. 2 Blacks in Rebellion* (Jamaica: Institute of Social and Economic Research, 1985), 309–10, 314.
11. This view was expressed to Revd William Copeland Hart by armed rebels who came to his house on October 13, 1865 in search of a 'gun and pistol'.
12. This statement was made to Richard Prendergast by Captain W. Astwood.
13. According to Henry Westmorland.
14. According to a report in the *Gleaner* October 21, 1865, 'Some of the rebels are giving up, and many committing suicide.'
15. Henry Ford, a merchant who headed a special volunteer unit, said on several instances while he conducted work on behalf of the suppressionists in St Thomas-in-the-East, 'the men took off their shirt, and said, 'Massa, I ready for flog.' They begged me to flog them, as a rule, in preference to sending them to Court-Martial....I have a clear recollection of dismissing a man after he had offered himself to be flogged' (Royal Commission 1866, 397).
16. A supple jack is a specially prepared and fashioned flexible stick used to hit mules, donkeys and horses and to punish people on estates and in prisons. It was still in use in Jericho, Hanover when I was a boy.

Factors Which Accounted for the Defeat of the People's Rising 225

17. Troops were sent to every parish in the island during October and November 1865. The *HMS Fawn* transported 40 troops to Savanna-La-Mar, Westmoreland, October 27, 1865 (*Gleaner* October 28, 1865); October 30, 1865 *HMS* 'Troopship' *Urgent* 'Left Port Royal late last evening for Port Maria, and other ports with troops under Command of Colonel Whitfield' (*Gleaner* October 31, 1865); Tuesday, October 7, 1865, 'One officer and fifty men...left Tuesday night, for the town of Mandeville' (*Gleaner* November 9, 1865).
18. The *HMS Wolverine* was one of the main vessels used to transport prisoners to St Thomas-in-the-East.
19. Middlesex and Surrey housed the seat of government and the military and, if the rising could have shifted the balance, especially in Surrey, the turn of events would have been different.
20. There was the Lucea meeting, October 20, 1865, attended by magistrates and other gentlemen 'For the purpose of adopting measures for the preservation of peace and order.' That meeting was chaired by Jacob Lyon and the gathering, 'Unanimously resolved that a Special Constabulary Force consisting of 200 respectable parishioners should be embodied....' and an 'immediate application be made to his Excellency the Governor...for a supply of arms and ammunition' (*Colonial Standard* October 27, 1865). The Mandeville meeting, October 18, 1865, which was attended by 'A number of the Magistracy, Planters and others interested in the welfare of the island,' agreed 'that the present Volunteers... be retained on duty at Mandeville' at the expense of the gathering (*Colonial Standard* October 24, 1865).

    The Kingston meeting, October 24, 1865, was attended by Custos Bowerbank and a 'number of highly respectable persons – Justices, Merchants and others', including Jonas Hart, Simon Soutar, Charles Levy, W.R. Myers, W.T. Jamison, Joseph Steins, A. De Roux and Arnold Malabre, enthusiastically received Major General O'Connor who was presented with a document 'the purport of which was to request that the officers of Volunteer be provided with pistols.' Altamont DeCordova also 'present a document' to O'Connor 'that he with others, to the number of 21, had volunteered their services to form a Mounted Volunteer Company' (*Colonial Standard* October 16, 1865).
21. One example of the serious differences between sections of the ruling classes and Governor Eyre found expression in the *Colonial Standard* which, reflecting the sentiment of the Merchant class, was convinced of 'the total unfitness of Mr. Eyre for the Government of this colony' (*Colonial Standard* October 13, 1865). On September 23, 1865, that paper printed the contents of a petition to Eyre which stated in part:

    > Mightier and greater minds than which Mr. Eyre possesses have before this have been made to quail under the force of public opinion. Let Mr. Eyre ponder on this. He is the last man needed by Jamaica in her transition state. All he has done for her is evil, which will leave no small

task for his successor to overcome whenever the happy day arrives on which we are to get rid of so unworthy a ruler.

22. As a result of these meetings, and also of the initiatives of state authorities at the parish level, arms were requested to bolster the power and authority of the ruling classes. From Portland W. Wemyss Anderson requested of Eyre 'a company of soldiers' to 'occupy the Port barracks' and 'that some supply of arms be sent for the well disposed' (Royal Commission 1966, 862). In the meantime, Westmoreland Custos Vickars 'suggest the propriety and expediency of sending down immediately 100 stand of the best description of arms available, with a moderate supply of ammunition, as a precautionary measure' (Royal Commission 1866, 862).
23. James Gall was a publisher and Quarter-master of the Volunteers unit, the Engineer Company.
24. Dr. Hamilton, member of the Executive Committee, sought to formalise the role of the Maroons when he presented a Bill to the Legislative Council calling for 'the formation of the Maroons of this island into Sects or Clans and their embodiment as a permanent military cops and for other purposes' (*Falmouth Post* December 8, 1865).
25. This referred to sticks, pikes and old muskets.
26. According to Captain Algernon de Horsey, Captain of the *Wolverine* (Royal Commission 1866, 206).
27. The *Gleaner* November 15, 1865, put the number of Maroons at 249, while the *Colonial Standard* November 15, 1865, stated that the number of Maroons in the procession amounted to 290, of which 163 were from Moore Town and 57 from Scott's Hall.
28. The November 15, 1865 issue of the *Colonial Standard* stated that each Maroon 'carried a rifle and side arm, with a canvas wallet across the shoulder.' Meanwhile, the *Gleaner* November 15, 1865, gave a more extensive and detailed description of the Maroons' appearance.
29. Among these merchants were Captain William Astwood, Captain Altamont DeCordova, 1st Lieutenant Charles Levy and Captain Arnold Malabre.
30. The trip to Accompong was deliberately organised by the authorities as an instrument to warn and to intimidate the black population across the island of the dire consequences they would encounter should they express any public indignation at the suppression or try in any way to repeat October 11, 1865.
31. How similar this statement is compared to the stereotype of white racist thought expressed by John Parry who 'saw the dangerous tendency of any association which had for its objects the discussion of social or political matters among a class of ignorant people, unable to judge for themselves, but ready to be guided by the evil counsels of designing men' (Royal Commission 1866, 866).
32. This meeting took place at Stony Gut according to Matthew Cresser who was present against his will. He was detained at Chigoe Foot Market by men ordered by Dacres, one of Bogle's deputies, on October 12, 1865 and taken to Stony Gut.

12 The Nature of the 'Negro Character' Determined the 'Character of Negro Insurrections':
The Philosophical and Ideological Justifications for the Suppression of the 'Morant Bay Rebellion'

> I cannot accept the negro as the equal of an English-man, nor admit that a negro insurrection and an English insurrection ought to be treated in the same way...if the falling into the hands of a Jamaican negro be a different thing from falling into the hands of an Englishman, then the conclusion is self-evident, that we are justified in going further to prevent the one calamity, than to prevent the other.
>
> – *John Tyndall*

The principal arguments that were advanced to support the savagery Eyre performed in Jamaica were derived from a body of ideas created and developed by Europeans since the sixteenth century to justify the enslavement and indefinite subjection of the black race by the white race. That body of ideas contended that the basis for and nature of the Morant Bay outbreak emanated from the ontology of the African who was from the beginning of human existence, an innately inferior being endowed with characteristics which made him/her a compulsively irrational insurrectionist, who could only be useful to civilisation if kept in a constant state of dystopian subjection by the civilising power of the European. Accordingly, legal writer and journalist William Francis Finlason noted that the 'causes...which had led to the insurrection were of long growth and operation, and widely spread and deeply seated in the whole character and condition of the Negro race' (Finlason Justice 1868, xxiii).

This theory held that from ancient time the African was 'the lowest man known to...civilisation' (Pim 1866, 3), who remained unchanged up to the time he revolted in Jamaica in 1865. He was incapable of changing what Bedford Pim called the African's 'innate cruelty...,his sensuality, his brutality under the influence of superstition or when excited or misled, his inbred sloth – in short, the almost total absence of those attributes which enable other races of mankind to advance in civilisation' (5). The innately cruel, revengeful, and brutal psychology assigned to the African by European intellectuals was said by them to be responsible for the diabolic nature of African insurrection and hence the justification for the prompt and energetic suppression in 1865.

Archibald Alison's view, that 'the insurrection of slaves is the most dreadful of all commotions' (qtd in Finlason 1868, vi 'Justice'), alluded to that racist contention. John Tyndall, eminent physicist, philosopher, professor and member of the Eyre Defence Aid Fund, was even more direct in his appraisal of black insurrections when he said at a public meeting in support of Eyre:

> I cannot accept the negro as the equal of an English-man, nor admit that a negro insurrection and an English insurrection ought to be treated in the same way...if the falling into the hands of a Jamaican negro be a different thing from falling into the hands of an Englishman, then the conclusion is self-evident, that we are justified in going further to prevent the one calamity, than to prevent the other (Finlason 1868, 368aaa, 'History').

Of course, Tyndall, Alison, Pim and others like them were right in asserting that back insurrections were different from white insurrections, but not for the racist reasons they gave. Black insurrectionists were different not because of their so-called uncivilised, savage traits, or their 'truly savage want of veneration for God or man', but primarily because the nature of their oppression and subjection by the white race rendered the objects of their outbreak different from whites who revolted against whites. In the first place, this difference was ontological. The African had to constantly assert his/her existence as a human being; an existence denied him/her by the European. This denial profoundly shaped the European sense of self and ontological compass.

Having established in thought that the nature of the 'Negro character' determined the character of 'Negro insurrections', these intellectuals proceeded on that basis to advance the theory that the 'historic antecedents' of the 'Morant Bay Rebellion' were proof enough to support the actions of Edward Eyre in Jamaica, because, even if the October outbreak were a 'local riot', a 'Negro rebellion is necessarily, sooner or later, a war of extermination'

The Nature of the 'Negro Character' Determined the 'Character of Negro Insurrections'

of white people (Finlason 1868, vi 'Justice'). Since the 'Negro rebellion is necessarily a war of extermination,' preventative and retaliatory measures like those employed by Eyre were deemed to be an appropriate response to the theoretical objects of black revolt against white people. The Africans were to be punished not on the basis of what they did, but more importantly, for what they might have done or theoretically expected to do. Hence Tyndall's formulation in Eyre's defence:

> The height and span of a bridge...must be regulated with reference to the larger floods, and the action of Governor Eyre had to be determined, not by the hypothesis of a local riot, but by the contemplation of the calamities which were certain to overwhelm the whole island if the insurrection were permitted to expand (Hume 1867, 274).

A main tenet of the ideas justifying the suppression of the Morant Bay outbreak was thus based on a racist epistemology of 'Negro rebellion'. In the raging ideological debate over the suppression,[1] advocates of the suppression drew heavily on works dealing with the history of black insurrections or the 'historical antecedents' of the Morant Bay War for arguments to support Eyre. The works most quoted by them were Archibald Alison's *History of Europe*, and Bryan Edwards's *History of the West Indies*, while the example most used to denote the character of black revolts was the Haitian Revolution as portrayed in Alison and Edwards.

The object of creating a theory of black insurrection was to prove several things. In the first place, the suppressionists were out to prove that the African who first rebelled against the European in the African diaspora was no different in natural cruelty and wickedness from the African who took to arms at Morant Bay in the second half of the nineteenth century. Hamilton Hume said as much in his defence of Eyre. He said, 'what the Negro was in 1795 so he is now' (113).[2] Hume's 1795 reference was the Haitian Revolution, while his 'now' was in reference to Morant Bay.

John Tyndall expressed similar views. Quoting Alison, he said African Jamaicans were people of the same 'race and temper' as those who 'marched with spiked infants on their spears instead of colours', 'sawed asunder the male prisoners, and violated the females on the dead bodies of their husbands' in Haiti in 1795 (269). Tyndall, like most of the intellectual defenders of Eyre, was of the view that the history of Black insurrections, 'written without reference to the Jamaica insurrection' was sufficient enough to justify the Governor's actions in Jamaica.

Secondly, the advocates of the suppression were seeking to prove that the example of black insurrections, especially the most feared of them all, the Haitian Revolution, deeply inspired Africans in Jamaica to fight for the establishment of a similar regime in the neighbouring British colony. They argued that the Jamaican outbreak would sooner rather than later replicate the Haitian Revolution if Eyre had not acted decisively to put it down. They argued that 'Jamaica is only one day's sail from St Domingo, where the horrors of negro insurrections had…achieved not only emancipation but independence, and had established a Negro state, which has ever since been a standing temptation to the blacks in Jamaica, and a standing terror to the Whites' (Finlason 1868, vi 'Justice').[3]

They also argued that where Africans disproportionately outnumbered Europeans in a colony, as was the case in St Domingue (Haiti), the chances of black unrest leading to a war of extermination of the ruling race were greatest and hence the need for colonial governors to act quickly and decisively with maximum terror to compensate for smallness in numbers and thus prevent the creation of another Haitian state of nature. Hence, no matter how small and localised a black Jamaican outbreak was, the logic of the theory of a preponderant African population required the maximum use of European terror to extinguish it before it necessarily became a war of extermination.

> Jamaica is the only negro colony where the number of negroes equals those in St. Domingo, and where the disproportion had even become greater. In St. Domingo, as in Jamaica, the negroes were near half a million in number, but the whites in the former colony were at least twice as numerous. The case of Jamaica, therefore, was of far greater peril (Finlason 1868, vi 'Justice').

Thirdly, the intellectual backers of Eyre were keen to prove that in order to ensure the successful suppression of the black insurrection, whites would need to use the proven methods employed by Europeans in the past to confront and defeat 'negro rebellions'. Those methods, it was argued, were understood and used by Eyre, in 1865, in the interest of Britain and civilisation. Some of those methods were alluded to by Pim when he commented on the means used by 'Colonel Spragge' in putting down the Tacky (Taki) led anti-slavery insurrection in St Mary, Jamaica in 1760: 'the prisoners, being tried and found guilty of rebellion, were put to death by a variety of tortures. Some were hanged, some beheaded, some burned, and some fixed alive upon gibbets' (Pim 1866, 48).

Pim was more explicit in expounding the necessity for Eyre's methods when he spoke about the objects of 'the first insurrection of the blacks' in the diaspora and its suppression.

The Nature of the 'Negro Character' Determined the
'Character of Negro Insurrections'

> In 1530, the first insurrection of the blacks occurred in Venezuela, and Herrera says their intention was to murder every white man, while the women were to be apportioned to the rebels. A certain Captain Santiago de Lassada, however, was equal to the emergency, and, with a vigour similar to that of Governor Eyre, stamped out the revolt (18).[4]

Fourthly, the supporters of the suppression were eager to prove that 'a negro rebellion' was nothing but 'a war of extermination'. The characterisation of black revolts as 'necessarily a war of extermination' ruled out any real or logical reason for any of those outbreaks to be categorised as a 'local riot' and hence rejected the argument that the amount of force employed against the black masses was excessive and criminal.

In Defence of Euro-Patriarchal Masculinity

When the intellectual supporters of the suppression spoke of black insurrection being 'a war of extermination', they usually meant a war waged by African men with the object of exterminating white men while reserving the white women as a group for a fate in which, according to Finlason, 'death would have been a mercy'. The fate that these intellectuals deemed to be worse than death was black men having sexual intercourse with and control over white women, should the Africans overthrow European patriarchal power. The *Colonial Standard* (October 16, 1865) noted, for example, that 'the slaughter of all the male portion of the white population and the children, and the partition among themselves of the lands and of the women' represented the principal aims of the outbreak in 1865. That newspaper asserted that the 'plan of the rebels is to murder all the white and coloured men first, then the children, and to keep the women as servants and for their own pleasure.'

The theory of the fate of European women under the regime of a black patriarchy arose as far back as the 1530 anti-slavery insurrection in Venezuela. Then, one of the two principal reasons advanced to support Captain Santiago de Lassada's use of excessive force to put down the outbreak was that he saved the dignity of Spanish women from black rebels. In the logic of suppressing black insurrection, excessive force was always deemed to be appropriate force.

Over 335 years later, Eyre was credited by Tyndall and others for saving 'the honour of 7000 British women, from the murder and the lust of black savages' in Jamaica (Hume 1867, 272). Tyndall held that the English women in Jamaica were saved 'from a fate which is left unexpressed by the term dishonour' (284).

Where Lassada or Eyre's methods were not employed, it was argued that the consequences for white women were worse than death. In Haiti, where the 'Paris Revolutionary Government's' declaration of liberty for blacks turned Africans into 'devils', the 'horrors inflicted on the women exceeded anything known even in the annals of Christian ferocity' (Finlason 1868, vi 'Justice'). According to Alison, 'virgins were immolated on the altar' (vi). He said black Haitian men 'violated the females on the dead bodies of their husbands' (Hume 1867, 113).

Bryan Edwards's views were similar to Alison's; he said the women 'were devoted to a more horrid fate' than white men 'and were carried away captives by assassins' (Finlason Justice X). He intimated that:

> On some few estates, indeed, the lives of the women were spared, but they were reserved only to gratify the brutal appetites of the ruffians, and many of them suffered violation on the dead bodies of their husbands and fathers (Finlason 1868, x 'Justice').

Edwards further said: 'Young women of all ranks were first violated by a whole troop of barbarians, and then gradually put to death. Some of them were indeed reserved for the further gratification of the lust of the savages' (x).

The harrowing descriptions of the sexual conquest and subjection of European women by African men, were only possible if Africans were allowed any semblance of a chance to remove themselves from the system of control that the Europeans designed for Africans when they did them the favour of removing them from what Georg Hegel called their 'zoological garden' in which they 'lived in an animal condition of innocence' (Eze 1997, 128). It was not good enough to remove Africans from the state of nature if the place designed for them in the European state of man (or the rational state), was not constantly monitored by whiteness, because the inherent traits of the Africans which prevented them from existing in the rational state on their own accord will reassert themselves, and cast them back into the state of nature.

It was little wonder therefore, that Eyre's intellectual backers concurred with Alison that 'The incipient civilization of the negro has been arrested by his emancipation with the cessation of forced labour, the tastes and habits which spring from and compensate it have disappeared, and savage habits and pleasures have resumed their ascendency over the sable race' (Pim 1866, 56).

One of the traits and habits which emancipation reawakened unblushingly in African Jamaicans in 1865, was what Hegel described decades before as

The Nature of the 'Negro Character' Determined the 'Character of Negro Insurrections'

'the enormous energy of sensuous arbitrariness which dominates their lives' so that 'morality has no determinate influence upon them' (Eze 1997, 142). This 'enormous energy of sensuous arbitrariness' was reasserting itself in Myaal/Native Baptist/Revival in an 'almost entirely unrestrained' manner, noted William Gardner. The result of all of this was 'rebellion' in the logic and explicit discourses of the suppression.

In the philosophy of Pim, Hume and Alison no attempt by Africans to be free and sovereign was just and rational, since such would indicate a resumption of their 'savage habits and pleasures' and a weakening of the benefits of the rational state of men on their identity. 'Thus, any attempt by the African man to be sovereign, equal and visible was viewed by white masculinity as a mission to rape white women, a mission realisable only with the extermination of the white man' (Hutton 2014, 30).

Real freedom for Africans then was not freedom from European control, but freedom from themselves, from their ontological state of nature, from the inherent flaws in their state of existence or being for which they lacked the agential capacity to overcome. European control in perpetuity was thus necessary to assist Africans to gradually manage their existential disabilities to the extent to which they could be useful in the state of man. Their innate flaws were to be found in their pathologically smaller brain conjoined with their pathologically larger genitalia.[5]

Clothed in the skin of primitive blackness, these and other signatures of humanity's cul-de-sac rendered the black body as the ontology of criminality, debauchery, profanity, irrationality, imprudence, impudence, ugliness, nastiness and laziness – the antithesis of civility, rationality, ingenuity, citizenship, independence, beauty and probity. These disabilities were antithetical to the making of civilisation (history) in general and political agency in particular.

In this logic, Africans had to be kept in a constant state of regimentation and proscription, even if slavery ended. Their innate traits which prevented them from exiting the state of nature on their own accord or staying in the European state of man similarly, must be ontologically restrained constantly. These traits denoted the character of 'Negro insurrections' which consequently required swift decisive force, to put them down, even if at first they appeared inconsequential, since they must necessarily lead to the extermination of white people, or more precisely, white men and the sexual enslavement of white women.

The plantocrats did not seem so hurt, indeed, so traumatised by other European men revolting against them and subjecting their women to sexual violation and control, because, even if those white men were not regarded as class equals by their opponents, they were certainly seen as racially equal. Rather than seeing English women falling into the hands of African men, or indeed, rather than having their pride hurt by black men having sexual relations with white women, thereby framing an equality with white men, Tyndall suggested the appropriateness of British men in Jamaica following the example of British officers in India if they were faced with defeat.

> I approve of the conduct of those British officers in India who shot their wives before blowing themselves to pieces, rather than allow what they loved and honoured to fall into the hands of the Sepoys. I should not approve of the shooting of wives through the fear of prospective insult in the case of an English insurrection (Hume 1867, 283).

Here, falling into the hands of the Sepoys was akin to falling into the hands of the Africans.

Of course, the actions of British officers and the ideology of plantation advocates were not just about the concern of their 'loved and honoured' women. Obviously, the so-called inherent inferiority of the African male made the character and effect of the black male sex complex different from the white man's as it made the character of 'Negro insurrection' different from 'white insurrection'.

Of all the power relations in plantation society, the one that appeared to have invoked the highest degree of emotion in the ruling patriarchy was the one in which the prospect of black men having sexual control over white women, the only receptacles for the regeneration of the European race and civilisation, was contemplated. Indeed, while it can be successfully argued that economic relation constituted the principal relation and primary source for other power relations in colonial society, sexual relation invoked the deepest emotion in the white patriarchy because it was considered to be at the heart of the existence and continued supremacy of the European over the African, the 'civilised' over the 'uncivilised', light over darkness.

The prospect of black males having sexual control over the women who were required to reproduce the race in which white men stood supreme and wielded power over the non-European world seemed to have triggered a visceral response in the racist patriarchy about its existential viability. It was, therefore, not hard to figure out why racist thinkers like Tyndall would prefer their 'loved and honoured' women to fall into the hands of white insurrectionists. Obviously, the sexual control of white insurrectionists over women of their own race was not considered a threat to or an invasion of the source from which the white race in general, and the European male in particular, were conceived, developed and given birth. To support that view,

The Nature of the 'Negro Character' Determined the 'Character of Negro Insurrections'

Tyndall reminded his audience of 'the story of the Sabine girls who were treacherously carried away by the Roman youth, and who, afterwards, when their fathers had collected to avenge the insult, threw themselves between the combatants, offering themselves to the spears of both' (283–84).

With this in mind, Tyndall asked 'the women of England' and 'the wives and daughters of our antagonists, whether it is likely the conduct of the Sabine maidens would have been the same had Jamaica negroes played the part of the Roman youth?' (284).[6] The antagonists of which Tyndall spoke above, were persons opposed to Eyre, especially those in the Jamaica Committee and their supporters.

The European patriarchal conception of the African as an inherent sensual being bespoke a fear of white men that white women might enjoy sexual intercourse with black men, an enjoyment that might ultimately lead to the destabilisation of the colonial order by undermining the power and authority of the white male. The logic of this theory was based on the notion that woman was the weaker sex, hence the European women constituted the weak link in the defence of the white race against the 'savage' black race and, if she could be conquered by the black man, the conquest of the European would be assured.

The African was the embodiment of uncensored/uncultured/uncivilised sexuality, the ontology of the arbitrary sexual will. He was the undiluted source of a peculiar kind of intense, seductive pleasure linked to the forbidden, the spirit(s) of the dark, the evil, sinful and irrational. Sensuality, like laziness and cruelty, was thus regarded as an innate feature of the African, which feature reasserted itself unblushingly whenever white society lost control and power over the black man. It was precisely this belief which led Hume to conclude that 'Emancipation had made him [the African] more lazy more cunning, more sensual, more profligate, more prone to mischief, and more dangerous' (113–14).

Africans Lacked the Capacity to Intellectualise Freedom

Colonial Plantation intellectuals also gave another important reason for supporting Eyre's handling of the outbreak. They argued that the outbreak had no legitimacy in law and natural motivation since the blacks did not and could not revolt on their own account but were led to do so by people who were inherently superior to them. The assumption was the same as discussed earlier: the inability of the African to extricate himself from the state of nature or the European state of man on his own accord, owing to the inherent flaws in his state of being which rendered him incapable of political agency. Hence, according to Edward Eyre, the outbreak was as a result of 'the misapprehensions and misrepresentations of pseudo-philanthropists in England and in this country [Jamaica]' (*Gleaner* November 8, 1865). Similarly, the *Gleaner* (October 20, 1865) stated:

> It is also apparent that "some mastermind" has to do with it as far as the planning goes. The Rebels seem to be acting "systematically," a strange fact, when we know that among themselves nothing like system could be suggested, much more acted upon.

The logic here is clear: there were some white people (pseudo-philanthropists) and some exceptional near white people, such as George William Gordon, who constituted the cognitive and intellectual foundations of the 'Morant Bay Rebellion' because, by themselves, black people were incapable of conceptualising freedom, rights, justice and sovereignty, since they lacked the cognitive and intellectual capacity to do so. Consequently, the usefulness of Africans to themselves and humankind as a whole rested not with guaranteeing them rights, freedom, justice and sovereignty, but in subjecting them to a regime of coercion in order to suppress their innate savage traits and impose on them a personality acceptable to the European state of man. With this regime of coercion, the African 'labours well, and becomes civilised and humanised to the extent of his small powers' (Pim 1866, 7). Without that regime the African 'becomes degraded, debauched, and depraved' (7). With that regime, he/she became 'capable of attachment' to his/her European master in much the same way a dog became attached to its master. Using this racist ideological construct, Anthony Trollope wrote in praise of the attached African Jamaican six years before the Morant Bay outbreak:

> We have all had dogs whom, we have well used, and have prided ourselves on their fidelity. We have seen them to be wretched when they loose (sic) us for a moment, and have smiled at their joy when they again discover us. We have noted their patience as they wait for food from the hand they know will feed them. We have seen with delight how their love for us glistens in their eyes. We trust them with our children as the safest playmates, and teach them in mocking sport the tricks of humanity. In return for this, the dear brutes give us all their hearts, but it is not given in gratitude; and they abstain with all their power from injury and offence, but they do not abstain from judgment. Let his master ill use his dog ever so cruelly, yet the animal has no anger against him when the pain is over. Let a stranger save him from such ill usage, and he has no thankfulness after the moment. Affection and fidelity are things of custom with him (Trollope 1860, 60–61).

The Nature of the 'Negro Character' Determined the 'Character of Negro Insurrections'

Six years later, the African Jamaican was back to his/her old savage self, according to the advocates of Edward Eyre. He/she revolted because the regime of coercion which was central to the creation and maintenance of the plantation state as well as the creation and maintenance of a subservient African personality was undermined by the notions of freedom, rights, and justice inherent in the abolition of slavery and the struggles to reform post-slavery society. Accordingly, Pim noted that the Africans:

> are capable of strong and earnest attachments to their superiors, and I honestly believe that if it were not for the pernicious influence so fatally exercised upon them by unscrupulous demagogues, by well-intentioned, but rash and enthusiastic philanthropists, but, above all, by those who, with diabolical hypocrisy, use religion as a cloak to carry out their levelling principles – to sow those seeds of hatred and disunion which produce bitter fruit, and so often lead to those terrible colonial tragedies, such as that recently enacted at Morant Bay,... the black man, as he exists in the West Indies, would develop into a good, and even an industrious citizen (Pim 1866, 56).

This so-called 'industrious citizen' of whom Pim spoke and whose 'fidelity' Trollope praise, was the product of perpetual white racist violence. The theory of violence against blacks was an indispensable tenet of plantation thought because 'the incipient civilization of the negro' could not be made industrious and loyal without subjecting the African to a perpetual regime of violence to tame his savage habits.

If the imposition of violence on blacks were essential to the normal day to day relationship between the African and European, how much so was violence needed to control black insurrectionists? The innate cruelty and barbarism that colonial plantation political theorists accused blacks of were exactly the same things that Europeans were practising against Africans. By creating an ideology demonising blacks, the whites were by the same token creating the reasons for behaving like the 'Negro' they created with their racist mind and methods of coercion. The essence of this creation, its raison d'être, was captured by US Navy Commander Andrew Hull Foote who wrote the following in 1854:

> if all that negroes of all generations have ever done were to be obliterated from recollection for ever, the world would lose no great truth, no profitable art, no exemplary form of life. The loss of all that is African would offer no memorable deduction from anything but the earth's black catalogue of crimes (Pim 1866, 9).

By relating to Africans on the basis of the above racist construct, Governor Eyre could commit no crime against African Jamaicans, and yet, the tradition of 'civilised' Europe which he represented, committed some of the most wanton, savage, barbarous and gruesome acts of cruelty ever visited on the Jamaican people.

Notes

1. A consequence of the Morant Bay outbreak and its suppression was the division of British society into two camps; one supporting the position of Edward John Eyre and the other opposing it. Organisationally, the division of British society found expression in the formation of the Jamaica Committee and the Eyre Defence Aid Fund. On the side of the Jamaica Committee were world renowned Utilitarian philosopher and Member of Parliament, John Stuart Mill, celebrated scientists Charles Darwin and Thomas Huxley, sociologist Herbert Spencer and left wing parliamentarian John Bright. On the side of Eyre were some of Britain's eminent men of letters – Thomas Carlyle, John Ruskin and Charles Dickens, Henry Kingsley and Lord Tennyson.

   Disagreements over the handling of the Morant Bay affairs led to one of the biggest and most intense ideological debate to envelope Britain since that country abolished slavery in 1834. For more read Bernard Semmel, *Jamaican Blood Victorian Conscience: The Governor Eyre Controversy* (West Port, Connecticut: Greenwood Press, 1962); Peter Zoller, 'A Study of Carlyle, Ruskin, Mill and Huxley.' PhD Dissertation, Claremont Graduate School, 1979; W[illiam] F[rancis] Finlason, *History of the Jamaica Case* (London, 1868) and John Gorrie, *Illustrations of Martial Law in Jamaica* (London, 1867).

2. Hamilton Hume (1797–1873) was the secretary of the Eyre Defence Aid Fund, an Australian explorer and a Fellow of the Royal Geographical Society.

3. Two specific ways in which this 'standing temptation' were said to have revealed themselves were in the constitutional provisions of the Haitian state which 'exclude the whites from any rights whatever', while opening up the country to the 'black man, who becomes a citizen at once' (Pim 1866, 50) and the 'sojourn' amongst Jamaicans of 'Haytian refugees – a black emperor, dukes, counts, generals, and colonels, who kept up quite an excitement by the expenditure of their ill-gotten wealth, naturally make each negro aspire to similar honours' (49).

4. José Luciano Franco noted that the 'first recorded black slave insurrection took place in Santo Domingo on December 26, 1522.' See John Henrik Clarke, 'African Cultural Continuity and Slave Revolts', in *African Studies Association of the West Indies*, Bulletin No. 8, Kingston, Jamaica 1976.

5. For more on the anti-black racist theory of black sexuality and its social, political and ontological implications, read Clinton Hutton, 'The Gyalification of Man: The Expression of Male-Male Conflict in Jamaica and the Roots of Homoeroticism in the Political Ideology, Ontology and Praxis of White Supremacy', *Caribbean*

Quarterly 60, no. 4 (December 2014): 21–45.

6. The legend of the wholesale kidnapping and raping of the Sabine women by Roman soldiers on orders from Romulus, the Roman king, as a strategy for populating the newly founded city state of Rome, was told by ancient writers such as Titus Livius, Ovid, Marcus Tullius Cicero, Dionysius and Plutarch of Chaeronea, a Greek philosopher who lived in the first century A.D. The Sabines were invited by Romulus to festivities in Rome to celebrate its founding around the eight century B.C. However, these festivities were an excuse to deliberately commit mass rape and control over the Sabine women.

   This led to the Sabine men going to war against the Romans. According to this legend, the Sabine women threw themselves and their children between the armies of their fathers and the Romans, their rapists cum husbands, to end the war. However, the Sabines were defeated, or rather, reconciled with the Romans, who went on to build a mighty empire.

   This ancestral story became an important narrative in the ontological framing of European masculinity, including the ideology of marriage and gender relations in the Columbian age and, as can be seen from Tyndall's use, justification to exterminate African Jamaican men in 1865. Diane Wolfthal noted that in Italy 'in the fourteenth through the seventeenth centuries', the story of the rape of the Sabine women 'was viewed as a heroic, patriotic act'. She said the 'Sabine women were revered as the mothers of the first Romans'. She further stated that their 'story adorned wedding banners, marriage chests, and the apartments of noblewomen'. Moreover, the 'name Talassius, that of a Roman who obtained an especially beautiful Sabine, became a wedding motto. The Sabine legend was considered essential to the founding of Roman family life and the future of the nation' (See *www.oneonta.edu/faculty/farberas/arth/arth200/Body/Heroic_Rape.html*). Excerpts from Diane Wolfthal Images of Rape... (Accessed 07/05/15).

   From the beginning of the Columbian age to the twentieth century, the rape of the Sabine women was an enduring theme in Western European art. These works of art seemed to almost always promote the 'sanitisation' and 'aestheticisation' of rape. Among the artists who painted or sculpted the rape of the Sabine women were Domenico Morone, 1490; Giovnni da Bologna, 1583; Peter Paul Rubens, 1635; Nicolas Poussin, 1637; and Jacques-Louis David, 1796.

References

Alleyne, Mervyn. 1988. *Roots of Jamaican Culture*. London: Pluto Press.
Anderson, William Wemyss. 1851. *Jamaica and the Americans*. New York.
Awolalu, J. Omosade. 1996. *Yoruba Beliefs & Sacrificial Rites*. New York: Athelia Henrietta Press, Inc.
———, and P. Adelumo Dopamu. 1979. *West African Traditional Religion*. Ibadan: Onibonoje Press & Book Industries (Nig.) Ltd.
Barnes, Sandra T., ed. 1997. *Africa's Ogun: Old World and New*. Bloomington and Indianapolis: Indiana University Press.
Barrett, Leonard E. 1977. *The Rastafarians: The Dreadlocks of Jamaica*. Kingston: Sangster's Book Stores in association with Heinemann.
Beckwith, Martha Warren. (1929) 1969. *Black Roadways: A Study of Jamaican Folk Life*. New York: Negro Universities Press.
Besson, Jean. 1995. Religion as Resistance in Jamaican Peasant Life: The Baptist Church, Revival Worldview and Rastafari Movement. In *Rastafari and Other African-Caribbean Worldviews*, ed. Barry Chevannes. New Brunswick, NJ: Rutgers University Press.
Bigelow, John. 1851. *Jamaica in 1850*. New York and London.
Bleby, Henry. 1866. *The Reign of Terror*. London.
Brodber, Erna. 1986. Afro-Jamaican Women of the Turn of the Century. *Social and Economic Studies* 35, no. 3 (September).
Brown, Karen McCarthy. 1995. Serving the Spirits: The Ritual Economy of Haitian Vodou. In *Sacred Arts of Haitian Vodou*, ed. Donald J. Cosentino. Los Angeles: UCLA Fowler Museum of Cultural History.
Bryan, Patrick. 1973. Émigrés, Conflict and Reconciliation: The French Émigrés in Nineteenth Century Jamaica. *Jamaica Journal* 7, no. 3 (September).
Campbell, Mavis C. 1990. *The Maroons of Jamaica 1655–1796: A History of Resistance, Collaboration & Betrayal*. Trenton, NJ: Africa World Press, Inc.
Carlyle, Thomas. 1971. In *The Nigger Question: The Negro Question*. Eugene R. August, ed. New York: Appleton-Century-Crofts.
Carnegie, Charles V., ed. 1987. *Afro-Caribbean Villages in Historical Perspective*. Jamaica: African-Caribbean Institute of Jamaica.
Chevannes, Alston [Barry]. 1971. Jamaican Lower Class Religion: Struggles Against Oppression. MSc Thesis, University of the West Indies.
Chevannes, Barry, ed. 1995. *Rastafari and Other African-Caribbean Worldviews*. 1998. New Brunswick, NJ: Rutgers University Press.
———. 1998. *Rastafari: Roots and Ideology*. Barbados. Jamaica. Trinidad: Syracuse University Press and The University of the West Indies Press.
———. 2006. *Betwix and Between: Explorations in an African-Caribbean Mindscape*. Kingston: Ian Randle Publishers.

Clarke, John Henrik. 1976. African Cultural Continuity and Slave Revolts. In *African Studies Association of the West Indies*. Bulletin No. 8.

Clerk, Astley. 1934. The Music and Song-words of Jamaica. No. 3. Kingston.

Colonial Standard and Jamaica Despatch. March 2, 1865–August 8, 1866.

Curtin, Philip D. 1955. *Two Jamaicas: The Role of Ideas in a Tropical Colony, 1830–1865*. Cambridge: Harvard University Press.

D'Costa, Jean, and Barbara Lalla, eds. 1989. *Voices in Exile: Jamaican Texts of the 18th and 19th Centuries*. Tuscaloosa and London: The University of Alabama Press.

Dick, Devon. 2009. *The Cross and the Machete: Native Baptists of Jamaica – Identity, Ministry and Legacy*. Kingston: Ian Randle Publishers.

Diop, Cheik Anta. 1952. *The Cultural Unity of Black Africa*. Paris: Presence Africaine (orig. pub. 1959).

Duncker, Sheila. 1856. The Free Coloured and Their Fight for Civil Rights in Jamaica 1800–1830. MA Thesis. London University.

Equiano, Alaudah. 1987. The Interesting Narratives of the Life of Olaudah Equiano or Gustavus Vassa, the African. In *Classic Slave Narratives*, ed. Henry Louis Gates, Jr. New York: A Mentor Book.

Eyre, Governor [Edward]. (1866) 1971. *Papers Laid Before the Royal Commission of Inquiry*. Shannon: Irish University Press.

Eze, Emmanuel Chukwudi, ed. 1997. *Race and the Enlightenment: A Reader*. Cambridge, Massachusetts and Oxford: Blackwell Publishers.

Falmouth Post and Jamaica General Advertiser. February 25, 1848–December 8, 1865.

Fick, Carolyn E. (1990) 1994. *The Making of Haiti: The Saint Domingue Revolution from Below*. Knoxville: The University of Tennessee Press (orig. pub. .

Finlason, W[illiam] F[rancis]. 1868. *Justice to a Colonial Governor: Or Some Consideration of the Case of Mr. Eyre Containing the Substance of All the Documents, Discussions, and Proceedings Relating Thereto*. London.

———. 1868. *History of the Jamaica Case*. London.

Fletcher, Duncan. 1867. *Personal Recollections of the Honourable George W. Gordon*. London.

Foner, Philip S., ed. 1972. *The Voice of Black America: Major Speeches by Negroes in the United States, 1797–1971*. New York: Simon and Schuster.

Gall, James, ed. 1879. *Who's Who 1879–80*. Jamaica.

Gibson, Kean. 2001. *Comfa Religion and Creole Language in a Caribbean Community*. New York: State University of New York Press.

Gleaner and DeCordova's Advertising Sheet. September 24, 1865–November 25, 1865.

Gorrie, John. 1867. *Illustrations of Martial Law in Jamaica*. London.

Great Britain. (1866) 1966. Report of the Jamaica Royal Commission, 1866 Part I: Minutes of Evidence and Appendix. Shannon: Irish University Press.

———. (1866) 1966. Report of the Jamaica Royal Commission, 1866 Part II: Minutes of Evidence and Appendix. Shannon: Irish University Press.

Hall, Douglas. 1959. *Free Jamaica 1838–1865: An Economic History*. New Haven: Yale University Press.

References

Harper's. 1872. *Harper's New Monthly Magazine* XLIV, no. CCLXII (March).
Hart, Ansell. n.d. *The Life of George William Gordon*. Jamaica: Institute of Jamaica.
Hart, Richard. 1974. *The Origin and Development of the People of Jamaica* (1952). Montreal: International Caribbean Service Bureau.
———. 1980. *Slaves Who Abolished Slavery: Volume 1 Blacks in Bondage*. Kingston: Institute of Social and Economic Research, University of the West Indies.
———. 1985. *Slaves Who Abolished Slavery: Volume 2 Blacks in Rebellion*. Kingston: Institute of Social and Economic Research, University of the West Indies.
Harvey, Thomas, and William Brewin. 1867. *Jamaica in 1866*. London.
Henriques, Fernando. (1933) 1968. *Family and colour in Jamaica*. London: MacGibbon and Kee.
———. 1974. *Children of Caliban: Miscegenation*. London: Secker & Warburg.
Heuman, Gad J. 1981. *Between Black and White: Race Politics, and the Free Coloreds in Jamaica, 1792–1865*. Westport, CT: Greenwood Press.
Higman, B.W. 1980. African and Creole Slave Family in Trinidad. In *Africa and the Caribbean: The Legacies of a Link*, ed. Margaret E. Crahan and Franklin W. Knight. Boston and London: Johns Hopkins University Press.
———. 1994. *'The Killing Time': The Morant Bay Rebellion in Jamaica*. London: MacMillan Caribbean.
———, ed. 1980. *The Jamaican Censuses of 1844 and 1861. A New Edition derived from the Manuscript and Printed Schedules in the Jamaica Archives*. Social History Project. Jamaica: Department of History, University of the West Indies.
Hume, Hamilton. 1867. *The Life of Edward John Eyre, Late Governor of Jamaica*. London.
Hutton, Clinton. 2005. *The Logic & Historical Significance of the Haitian Revolution & the Cosmological Roots of Haitian Freedom*. Kingston: Arawak Publications.
———. 2007. The Creative Ethos of the African Diaspora: Performance Aesthetics and the Fight for Freedom and Identity. *Caribbean Quarterly* 53, nos. 1–2 (March–June).
———. 2009. The Revival Table: Feasting with the Ancestors and Spirits. *Jamaica Journal* 32, nos. 1–2 (August).
———. 2014. The Gyalification of Man: The Expression of Male-Male Conflict in Jamaica and the Roots of Homoeroticism in the Political Ideology, Ontology and Praxis of White Supremacy. *Caribbean Quarterly* 60, no. 4. (December).
Jamaica. 'C' MDCCCLXIV. *Laws of Jamaica, Chapt. 1 of 1847 to Chapt. 45 of 1855*. Jamaica.
———. 1846/1865MDCCCLXIV. *Laws of Jamaica, Chapts. 1–45 of 1864–1865*. Jamaica
———. 1863/1864 MDCCCLXIV. *Laws of Jamaica, 1863–1864, Chapt.7*. Jamaica.
———. 1863. *Parliamentary Debates of Jamaica* Vol. VIII. Comprising the Session Commencing on the 24th Day of March 1863, and Terminating on the 6th Day of May 1863. Kingston.
———. 1865. *Parliamentary Debates of Jamaica* Vol. IX. Comprising the Session

Commencing on the 27th Day of October 1863, and Terminating on the 22nd Day of February 1864. Spanish Town.

———. 1859. *Laws of Jamaica, 1858–1859*. Jamaica.

———. 1877. *Laws of Jamaica, Vol. IV. 1857–1865*. Jamaica.

———. 1877. *Laws of Jamaica, 1858–1859*. Jamaica.

———. 1912. *Laws of Jamaica, Vol. IV. 1857–1865. (1889)*. Jamaica.

Jamaica Committee. 1866. *Jamaica Paper No1. Facts and Documents Relating to the Alleged Rebellion in Jamaica and the Measures of Repression Including Notes of the Trial of Mr. Gordon*. London.

Jamaica Despatch and Kingston Chronicle. 1838. August 17.

Jamaica Information Service. 'C' 1965. *The Morant Bay Rebellion*. Kingston: Jamaica Information Service.

Jamaica Tribune. 1865. October 18 and October 23.

Kanogo, Tabitha. 1987. *Squatters & the Roots of Mau Mau*. London. Nairobi. Athens, Ohio: James Currey, Heinemann Kenya and Ohio University Press.

Lan, David. 1985. *Guns & Rain: Guerrillas & Spirit Mediums in Zimbabwe*. London. Berkeley and Los Angeles: James Currey and University of California Press.

Livingstone, W.P. 1899. *Black Jamaica: A Study in Evolution*. Fleet Street, E.C.

Locke, John. 1960. *Two Treatises of Government*. Peter Laslett, introduction and apparatus criticus. 1690 and 1706. New York; Scarborough; Ontario and London: A Mentor Book.

MacLean, Isabel Cranstoun. 1910. *Children of Jamaica*. Edinburgh and London: Oliphant, Anderson and Ferrier.

Marx, Karl, and Friedrich Engels. (1850–88)1978. *On Colonialism*. Moscow: Progress Publishers.

Menard, Edith. 1964. John Willis Menard First Negro Elected to the US Congress First Negro to Speak in the US Congress. In *Negro History Bulletin* XXXVIII, no.3.

Murphy, Joseph M. 1994. *Working the Spirit: Ceremonies of the African Diaspora*. Boston: Beacon Press.

New York Daily Tribune. 1865. November 17.

New-York Daily Times. 1865. November 17.

Olivier, Lord [Sydney]. 1833. *The Myth of Governor Eyre*. London: Leonard and Virginia Woolf at the Hogarth Press.

Owen, Joseph. 1976. *Dread: The Rastafarians of Jamaica*. Kingston: Sangster's Book Stores Ltd.

Peel, J. 1867. War Office, 11 February, 1867 'Copy or Extracts of Correspondence between the House Guards and General O'Connor on the Conduct of Military Officers during the Recent Deplorable Occurrences in Jamaica.' (Ordered by the House of Commons, to be printed, 12 February).

Pigou, Beverley Elizabeth. 1985. Attitudes to Death in Jamaica from the Seventeenth Century to the Twentieth Century. MPhil Thesis, University of the West Indies.

Pim, Bedford. 1866. *The Negros & Jamaica*. London.

References

Rankin, David C. 1974. The Origins of Black Leadership in New Orleans during Reconstruction. *The Journal of Southern History* 40.

Ripley, C. Peter, ed. 1985. *The Black Abolitionist Papers – Volume 1: The British Isles, 1830–1865*. Chapel Hill and London: The University of North Carolina Press.

Roberts, Walter Adolphe. 1952. *Six Great Jamaicans*. Biographical Sketches. Kingston: Pioneer Press.

Robotham, Don. 1981. *'The Notorious Riot': The Socio-Economic and Political Bases of Paul Bogle's Revolt*. Jamaica: Institute of Social and Economic Research, University of the West Indies.

Rogers, J.A. 1972. *World's Great men of Color*. Vol. II. John Henrik Clarke, introduction, commentary, new bibliographical notes. 1947. New York & London: Collier MacMillan Publishers.

Schuler, Monica. 1980. *'Alas, Alas Kongo': A Social History of Indentured African Immigration in Jamaica, 1841–1865*. Baltimore and London: Johns Hopkins University Press.

Semmel, Bernard. 1962. *Jamaica Blood Victorian Conscience: The Governor Eyre Controversy*. Connecticut: Greenwood Press.

Sentinel. 1865. January 19, 1865–April 27, 1865.

Shirley, Gordon. 1971. *A Century of West Indian Education*. Reprint. London: Longman Group Ltd.

Sibley, Inez Knibb. 1965. *The Baptist of Jamaica 1793 to 1965*. Kingston: The Jamaica Baptist Union.

St John, Spenser. 1971. *Hayti or the Black Republic*. 1884/1889. London: Frank Cass & Co. Ltd.

Stewart, Dianne M. 2005. *Three Eyes for the Journey: African Dimensions of the Jamaican Religious Experience*. Oxford. New York: Oxford University Press.

Stewart, Robert J. 1995. Reporting Morant Bay: The 1865 Jamaican Insurrection as Reported and Interpreted in The *New York Herald*, *Daily Tribune*, and *Times*. Presented at the Twenty-Seventy annual Conference of the Association of Caribbean Historian. Georgetown, Guyana, April 2–7.

Stuckey, Sterling. 1987. *Slave Culture: Nationalist Theory & the Foundations of Black America*. New York and Oxford: Oxford University Press.

Swell, William Grant. 1861. *The Ordeal of Free Labor in the British West Indies*. New York.

Thompson, Robert Farris. 1993. *Face of the Gods: Art and Altars of Africa and the African Americas*. New York and Prestel, Munich: The Museum for African Art.

———. 1984. *Flash of the Spirit: African & Afro-American Art & Philosophy*. New York: Vintage Books.

Throup, David. 1987. *Economic & Social Origins of Mau Mau 1945–53*. London. Nairobi. Athens, Ohio: James Currey, Heinemann and Ohio University Press.

Trollope, Anthony. 1860. *The West Indies and the Spanish Main*. London.

Underhill, Edward B. 1865. *Dr Underhill's Letter: A Letter Addressed to the Rt Honourable E. Cardwell with Illustrated Documents on the Condition of Jamaica*. London.

———. (1862) 1970. *The West Indies: Their Social and Religious Condition*. Westport, CT: Negro University Press.

———. (1895) 1971. *The Tragedy of Morant Bay*. New York: Book for Libraries Press.

US Government. 1868. Papers Relating to Foreign Affairs Accompanying the Annual Message of the President to the Second Session of the Fortieth Congress, 1867, Part 1. Washington, DC: Government Printing Office.

Warner-Lewis, Maureen. 2003. *Central Africa in the Caribbean: Transcending Time, Transforming Cultures*. Barbados. Jamaica. Trinidad and Tobago: University of the West Indies Press.

———. 1991. *Guinea's Other Suns: The African Dynamic in Trinidad Culture*. Dover, MA: The Majority Press.

Watts, Isaac. 1718. *Psalm, Hymns & Spiritual Songs*. London.

The West Indian. 1838. January 20.

Williams, Eric. (1944) 1994. *Capitalism & Slavery*. Chapel Hill: University of North Carolina Press; 2005. Kingston: Ian Randle Publishers.

Wilmot, Swithin. 1977. Political Development in Jamaica in the Post Emancipation Period: 1838–1854. PhD Thesis, Oxford University.

———. 1986. Baptist Missionaries and Jamaican Politics, 1838–1854. In *A Selection of Papers Presented at the Twelfth Conference of the Association of Caribbean Historians 1980*, ed. K.O. Laurence. Trinidad: Association of Caribbean Historians.

———. 1987. Women and Protest in Jamaica 1838–1865. Paper presented at the Nineteenth Annual Conference of Caribbean Historians, Martinique, April 13–17.

———. 1996. The Politics of Samuel Clarke: Black Political Martyr in Jamaica 1851–1865. *The Jamaican Historical Review* XIX.

Wolfthal, Diane. n.d. Excerpts from Diane Wolfthal Images of Rape: The "Heroic" Tradition and its Alternatives, from www.oneonta.edu/faculty/faberas/arth/ARTH200/Heroic_Rape.

Zoller, Peter. 1979. *A Study of Carlyle, Ruskin, Mill and Huxley*. PhD Diss., Claremont Graduate School.

Communion with the Spirits

The assemblage, an altar or seal, depicts seven cutlasses stuck into the earth in a semi-circle at the root of a huge silk cotton tree. The semi-circle is made whole with seven red candles, lit. In the centre of the circle is a basin with water in which are placed stems of the leaf of life plant (medicinal plant), croton leaves (spirit plant), a grape fruit, marbles, red, black and white beads (denoting Kongo spirituality) and some coins.

The basin with its contents dominated by the colour yellow, symbolises the river spirit (Riva Muma in Jamaica), bringer of health, wealth and at times, destruction – since this healer spirit, patron of the medicine seal, is also a warrior spirit who is sometimes depicted with a cutlass or sword in Revival.

Enslaved Africans in Jamaica did find a path through George Leile's African American Baptist complex and later Europeanised Christianity, to serve their interests. Christianity's symbols of baptism became a way in which the African age old embrace of water spirits in the ancestral pantheon, became a bridge to the fashioning of the Native Baptist. The gathering of spirits (including non-African spirits) to serve the cause of freedom, dignity, redemption and sovereignty, is a modus operandi of the African diaspora.

The cutlasses and candles denote a warrior spirit or spirits of the Ogun/Archangel Michael type. The bottle of rum behind the basin is to feed the spirit(s). Behind the circle is a recreation of the flag of the Paul Bogle led movement, hanging from the trunk of the silk cotton tree. They both provide a backdrop to the circle. The coconut in front of the basin is a symbol of three eyes (a similar concept to that of the 'four eye man'). The coconut when shattered into bits in rituals, requires the special sight or reading ability of the divinatory to make sense of its signs and symbols.

This assemblage symbolises the world of the living in communion with the world of the spirits denoted in the oath-taking ceremony presided over by Paul Bogle in Stony Gut and the final meeting of Bogle and his followers under a very big silk cotton tree, just before they entered Morant Bay on that afternoon of October 11, 1865.

Clinton Hutton, September 6, 2015

Index

17th Regiment (from Halifax), 209, 219
1st West India Regiment, 209, 219, 224
6th Royal Regiment, 198, 209

A Son of Africa, 102, 141, 142, 147
abject poverty, 20
Abolitionist, 8, 82, 86, 89, 94, 95, 103, 123, 137, 205
Accompong, 105, 117, 220, 226
activist leaders, 49
Aesthetic culture, 127, 147
aesthetic, 100, 127, 147, 152, 158, 165
African Americans, 81, 82, 89, 170
African ancestral orders, 100
African descent, xiv, 7, 57, 77, 79, 80, 93, 102, 168, 213, 220
African diaspora warrior spirits, 152
African family, 184, 189, 196
African Jamaican Spirituality, 77, 156, 168
Africans, xv, 1, 4, 5, 7, 8, 11, 27, 32, 44, 46, 53, 56, 57, 58, 59, 73, 77, 79, 80, 81, 82, 85, 88, 89, 95, 100, 103, 104, 106, 126, 127, 128, 139, 151, 154, 155, 156, 157, 158, 159, 160, 161, 162, 163, 164, 165, 166, 168, 169, 184, 188, 204, 205, 209, 216, 220, 229, 230, 231, 232, 233, 234, 236, 237
aggressive medicine, 149, 150, 157
Alberga, H.A., 2
American vessel, the Re-Union, 207
American war steamer, 207
Amity Hall Estate, 55, 66, 67
Ancestral, iii, 100, 101, 130, 142, 148, 154, 155, 156, 157, 158, 160, 163, 170, 188, 239
Ancient conservatism, 90, 91
Anderson, John, 40, 42, 80, 107, 110, 127

Anderson, Wellwood, 5, 45
Anglican Church, 15, 60, 134
Anglophone Caribbean, 2
antagonistic social groups, 46
Anti-Slavery Reporter, 17, 24, 141
apprentices, 6
Armed private civilians, 209
Arnold Malabre and Company, 215
artillery pieces, 209, 212
Assembly, 2, 18, 21, 25, 26, 28, 29, 30, 31, 45, 46, 51, 60, 70, 96, 98, 116, 127, 129, 133, 135, 137, 142, 144, 145, 203, 207, 214, 218, 224
Astwood, Captain, 93
awful stench, 176
Awolalu, J. Omosade, 169

Bailey, E.K./Edward K. Bailey, xiii, 103, 107, 109, 118
Banquet style Revival, 158
Baptist Ministers' Report, 16
Baptist ministers, 7, 16, 19, 142
Barbados, 1, 51, 142, 170, 209, 212
Bartley, John, 157
Bath, viii, ix, 2, 21, 61, 63, 64, 65, 66, 67, 68, 69, 70, 93, 110, 124, 178, 199, 200, 216
Beckwith, Martha, 147, 167
Bedward, Alexander, 100, 147, 165, 167
Bell Castle Chapel, 155
Belle Castle, 61, 201
Benuzzi, Maximilliam Carto, 210
Berry, Eliza, 194, 195
Berry, Elizabeth, 180
Bible, 2, 102, 103, 125, 141, 149, 152
Bigelow, John, 7, 54, 62
Bigotry, 127, 128
black American Baptist Minister, 123
black consciousness, 85, 100
black entrepreneurial efforts, 11

black family, 19, 185, 186, 188, 189, 199, 200
black females, 192, 193
black masses, 2, 101, 103, 111, 114, 124, 125, 129, 130, 131, 134, 146, 148, 152, 161, 191, 200, 209, 212, 213, 215, 216, 231
Black Nationalist ethos, 89
black patriarchy, 187, 231
black people too fool, 59, 74, 220
black policemen, 45
black progressives, 94
Black River, 10, 45, 47, 137
black thought, 109
black women, 184, 185, 186, 187, 189, 190, 191, 192, 193, 196, 198, 199, 201, 203
Bleby, Henry, 174
Blue Jacket, 176, 209
Bob Marley, xv
Bogle's Chapel, viii, 101, 124, 151, 152, 155, 167, 180
Bogle, Elizabeth, 116
Bogle, Henry Theophilus, 110
Bogle, Moses, 80, 99, 107, 113, 116, 118
Bogle, William, 73, 74, 107, 113, 116, 119
Bois Caïman, 156
Bongo Seal, 150
bourgeoisie, 3, 4, 5, 14
Bowden, 212
Bowerbank, Custos Lewis, 219
Bowie, James (Old Bowie), 111, 223
Bowie, William, v, 73, 80, 111
Bright, John, 141, 238
British and Foreign Anti-Slavery Society, 8
British colonialism, 2, 5, 18, 169, 198
British economy, 14, 24
British Foreign Office, 89, 90
British Honduras, 81
British military command, 206
British West Indian interests, 13
Brown, Karen McCarthy, v, 73, 80, 111

browns (coloureds), 78, 95, 115, 126, 127, 128, 129, 130, 144, 184, 216
Bruce, Dr Robert, 46, 210
Buckra country, 222
Buckra has gun, negro has fire stick, vii, 29
buckra, 43, 45
Buncher, J.H., 155–56
Burchell, Thomas, 139
Burke, Samuel Constantine, 126

Callagan, Daniel, 44
campaign of terror, 175
Campbell, Revd Duncan, 120
cane sugar, vii, xiv, 13, 48, 49, 58
Captain of the French Steamer, 207, 224
Cardwell, Edward, 1, 11
Carlyle, Thomas, 13, 54, 62, 238
Carlylean, 88, 114
Carlylean philosophy, 114
Carr, William, 51, 58, 65
Chamerovow, Louis Alexis, 8
Chevannes, Barry, 100, 116, 165
Chigoe Foot Market, 177, 226
Children, 13, 15, 16, 17, 18, 19, 20, 21, 78, 85, 86, 98, 99, 106, 110, 116, 117, 135, 141, 142, 174, 177, 181, 184, 185, 187, 189, 192, 193, 194, 195, 196, 197, 198, 199, 201, 222, 231, 236, 239
Chisholm, William, 74, 75, 114
Christie, Bishop Raleigh, 163
Church Corner, 107, 113, 117
Church Establishment, 15
Churchill, Alfred S., 196
Clarke, George, 97, 98, 113, 116
Clarke, Richard, 140, 181, 197
Clarke, Samuel, 40, 46, 77, 80, 81, 88, 92, 93, 94, 95, 96, 97, 98, 114, 115, 116, 136, 140
Clergy Law, 31
Clyne, Henry, 43, 74, 75, 80, 107, 108, 109, 110, 111, 112
coercive labour, 17, 200

Index

coffee, 6, 7, 8, 9, 11, 24, 31, 32, 56, 57, 59, 107, 108, 136, 182
Coley Estate, 108, 109
Collins, Elizabeth, 177
Colonial Standard, 20, 21, 29, 33, 34, 39, 42, 43, 78, 93, 99, 118, 129, 130, 132, 134, 138, 143, 146, 173, 175, 183, 196, 205, 206, 208, 211, 212, 215, 217, 218, 220, 221, 223, 224, 225, 226, 231
Complainants, ix, 21, 63, 64, 65, 66, 67, 69, 70, 76
conservatism, 90, 91, 139, 142, 143, 216
Cooke, Stephen (Clerk of the Peace and 1st Lieutenant of the No. 2 Rifle Volunteers), 96, 106
Corn Laws, 4
corporal punishment, 22, 23
cosmological roots of freedom, 159, 160, 161
County Union, 19, 46, 78, 141, 210, 211, 223
Cousins, Thomas, 221
Craddock, George, 106, 112, 113, 114, 149, 155, 223
Crole, Revd J.H., 124
Crown Colony rule, 26
Crown Lands, 6
Cuba, 1, 111, 118, 205, 206, 207, 209, 223
Cuniffe, 33, 34

Dacres, James, 80
Dalling, Revd, 18
Darwin, Charles, 141, 238
Davidson, Colthirst and Company, 215
Davidson, Richard, 57
Davis, Sophia, 181
Dawkins, Ellen, 195
Decapitated, viii, 21, 157, 161, 183
DeCordova, Altamont, 214, 225, 226
DeCordova's Irregular Cavalry, 214
Defendants, ix, 21, 63, 64, 65, 68, 69, 70, 76

Dick, Devon, 152, 161, 162
dirty niggers, 127
dispute with white sailors, 45
disturbances, 36, 37, 45, 55, 205
Dompédre, 150
Druggist Store of Mr. Charles Delgado, 36
Duckett, Angus, 71
Duncker, Sheila, 126
duppy (dopi), 151, 153, 155, 157, 159, 160
Dux, 140, 141

East, Revd D.J., 61
economic nationalism, 136
Edna Manley's sculptural depiction, 165
Education, 13, 15, 30, 42, 77, 78, 83, 84, 85, 86, 88, 95, 114, 125, 126, 128, 129, 135, 139, 145, 185, 190, 220, 221
Edwards, John, 59, 107, 110
election campaigns, 27
Election Law, 29, 30, 42
elementary education, 13, 85
Elkington, Lieutenant Colonel, 174
emancipation, 4, 5, 6, 7, 13, 14, 18, 23, 25, 28, 29, 30, 37, 53, 77, 78, 79, 81, 82, 88, 126, 139, 144, 181, 185, 186, 207, 217, 230, 232, 235
Emancipation Day, 53, 82
Engels, Frederick, 194
English Baptist Church, 60
English Baptist Missionaries, 61
English education, 126, 129
episteme, 53, 77, 84, 85, 91, 147, 165, 170
epistemic wellspring, 12
epistemology, 80, 84, 85, 229
Espeut, Peter, 51, 202
Established Church, 135, 139, 161, 192
estates, 6, 7, 14, 15, 16, 17, 24, 25, 35, 38, 39, 40, 44, 49, 51, 55, 56, 57, 58, 63, 65, 66, 67, 68, 69, 71, 73, 77, 91, 92, 104, 137, 138, 180, 185, 187, 214, 215, 232

executions, 175, 176, 193
Executive Committee, 21, 45, 129, 205, 207, 215, 226
exploitation, 75
ex-slave owners, 6, 25, 27
extreme poverty, 19
Eyre Defence Aid Fund, 228, 238
Eyre, Edward John, viii, xiv, 205, 238

Falmouth, 16, 35, 117, 215
Falmouth Post, 9, 20, 21, 22, 23, 24, 28, 29, 30, 31, 32, 33, 35, 36, 37, 38, 39, 41, 42, 56, 135, 138, 140, 141, 143, 185, 204, 211, 215, 223, 226
females, 19, 20, 21, 35, 69, 153, 159, 184, 185, 187, 191, 192, 193, 195, 229, 232
Fenians, 141
Finlason, William Francis, 227
Fletcher, Duncan, 123, 124, 125
flogging, 95, 142, 173, 177, 178, 179, 198, 200, 202, 203
Florence Hall Pen, 35
Foote, Reverend Alexander, 178
Ford, Capt. Henry, 182, 214, 224
Ford's Special Volunteers, 214
Foreign markets, 14
Foster, James (policeman), 149, 151, 152, 154
Fouche, George, 41, 95
Francis, Mary Ann, 195
Free Trade Ideology, 4
Freedom, v, 4, 5, 6, 21, 23, 28, 29, 51, 58, 78, 79, 87, 88, 91, 103, 104, 109, 114, 126, 129, 144, 147, 156, 159, 160, 161, 163, 184, 186, 189, 199, 205, 221, 233, 235, 236, 237
freeholders, 10, 12, 30, 56, 57, 58, 59, 114, 122, 148
Freeholdership, 12, 51, 52, 58, 101
Fuller, William, 149
funeral dirge, 160
funeral rituals, 158, 159, 160
Fyfe, Alexander Gordon, 27, 32, 106, 208

Gardner, William, 162, 233
Garnet, Henry Highland, 8, 82, 95, 103
Garrisonian Abolitionist, 95
Garvey, Marcus, 103
Garveyite consciousness, xiv
General Penitentiary, 22, 24, 178, 179
General taxation, 15, 103
Geoghegan, James, 3, 195
Geoghegan, Letitia, v, 195
George Delisser and Son, 36
George Leilean tradition of Christianity, 152
Georges, William P., 93
Glenelg, Lord, 6
Goldson, Emanuel, 41, 136
Goldson, Joseph Emanuel, 96, 116, 210
Gordon, George William, vii, 137, 138, 140, 142, 143, 145, 146, 166, 210, 211, 213, 236
Gordon's Tabernacle, 40
Grant, John Elisha, 198
Grant, William, 43, 59, 80, 107, 110, 111, 127
Grey, Charles, 25
guerrilla warfare, 104, 207
gunpowder and rum, 2, 150, 155
Guthrie, Bishop, 171

Haitian exiles, 210
Haitian Revolution, 141, 146, 156, 169, 229, 230
Hall, Douglas, 12, 114, 115
Hamilton, George, 57, 181
Hampden, 20, 56
Hanover, 33, 36, 39, 41, 45, 79, 141, 215
Harris, Henry, 61, 201
Harris, Richard, 57
Harrison, James, 67
Hart, Richard, 12, 117, 169
Harvey, Thomas and William Brewin, 7, 76
heads shaven, 202
heavy with child, 199

Index

Hebrew Benevolent Society, 9
Henderson, Revd, 15, 18, 61
Henriques, Fernando, 188
Henry, Claudius 'Cyrus', 100
Her Majesty's representatives, 18
Herschell, Revd V., 2
Heslop, Alexander, 10, 96, 126, 128, 129
Heuman, Gad, 89
Higman, Barry, 188
Hindu cosmology, 165
Hire, Augustus, 66, 67, 76
Hitchins, Captain E.W., 2
HMS Wolverine, 208, 212, 225
Hobbs, Col. Francis, viii, 58, 59, 111, 175
Hobbs, Colonel Francis, 157, 161
Hole, Captain, 179
Holland Estate, 52, 200
Holt, Samuel, 136
Home Circuit Court, 20
homeless, 180, 182, 183, 196, 199, 200
Hope, Sir James, 1, 219
House of Assembly, 28, 29, 31, 45, 60, 127, 129, 130, 131, 132, 135, 137, 142, 144, 145, 218
House of Commons, 4, 244
House of Lords, 4, 108
houses, 5, 35, 56, 58, 140, 144, 180, 181, 192, 199, 201, 219
Howell, Leonard, 100
Hutton, Clinton, 50, 66, 81, 151, 164, 171, 172, 175, 179, 238

Immigration Bill, 23, 28, 29
impending showdown, 36
Indian fighters for nation liberation, 208
Indian mutiny, 141, 208
industrial bourgeoisie, 3, 4, 5, 14
inferiority, 28, 234
injustice, 3, 7, 32, 75, 91, 92, 140
Inspector General of Prisons, 21, 22
International Peace Makers Association, xi, 100

Island Collegiate Institution, 31
Itals, xv

J.W.M., 83, 84
Jamaica, 84, 85, 86, 87, 88, 89, 90, 91, 92, 94, 95, 96, 99, 100, 103, 104, 106, 113, 114, 115, 116, 117, 118, 121, 123, 124, 126, 127, 128, 129, 131, 132, 133, 134, 135, 136, 137, 139, 140, 141, 143, 144, 145, 146, 148, 149, 150, 152, 154, 155, 158, 159, 160, 161, 162, 163, 164, 165, 166, 167, 168, 169, 170, 171, 173, 174, 175, 184, 186, 190, 193, 194, 196, 200, 203, 205, 206, 207, 208, 209, 211, 212, 213, 215, 217, 222, 223, 224, 225, 227, 228, 229, 230, 231, 234, 235, 236, 238
Jamaica Committee, 121, 222, 235, 238
Jamaica Despatch and Kingston Chronicle, 53, 242, 244
Jamaica Native Baptist Free Church, 100, 165
Jamaica Tribune, 9, 104, 117, 131, 217, 244
Jamaican interest, 25, 129, 130, 134
Jamaican masses, vii, 83, 130, 139, 161, 172, 184
Jamaican popular music, xv, 109
James Garfield's motion, 93
Jewish Society, 9
John Willis Menard, viii, 42, 77, 80, 81, 83, 87, 89, 114
Johnson, Revd R.A., 29, 42
Jordan, Edward, 29, 78, 119, 219
juxtaposition of opposing beliefs, 162, 163, 168

Kalunga, 153
Kerr, Justice Allan, 49, 64
Ketelholdt, Maximilian Augustus von, 2, 3, 97, 132, 138, 145
Ki-kongo, 151

King's House, 10, 206
Kingston, 19, 20, 22, 29, 37, 38, 40, 41, 42, 44, 45, 53, 62, 71, 81, 89, 93, 95, 96, 115, 116, 117, 123, 124, 127, 134, 145, 146, 165, 169, 176, 179, 186, 200, 201, 205, 206, 207, 209, 210, 214, 215, 217, 218, 219, 225, 238
Kingston Volunteer Troop, 93
Kitchen, John, 70, 71
Knibb, William, 139
Kongo spirituality, 154
Kongo tradition, 149
Kumfa, 168
Kumina and Revival cosmologies, 153
Kumina, viii, xiii, xiv, 150, 152, 153, 156, 164, 165, 169, 204

Labouring masses, 15, 18, 73, 110, 131
Labourers, ix, 1, 11, 16, 17, 18, 21, 24, 26, 31, 34, 35, 39, 41, 44, 48, 49, 51, 52, 53, 55, 56, 57, 58, 59, 60, 61, 63, 64, 65, 66, 67, 68, 69, 70, 71, 73, 76, 88, 105, 110, 118, 148, 151, 166
Lake, Augustus, 175
Lake, William, 151
Lan, David, 170
Lawrence, Henry, 97, 113
Lee, Revd Thomas, 12, 42, 146
Lemba-Petro order, 150
Leslie, C., 160
Letter Hill, 72, 73
Levien, Sidney, 78, 116, 205, 210, 211
Levingston, Polly, 195
Levy, George, 78
liberal reformers, 143
liberalism, 139, 142, 143
Liberation Society, 42, 43, 79
Liberation Theology, 103
Lincoln, Abraham, 81, 141
Lindsay, Emily, 177
Locke, John, 133
looting of wedding rings, 181

Lord, John Ashley (Inspector of Police), 98
low radicalism, 35
Lucea, 33, 38, 39, 41, 102, 141, 215, 225
Lukumi, 168
Lutus, John, 176

magisterial oppression, vii, 63, 68, 72
magistrates, xi, 35, 40, 56, 65, 66, 67, 68, 71, 72, 76, 94, 98, 142, 147, 211, 214, 225
Makindo, Sarah, 181, 199, 202
making images, 112, 157
Manbo, 156
Manchioneal, 61, 73, 118, 155, 174, 178, 179, 197
Manning Toll-gate, 35
manufacturing class, 14
Maroons, 32, 103, 104, 105, 110, 117, 194, 195, 200, 201, 209, 214, 216, 217, 218, 219, 223, 226
Maroons addressed by Governor, 219
Maroons welcomed at the Kingston Courthouse, 219
Maroons, fully armed and dressed in camouflage battle outfit, 218
Marshall, George, 175
Marx, Karl, 194
Masculinity, 174, 193, 231, 233, 239
mass terror and humiliation, 177
massive redundancies, 18
Mau Mau uprising in Kenya, 169
McClintock, Commodore, 173
McIntosh, George, 43, 59, 80, 97, 107, 111, 112
McKay, William, 66, 67
McLaren, James, v, 80, 97, 103, 107, 108, 109, 111, 114, 117
McLaren, John, 107
McLean, Charles, 94, 115
Maclean, Isabel, 190
meagre wages, 17

Index

Mendes, John, 105, 202, 203
Mercantile Agency Association, 10
mercantile firms, 10, 215
Middle Passage, 164
Middleton property, 5
military rule, 200
military tactics, 209
Militia, 1, 32, 75, 99, 110, 135, 209, 212, 213
Miller, William, 73
Minknot, W.C., 72
Mitchell, Ann, 196
Monklands, 175, 202
Montego Bay, 18, 20, 38, 41, 47, 126, 144, 210, 211, 215
Morant Bay, vii, viii, xiii, xiv, xv, 1, 2, 3, 33, 37, 40, 41, 43, 44, 55, 57, 58, 59, 61, 74, 77, 80, 84, 89, 92, 93, 95, 96, 97, 98, 99, 101, 102, 105, 106, 107, 108, 109, 110, 111, 112, 113, 114, 116, 117, 118, 124, 128, 147, 148, 149, 151, 154, 156, 157, 158, 161, 163, 170, 172, 176, 178, 179, 181, 191, 192, 193, 195, 198, 204, 205, 207, 208, 209, 210, 211, 214, 216, 218, 220, 221, 223, 224, 227, 228, 229, 236, 237, 238
Morant Bay police station, 111, 209
Morant Bay Rebellion, vii, xiii, xv, 1, 37, 57, 58, 77, 101, 109, 114, 220, 227, 228, 236
Morant Bay War, 80, 99, 105, 109, 128, 147, 149, 151, 154, 157, 158, 170, 191, 229
Morant War, 1, 74, 165, 167
Mount Lebanus, 161, 175, 196, 200
Munro, Chloe, 201
Mutual loan societies, 11
Myaal liturgical complex, 155
Myaal upsurges, 170
Myaalists, 38
Myombe, 168

Nassau, Bahamas, 209
Native Baptist Church, 44, 60, 100, 101, 152, 161, 162, 167, 168
Native Baptist Communion, 125, 166
Native Baptist Missionary Society, 123, 124, 163, 166
Nelson, Brigadier-General A.A., 176
neo-slaveocracy, 139
New Agitation Movement, 37, 148
New York Daily Tribune, 59, 74, 176, 205, 220, 222
New York Times, 63
No. 1 Volunteer Troops, 3
Nunes, Robert, 61
Nutts River, 107, 118

O'Connor, Major General, 93, 206, 208, 212, 219, 225
oath, 2, 3, 89, 93, 101, 111, 112, 148, 149, 150, 151, 152, 154, 155, 157, 163, 165, 168, 169, 174, 191
oath-taking ceremony, 2, 3, 89, 93, 101, 107, 111, 112, 148, 149, 150, 152, 154, 163, 165, 168, 174, 191
Obeah, 111, 112, 118, 157, 158, 202
Obeahism, 142
Obeahman, 111, 112, 118, 157, 158, 161, 202
Occasional Discourse on the Nigger Question, 54
Ogou (Ogoun/Ogun), 151, 152, 153
Ogoun-like/Shango-like spirit, 152, 153
Olivier, Lord, 182
Onslow, William, 113, 177
ontological construction of blackness, 166
ontological evolution, 127
oppressive tax regime, 15, 16
Orisha, 168
Orthodox Christianity, 162, 166, 167
Osborn, Robert, 29, 78, 120, 127, 129, 130, 137

Oungan, 150, 156
own-account, 26, 30, 46, 48, 57, 58, 59, 60, 80, 100, 114, 136, 199

pacification of the peasantry, 213
Pan-African Jamaican episteme, 147
para-military forces, 192, 195
parish militia, 212
Payne, Daniel, 103, 117
people's court, 71, 72, 73, 116
Phillips, Wendell, 141
pillage and looting, 181
Pim, Commander Bedford, 143, 146, 228
Pimento, 8, 9, 24, 136
Pink, Caroline, 210
pistols, 215, 225
Plaine-du-Nord, 156
Plantain Garden River district, viii, 50, 214
Plantation economy, 91
Planters, vii, 1, 7, 8, 9, 11, 13, 14, 143, 180, 199, 213, 214, 215, 225
plantocracy, 2, 4, 6, 7, 8, 11, 12, 13, 14, 18, 23, 25, 29, 32, 34, 37, 38, 39, 45, 49, 51, 52, 54, 55, 58, 59, 60, 63, 65, 68, 80, 86, 94, 95, 99, 100, 101, 103, 108, 114, 115, 117, 139, 142, 144, 145, 146, 155, 181, 190, 199, 200
Poko leader, 152
Poko-Kumina (Pukkumina), xiii, 152
Political ontology, 109
Popular Education, 83, 84, 85, 86
Port Antonio, 34, 117, 174, 179, 197, 198, 217
Port Royal, 81, 207, 209, 214, 225
Portland, 207, 209, 210, 212, 217
post-emancipation newspapers, 78
post-slavery society, vii, 6, 12, 48, 58, 79, 80, 84, 88, 92, 109, 126, 129, 136, 142, 147, 163, 184, 185, 186, 187, 189, 191, 205, 221
poverty, 18, 19, 20, 37, 38, 39, 109, 114, 125, 185

pregnant, 81, 181, 192, 198, 199
Price, Charles, 2, 118
Prospect, 199
prostitution, 19
proto-reparation vision, 11
Psalms of David, 101, 102

race conscious, 75, 95, 221
racial oppression, 68
racist episteme, 85
racist theory of knowledge, 84
radical ideological position, 138
Ramsay, Gordon (Provost Marshall), 182, 208, 212
rape, 20, 21, 202, 233, 239
rape cases, 20
Rastafari, xiv, 103, 166, 241
Reparation, 7, 11, 32
Report of Sterling, 88
Representative democracy, 30, 32
Republican Party, 90
Revival, viii, xiii, xiv, xv, 37, 38, 74, 75, 77, 102, 123, 138, 141, 146, 147, 148, 150, 152, 153, 156, 158, 163, 164, 165, 166, 167, 168, 169, 170, 171, 233, 241
revolutionism, 139
Richard, David, 113
Ricketts, John, 179
Rio Bueno, 143
riots, 35, 36, 37, 81, 138, 140, 148
Roach, Revd James, 30, 46, 96, 116
Robinson, Maria, 200
Rock Fort, 218
Rose, Joseph, 155
Rosseau, Jean-Jacques, 141
Round Hill Estate, 33
Rowe, Archdeacon, 22, 46
Royal Artillery Detachment, 176
Royal Artillery, 176, 209, 211
Royal Commission, 5, 19, 22, 24, 26, 30, 32, 33, 40, 41, 43, 49, 51, 52, 53, 57, 61, 63, 64, 66, 67, 68, 70, 74, 76, 92, 93, 95, 96, 98, 99, 100, 104, 105,

Index

106, 107, 109, 110, 111, 112, 113, 115, 116, 117, 118, 119, 120, 121, 124, 125, 128, 141, 144, 145, 146, 149, 155, 157, 162, 167, 168, 169, 173, 174, 177, 180, 181, 183, 191, 193, 194, 196, 197, 200, 201, 203, 205, 206, 208, 209, 212, 213, 214, 216, 221, 222, 223, 224, 226
Royal Marine, 209, 212
Royal Marines used artillery pieces, 212
Ruling classes, 10, 22, 24, 25, 27, 28, 29, 30, 31, 32, 33, 34, 35, 36, 37, 39, 46, 50, 63, 68, 73, 90, 96, 101, 104, 106, 143, 173, 176, 191, 300, 207, 212, 213, 214, 215, 216, 218, 222, 225, 226
rural militia, 209

Saint Domingo (Saint Domingue), 36, 150
Saint-Méry, Moreau de, 150, 155
Salmon, Custos John, 10, 11, 47
Savanna-la-Mar, 35, 37, 38, 47, 225
Schuler, Monica, 245
Scott, Benjamin, 1
Scott, Charlotte, 177, 197, 198
Sebastopol, 141, 208
sedition-mongers, 32
Seditious Society, 9
Seilas, Revd John, 24
Sentinel, 30, 41, 42, 78, 80, 82, 83, 84, 85, 86, 87, 90, 91, 92, 95, 132, 133, 146, 210, 211
Serf labour(er), 6, 23
seven cutlasses, 151
sex and sexual relations, 19
sexual favours, 19
Sharpe, Sam, 32, 104, 139, 170, 208
Shot and beheaded, 112
shot-drill, 22
Slavery, 44, 46, 54, 55, 57, 74, 77, 78, 79, 82, 84, 85, 87, 88, 90, 91, 99, 103, 109
Sligo, Lord, 6
small settlers, 10, 56, 135, 136

Smith, Rayne, 45
Smith, Sir Lionel, 185
Smith, William Kelly, 96, 116, 136, 210, 211
Smithfield Wharf, 35
Social and political polarization, 57
Social explosion, 32
Society of Friends, 43, 109, 111, 112, 113
Somerset, 111, 112, 157, 161, 180, 181, 182, 201
Sovereign capacity, 130
Sovereignty, v, 185, 186, 188, 204, 206, 213, 221, 236
Spanish Consul in Kingston, 206
Spanish forces from Cuba, 1
Spanish men of war, 205
Spanish military vessels, 205
Spanish Town, 2, 38, 112, 118, 119, 123, 136, 214, 218, 219
Spirits, iii, vii, xiv, xv, 100, 147, 148, 150, 151, 152, 153, 154, 155, 156, 157, 158, 161, 163, 165, 169, 171
Spiritual Baptist, 168
Spring Estate, 33
St David, 2, 12, 40, 42, 43, 79, 80, 81, 82, 86, 89, 92, 93, 94, 95, 96, 97, 98, 106, 115, 202, 209, 210, 212, 213
St Domingue (Haiti), 150, 230
St George of Lydda, 152
St John, Spenser, 245
St Lucia and the Andaluzia, 205
St Mary, 45, 141, 150, 210, 230
St Michael or Archangel Michael, 152, 153
St Michael Order of Revival, 165
St Thomas-in-the-East, vii, ix, xiii, xiv, 1, 2, 3, 5, 14, 17, 21, 31, 32, 42, 43, 44, 45, 46, 48, 49, 50, 51, 52, 55, 57, 59, 60, 61, 63, 64, 65, 66, 67, 68, 70, 71, 72, 73, 74, 75, 80, 92, 93, 96, 97, 98, 99, 100, 103, 106, 107, 109, 110, 111, 112, 113, 116, 119, 120, 121, 124, 132, 133, 137, 138, 140, 141, 145, 148, 149,

151, 161, 166, 173, 180, 184, 194, 196, 198, 202, 206, 209, 210, 211, 212, 213, 214, 217, 218, 220, 224, 225
St Thomas-in-the-Vale, 31, 51, 65, 76
Stanley, Lord, 5, 89
Stanton Road, 113
State Department, 89, 90, 207
status symbol, 70
Stephen, Captain Thomas, 34
Sterling, James (Major Hayfield Maroons), 105
Stewart, Dianne, 169, 245
Stewart, James, 159, 160
Stony Gut, viii, 2, 3, 44, 55, 98, 101, 102, 106, 111, 113, 118, 119, 121, 122, 124, 149, 151, 152, 153, 155, 156, 163, 167, 177, 180, 195, 198, 201, 226
struggle, vii, xiv, 3, 4, 5, 12, 14, 25, 27, 29, 30, 31, 32, 33, 37, 38, 39, 42, 43, 44, 46, 48, 50, 65, 80, 85, 91, 99, 100, 102, 103, 104, 107, 108, 109, 114, 116, 124, 127, 129, 139, 141, 144, 148, 150, 178, 186, 204, 213, 222, 237
Stuckey, Sterling, 158, 170
Sugar Duties Act, 13, 14, 39
sugar estates, 14, 17, 49, 56, 65, 66, 68, 138, 180
Suppression, vii, xiii, 1, 36, 37, 43, 57, 58, 59, 89, 105, 110, 113, 117, 118, 141, 143, 167, 172, 173, 174, 181, 183, 184, 192, 196, 198, 200, 201, 202, 204, 205, 207, 208, 209, 210, 211, 212, 214, 215, 216, 217, 218, 224, 226, 227, 228, 229, 230, 231, 233, 238
Swell, W.G., 245

Tacky (Taki), 150, 230
Tax-free articles, 15
Taylor, Henry, 25
Taylor, John, 158, 160
Taylor, Justina, 195
Telford, Stephen, 57
Tharp Estates, 16
the crank, 22
the flag of the movement, 152
The Gleaner, 1, 23, 93, 102, 111, 116, 143, 173, 207, 211, 218, 219, 224, 226, 236
The Jamaica Reform Association, 29, 42, 96, 116
The St. David's Joint-Stock Company and Societies of Arts, 12
the thread-wheel, 22
Thompson, Robert Farris, 153, 170
Toll-Gates Riots, 35
Trelawny, 9, 10, 17, 20, 35, 36, 38, 42, 49, 57, 61, 70, 71, 78, 117, 138, 143, 215
Trinity Village, 199
Trollope, Anthony, 127, 236
Truro protestors, 35
Tyndall, John, 227, 228, 229, 238

uncivilised sexuality, 235
Underhill Convocations, 37
Underhill Letter, 37, 43, 97
Underhill, Edward, 6, 37, 78
undisguised display of disrespect, 46
Up-Park Camp, 93, 182
upper class, 15, 26, 34, 37, 38, 64, 95, 144, 180
US military assistance, 89

Vaz, Isaac, 78, 210, 211
Vere, 21, 33, 40, 44, 50, 51, 61, 63, 71, 75, 210
Vestry, 30, 40, 60, 70, 94, 97, 98, 115, 131
Vestryman, 92, 93, 94, 95, 96, 98, 113
Vickars, Edward, 127
Victoria, Queen, 11, 115, 139
Violence, 32, 33, 34, 35, 60, 143, 173, 192, 201, 237
violent confrontation, 2, 48, 49, 55, 57, 207
Vodun, 150, 153, 155, 156, 162, 168
Voltaire, Francois-marie, 141

Index

Wages, 1, 5, 7, 8, 11, 13, 16, 17, 18, 23, 28, 40, 45, 49, 52, 53, 54, 55, 62, 105, 110, 162, 187, 200
Wailers, xv, 109
wake rituals, 159, 161
Walcott, Magistrate Robert, 22
Walton, John, 2, 3
Ward, Samuel Ringgold, 82, 94, 95, 96, 115
Warner tradition, 141, 142
Warner-Lewis, Maureen, 169, 170
Warrant, 3, 76, 89
Warren, Revd Richard, 74, 123, 124, 125, 166
warrior spirit, 149, 150, 152, 153, 165
Watchman newspaper, 23, 26, 94, 101, 210
weaker sex, 193, 235
Wedderman, Anne, 52
Wellington, Arthur, v, viii, 59, 107, 111, 157, 161, 182, 183
Westmoreland, 8, 22, 24, 35, 36, 45, 49, 57, 61, 138, 140, 225, 226
whip, viii, 7, 23, 27, 54, 92, 109, 153, 177, 198, 210

whipped victim, 177, 178
Whipping Bill, 24, 142
White, Alexander, 3
White, Colonel, 105
White, Peggy, 200
widespread fear, 24
Williams, Catherine, 202
Williams, Esther, 198
Williams, Mary, 52, 200
Wilmot, Swithin, xi, 12, 94, 115, 146
Wilson, Simon, 177, 196
Women, 3, 7, 16, 17, 18, 19, 20, 21, 26, 35, 106, 117, 126, 157, 158, 162, 174, 177, 181, 182, 184, 185, 186, 187, 188, 189, 190, 191, 192, 193, 194, 195, 196, 197, 198, 199, 200, 201, 202, 203, 231, 232, 233, 234, 235, 239
Woollett, Joseph, 22
Workingmen's Literary Society of St. David, 42, 79, 82, 83, 86, 92, 93, 94

Yoruba, 152, 169

Zion, xiii, xiv, xv, 78, 148

www.ingramcontent.com/pod-product-compliance
Lightning Source LLC
Chambersburg PA
CBHW032038150426
43194CB00006B/327